# PROGRESSIVE ROCK GUITAR BIBLE

AUTHENTIC TRANSCRIPTIONS
WITH NOTES AND TABLATURE

T0040839

ISBN 978-0-634-06119-6

HAL•LEONARD®
CORPORATION
7777 W. BLUEMOUND RD. P.O. BOX 13819 MILWAUKEE, WI 53213

Visit Hal Leonard Online at
**www.halleonard.com**

from Coheed and Cambria - *Good Apollo, I'm Burning Star IV, Volume One:*
*From Fear Through the Eyes of Madness*

# Apollo I: The Writing Writer

**Words and Music by Claudio Sanchez, Michael Todd, Joshua Eppard and Travis Stever**

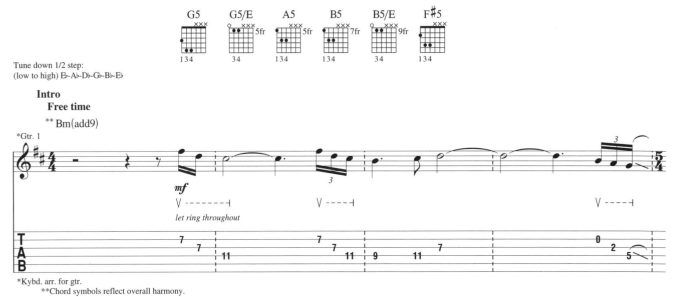

Tune down 1/2 step:
(low to high) E♭-A♭-D♭-G♭-B♭-E♭

**Intro**
**Free time**

*Kybd. arr. for gtr.
**Chord symbols reflect overall harmony.

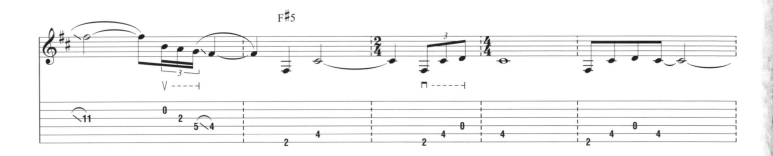

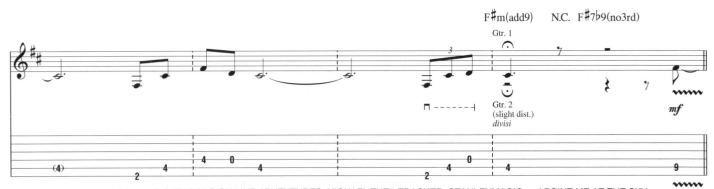

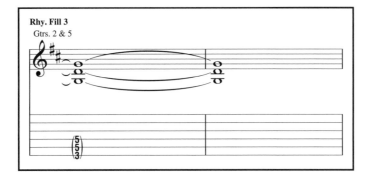

stom - ach this \_\_ in fear. _____ With the turn \_\_
fic - tion I \_\_\_\_\_ must fake _____ your death \_\_

1st time, Gtr. 2: w/ Riff A
1st time, Gtr. 3: w/ Riff A1 (1st 7 meas.)
Gtr. 4: w/ Riff A2
2nd time, Gtr. 3: w/ Riff A1

\_\_ I gath - ered name \_\_ as the bas - tard's \_\_ son, who by
\_\_ to grace \_\_ the face \_\_ of my char - ac - ter. _____ With these

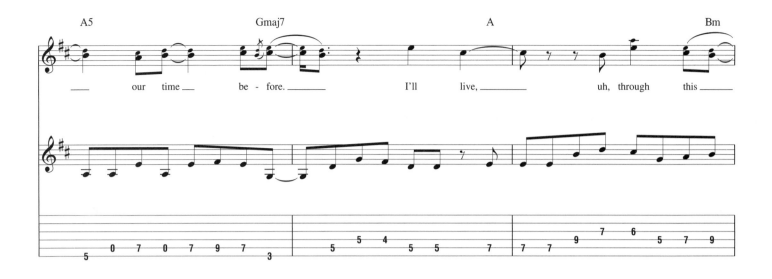

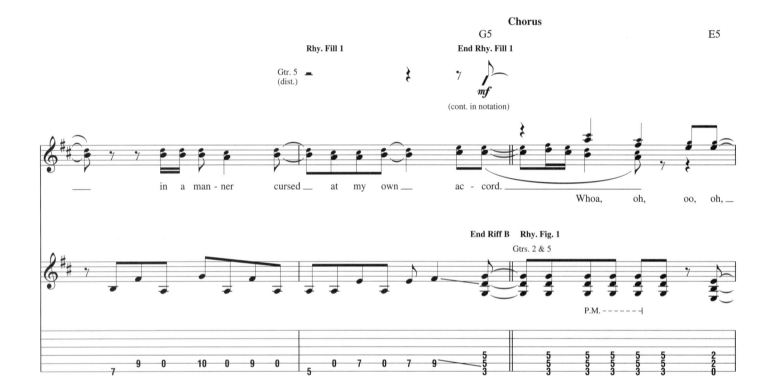

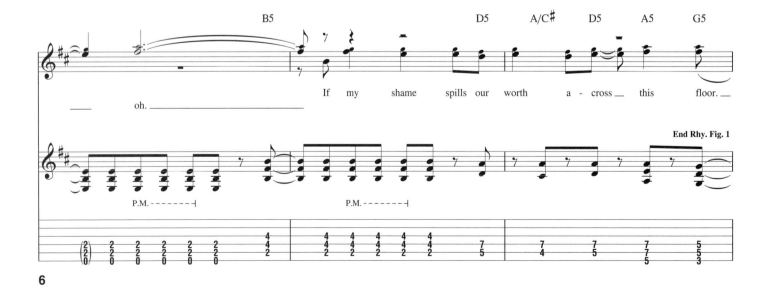

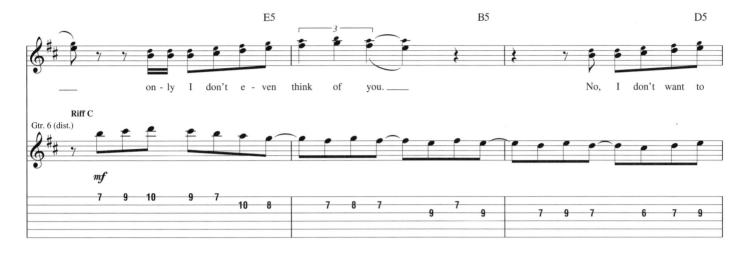

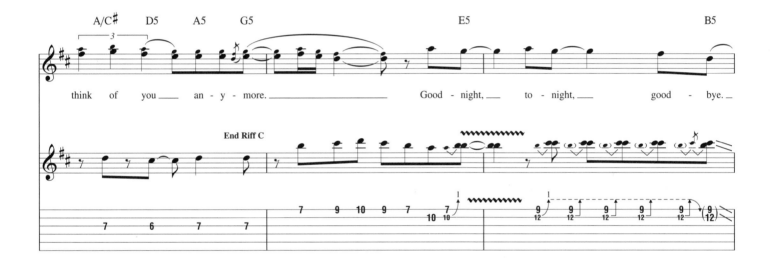

*D.S. al Coda*

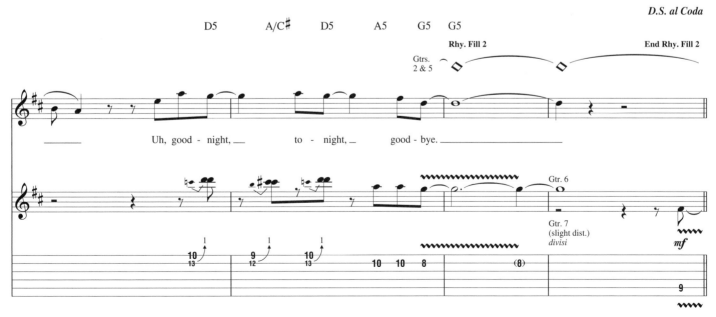

Interlude

Gtrs. 5 & 7: w/ Rhy. Fill 2          Gtr. 6 tacet          Gtr. 2: w/ Riff A (1 7/8 times)
                                                           Gtr. 3: w/ Riff A1 (2 times)
                                                           1st time, Gtrs. 5 & 7: w/ Rhy. Fill 3

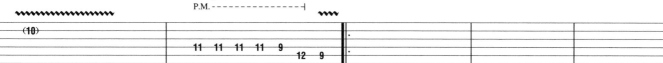

**Pre-Chorus**

**Bridge**

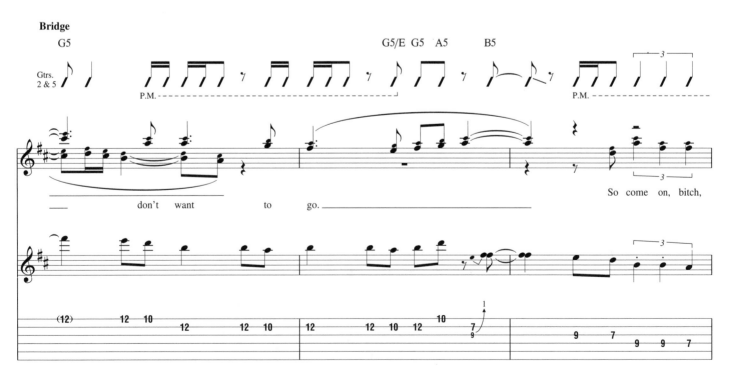

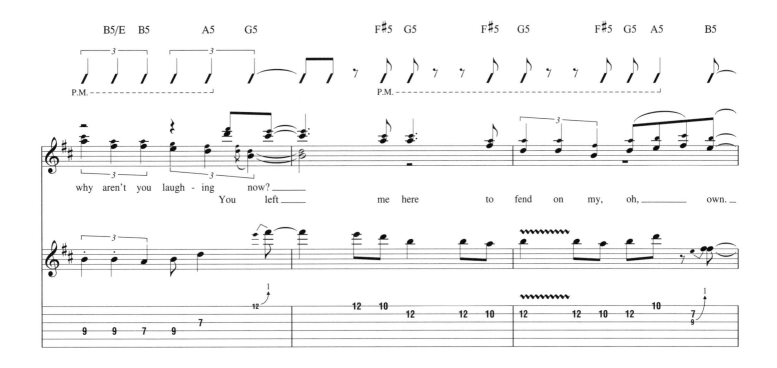

why aren't you laugh-ing now? You left ____ me here to fend on my, oh, ____ own. ____

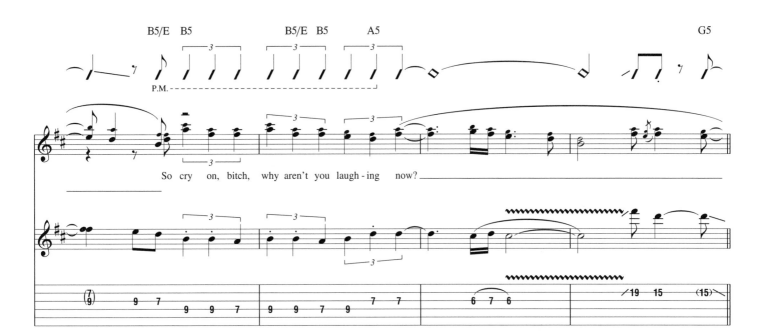

So cry on, bitch, why aren't you laugh-ing now? ____

**Chorus**

Gtrs. 2 & 5: w/ Rhy. Fig. 1 (7 1/2 times)
Gtr. 6: w/ Riff C (1 3/4 times)

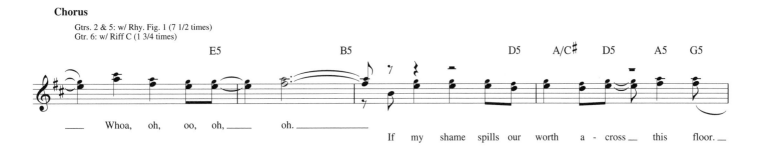

E5    B5    D5    A/C#    D5    A5    G5

____ Whoa, oh, oo, oh, ____ oh. ____    If my shame spills our worth a - cross ____ this floor.

Gtr. 6: w/ Riff D

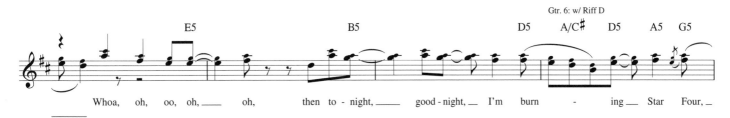

E5    B5    D5    A/C#    D5    A5    G5

Whoa, oh, oo, oh, ____ oh,    then to - night, ____ good - night, ____ I'm burn - ing ____ Star Four, ____

11

on - ly I don't e - ven think of you.___ No, I don't want to think of you___ an - y - more.

Good - night, ___ to - night, ___ good - bye. _____ Uh, good - night, ___

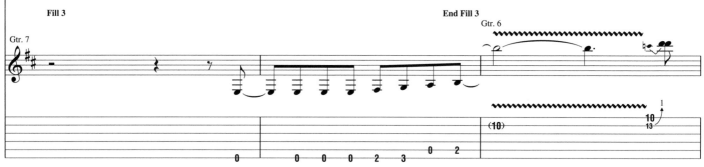

to - night, ___ good - bye. ___

Whoa, oh, oo, oh, ___ whoa, oh, oo, oh, ___

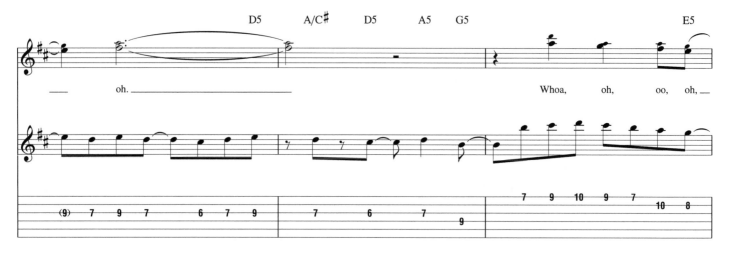

oh.

Whoa, oh, oo, oh,

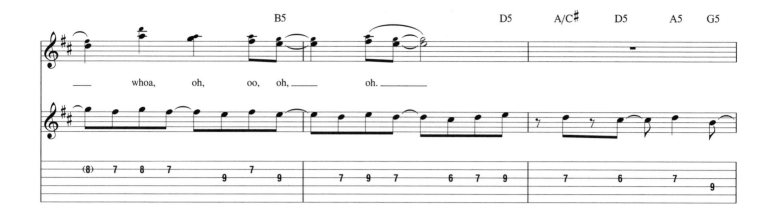

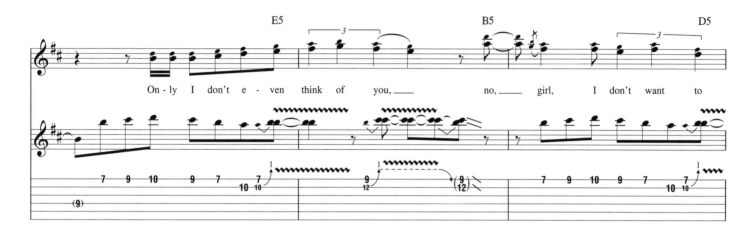

# Assassing

**Words and Music by Derek Dick, Mark Kelly, Michael Pointer, Peter Trewavas and Steve Rothery**

*w/ echo set for half-note regeneration w/ 4 repeats.

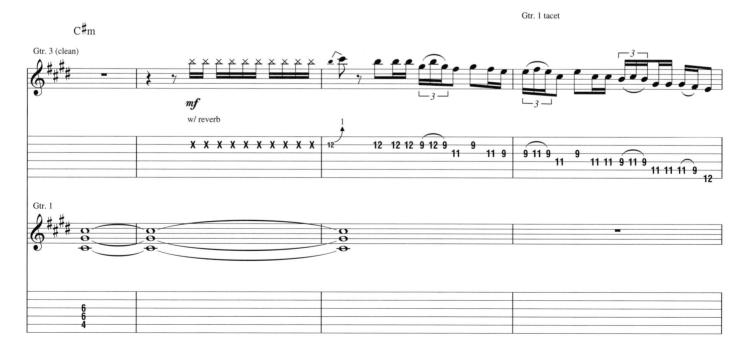

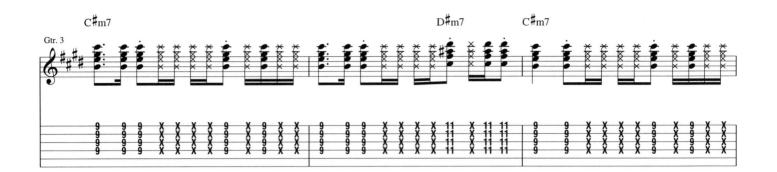

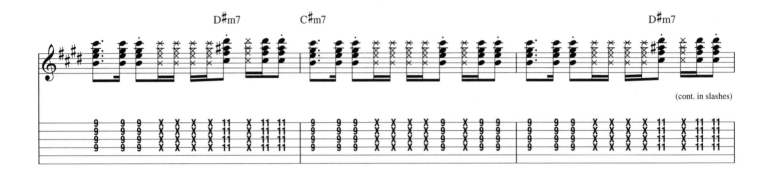

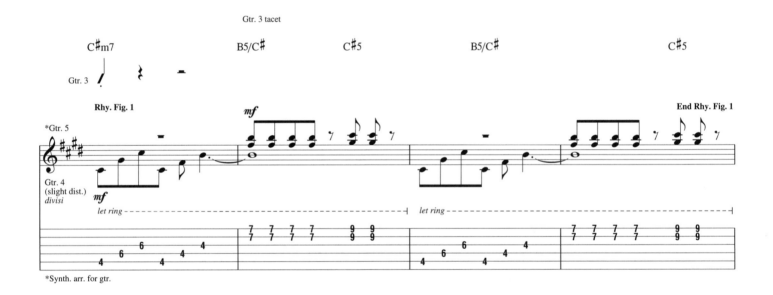

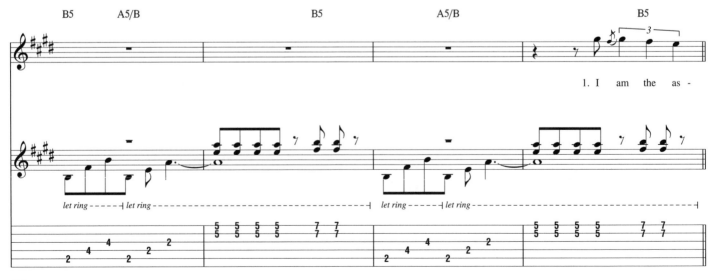

**Verse**

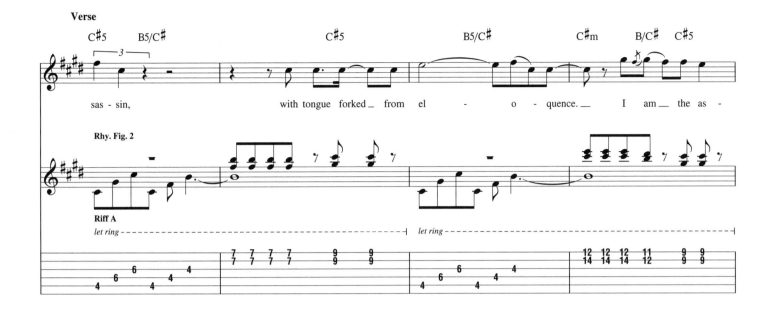

sas - sin,     with tongue forked _ from el - o - quence. _ I am _ the as -

sas - sin,     pro - vid - ing your nem - e - sis. ___ On the

**Chorus**

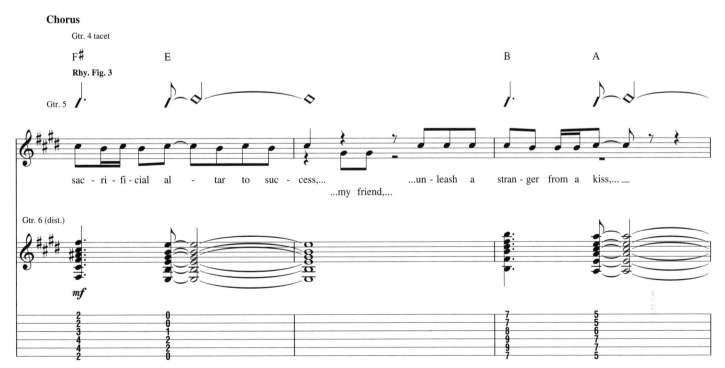

sac - ri - fi - cial al - tar to suc - cess,... ...un - leash a stran - ger from a kiss,...

...my friend,...

**Interlude**

Gtr. 4: w/ Riff A
Gtr. 5: w/ Rhy. Fig. 2
Gtr. 6 tacet

*w/ echo set for half-note regeneration w/ 3 repeats.
**w/ echo set for half-note regeneration w/ 3 repeats.

**Verse**

Gtr. 4: w/ Riff A
Gtr. 5: w/ Rhy. Fig. 2

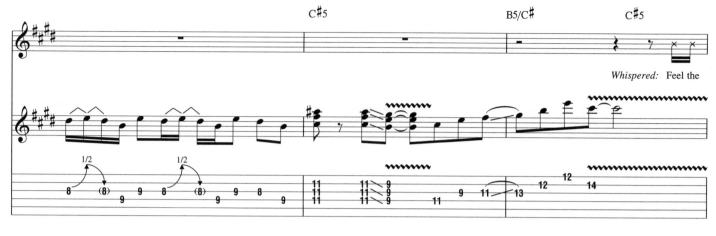

**Interlude**

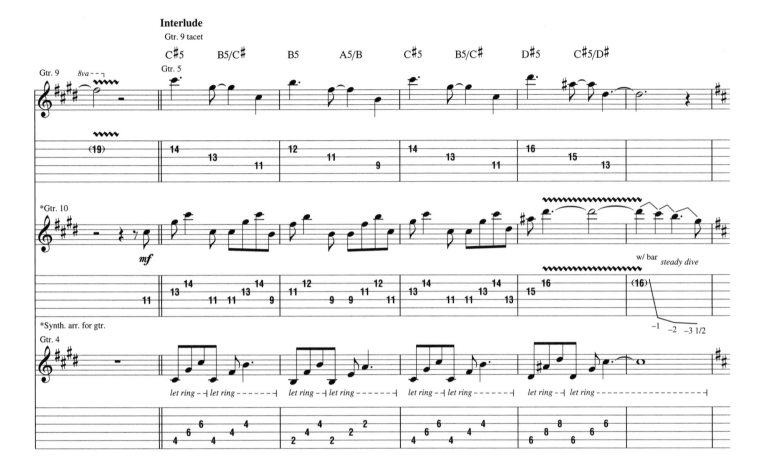

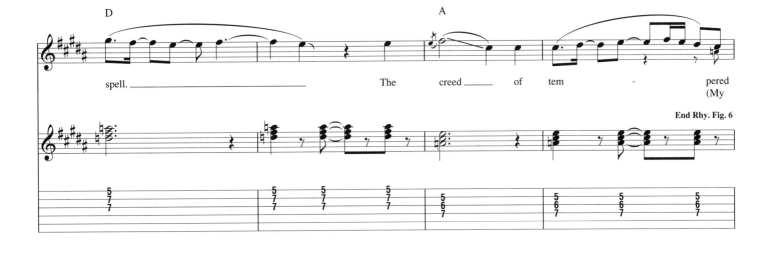

spell. _____ The creed _____ of tem - pered (My

**End Rhy. Fig. 6**

Gtr. 5: w/ Rhy. Fig. 6

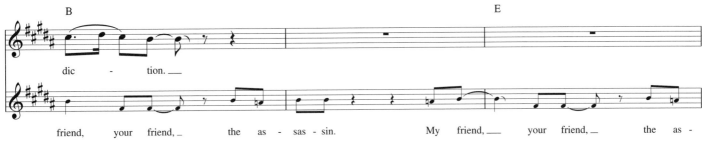

dic - tion. _____

friend, your friend, _____ the as - sas - sin. My friend, _____ your friend, _____ the as -

sas - sin. My friend, _____ your friend, _____ the as - sas - sin. My friend, _____

friend in need _____ is a friend that bleeds. _____ Let bit - ter

_____ your friend, _____ the as - sas - sin.)

si - lence in - fect the wound. _____ Let bit - ter si - lence in - fect _____ the wound.

Gtr. 5

**F#**

I am the as-sas-sin. (Your friend, I am the as-sas-sin. your friend, I am the as-

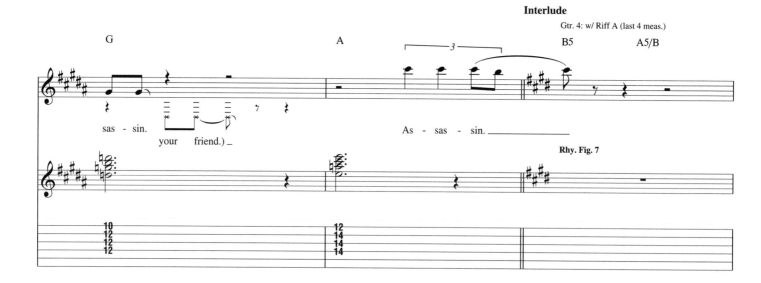

**Interlude**

Gtr. 4: w/ Riff A (last 4 meas.)

**G**                    **A**                    **B5**    **A5/B**

sas-sin. your friend.) As-sas-sin.

**Rhy. Fig. 7**

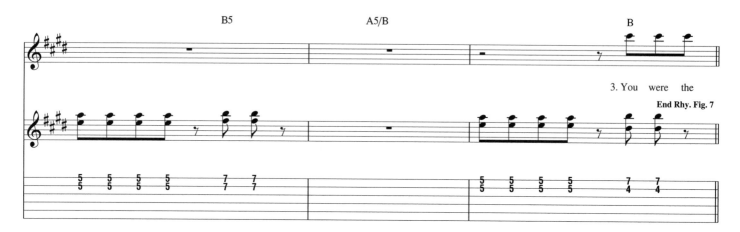

**B5**                    **A5/B**                    **B**

3. You were the

**End Rhy. Fig. 7**

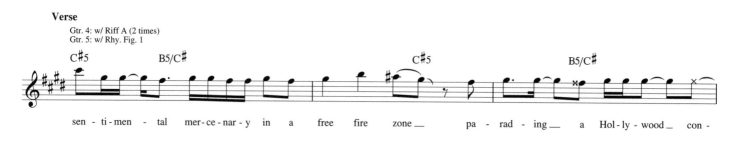

**Verse**

Gtr. 4: w/ Riff A (2 times)
Gtr. 5: w/ Rhy. Fig. 1

**C#5**         **B5/C#**                    **C#5**         **B5/C#**

sen-ti-men-tal mer-ce-nar-y in a free fire zone pa-rad-ing a Hol-ly-wood con-

Gtr. 5: w/ Rhy. Fig. 7

**C#5**         **B5**         **A5/B**                    **B5**

-science. You were a fash-ion-a-ble ob-ject-or with a u-ni-form fet-ish, Pav-

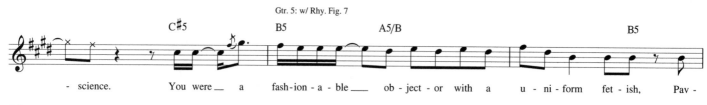

# Astronomy Dominé

**Words and Music by Syd Barrett**

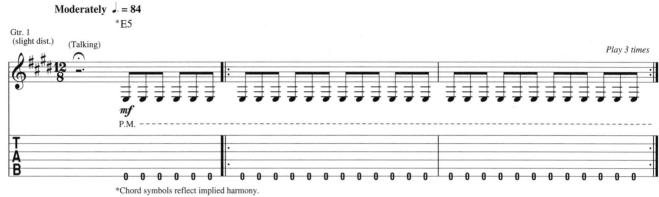

*Chord symbols reflect implied harmony.

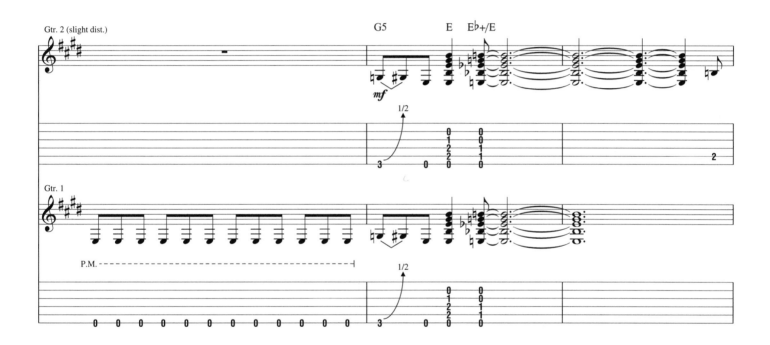

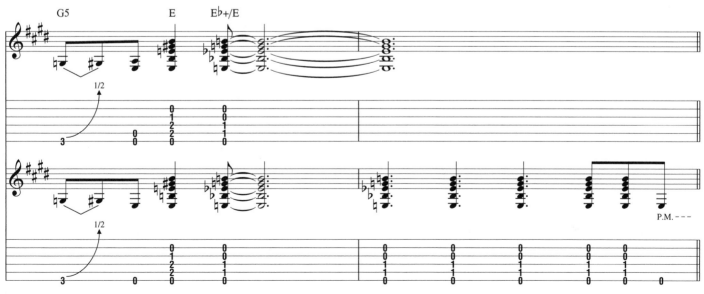

**Verse**

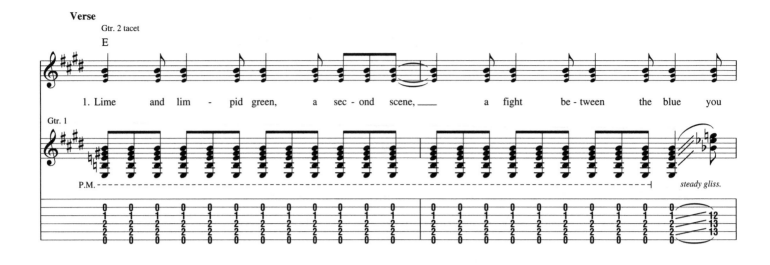

**28**

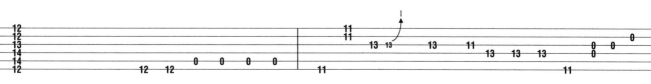

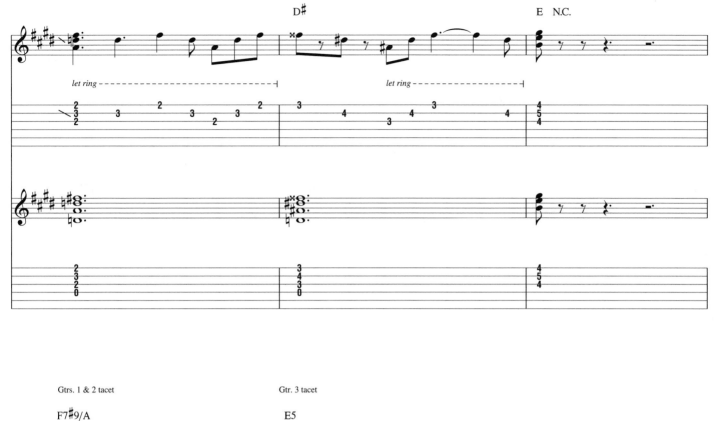

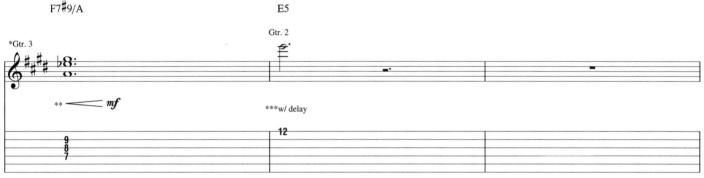

Gtrs. 1 & 2 tacet

Gtr. 3 tacet

F7#9/A

E5

Gtr. 2

*Gtr. 3

***w/ delay

**Vol. swell

*Organ arr. for gtr.

***Set for eighth-note regeneration. Repeats rapidly fade,
then gradually fade back in over next 1 1/2 meas.

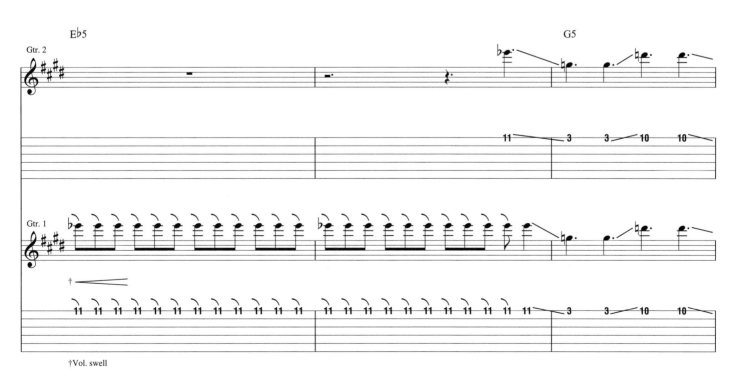

Eb5

G5

Gtr. 2

Gtr. 1

†Vol. swell

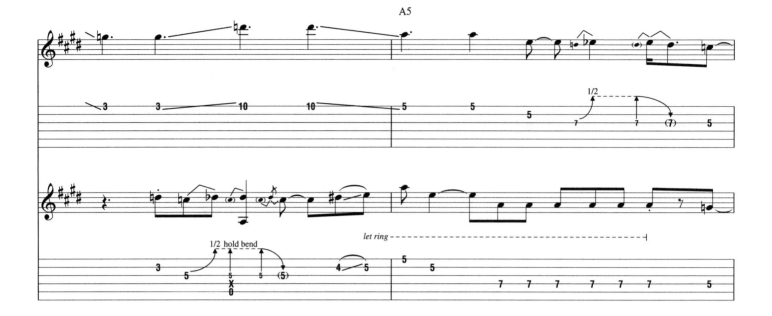

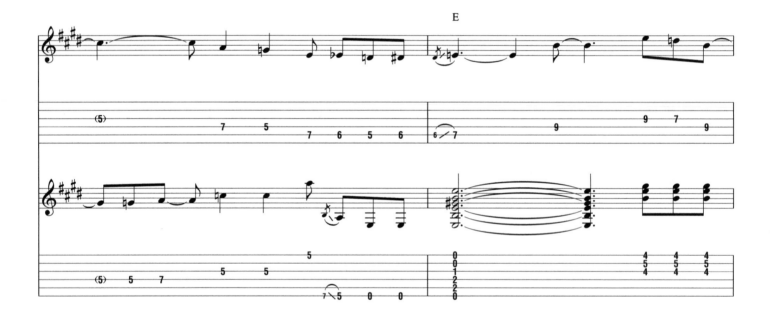

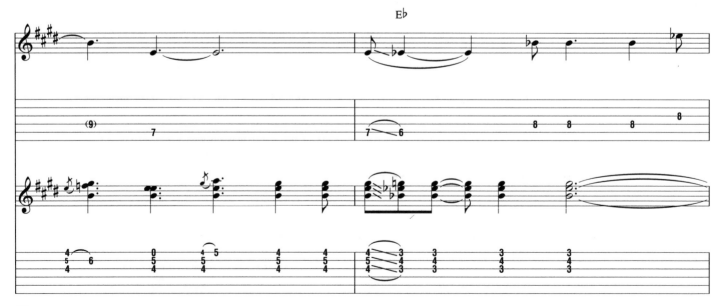

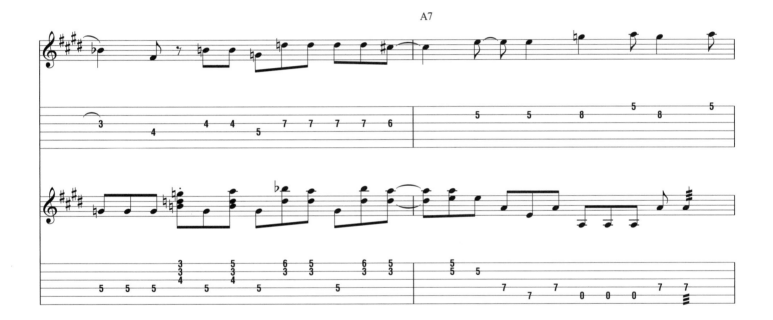

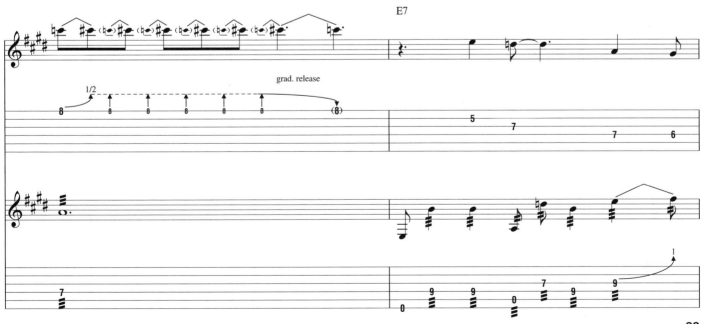

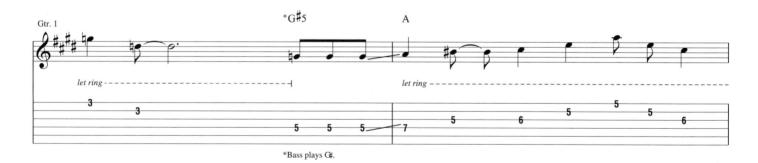

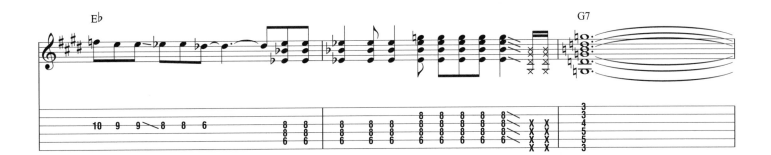

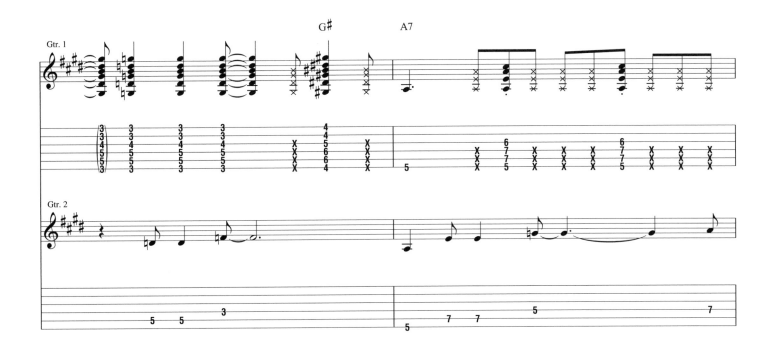

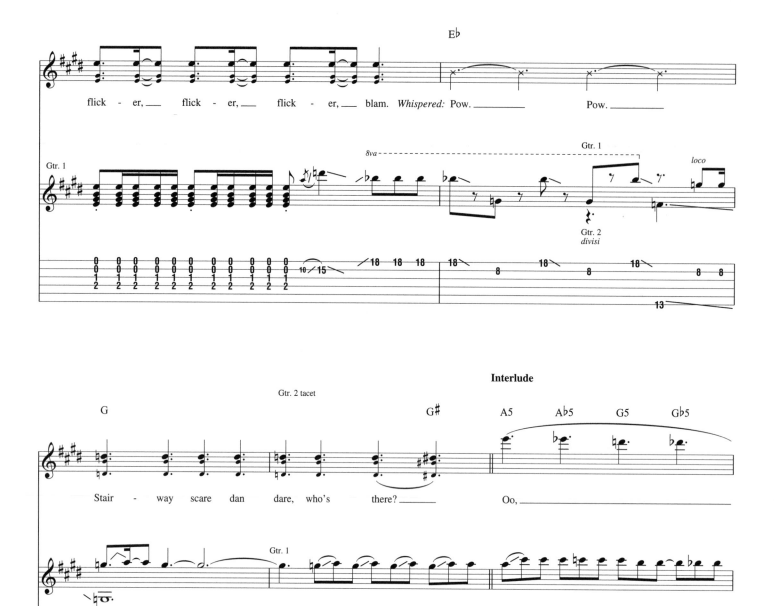

flick - er,___ flick - er,___ flick - er,___ blam. *Whispered:* Pow._____ Pow._____

**Interlude**

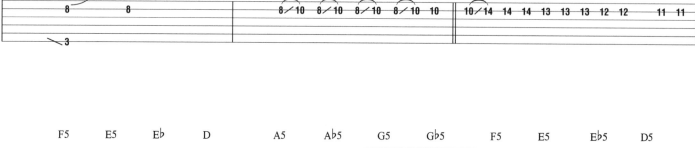

Stair - way scare dan dare, who's there? _____ Oo, _____

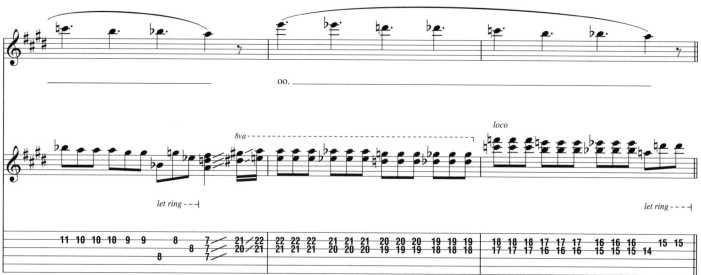

_____ oo. _____

**Outro**

*Gtr. 4 to left of slash in tab.

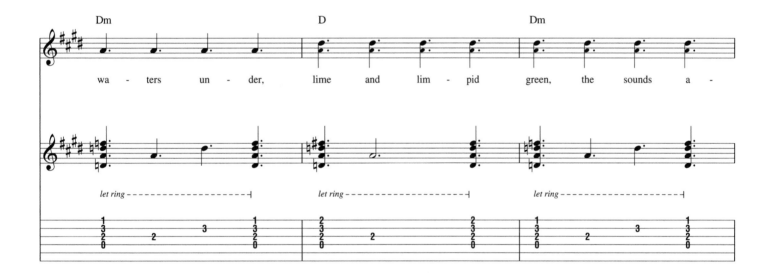

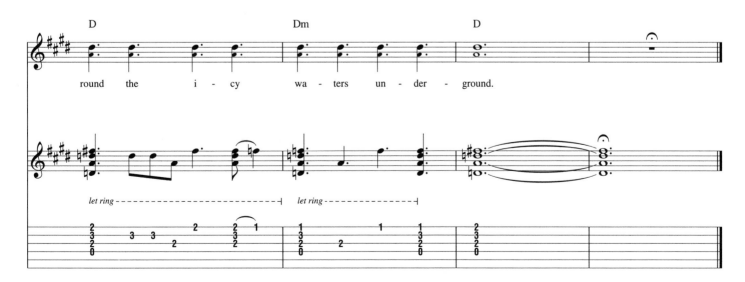

# Carry On Wayward Son

**Words and Music by Kerry Livgren**

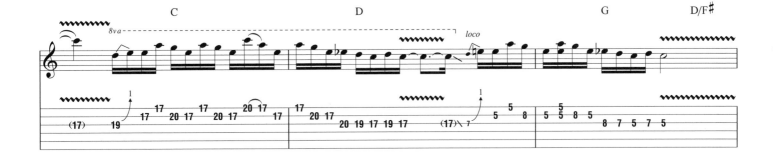

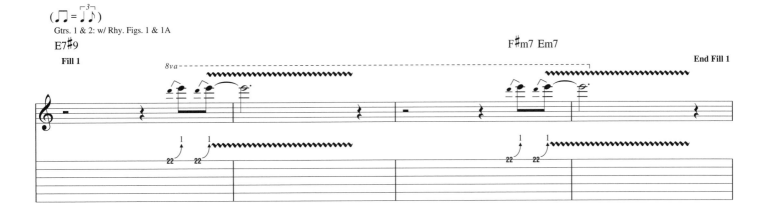

1. Once I rose a - bove the noise and con - fu - sion, just to get a glimpse be - yond this il - lu - sion.
2. Mas - quer - ad - ing as a man with a rea - son. My cha - rade is the e - vent of the sea - son.

I was soar - ing ev - er high - er, but I flew too high.
And if I claim to be a wise man, well, it sure - ly means that I don't know.

*Played as even eighth notes.

from Queensrÿche - *Empire*

# Empire

### Words and Music by Geoff Tate and Michael Wilton

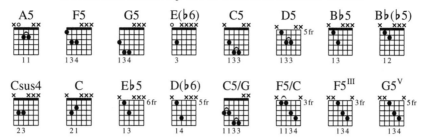

**Intro**

**Moderately slow rock**  ♩ = 80

*Next message, saved, Saturday at 9:24 P.M. "Sorry, I'm just...it's starting to hit me like a, um, um, two ton heavy thing."*

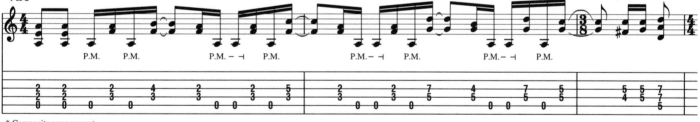

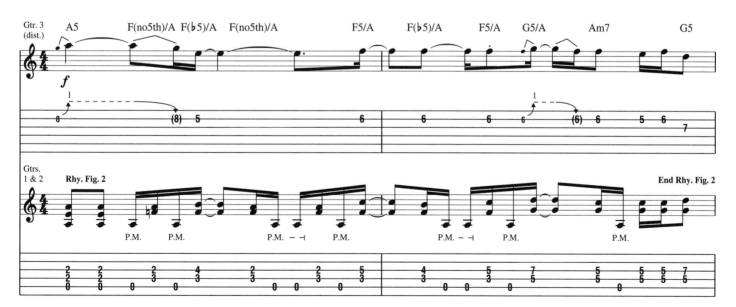

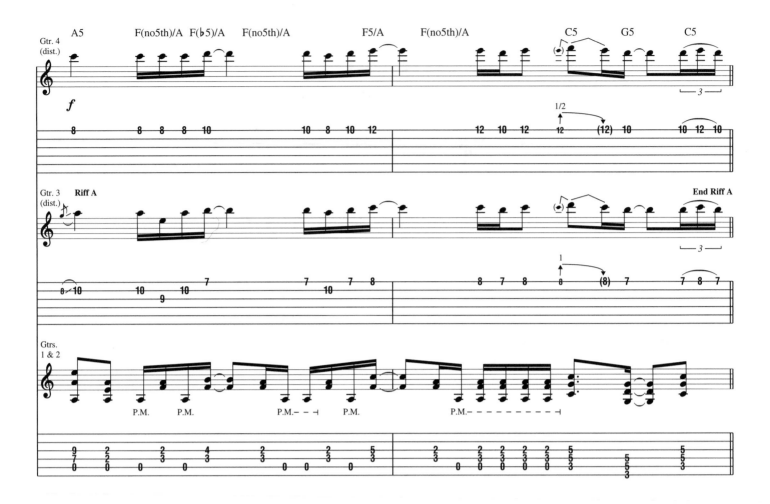

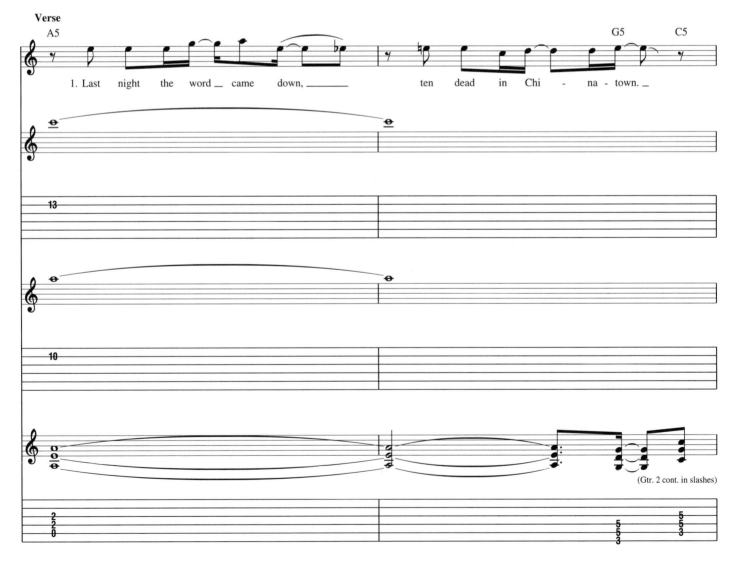

at the cin-e-ma show. ___ Got-ta hus-tle if he wants an ed-u-ca-tion, ___

yeah, he's got-ta long way to go. ___ Now he's out on the streets ___ all day ___ sell-ing

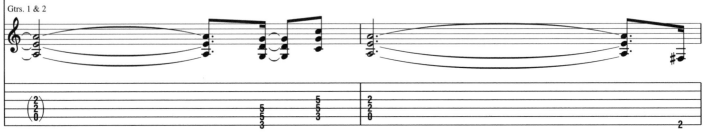

crack to the peo-ple who pay. ___ Got an A- K- for-ty- sev-en for his best friend,

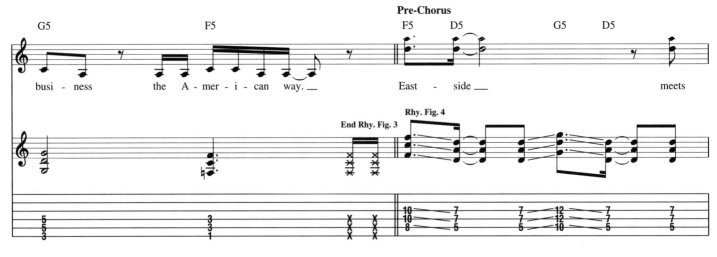

**Pre-Chorus**

busi- ness the A-mer-i-can way. ___ East - side ___ meets

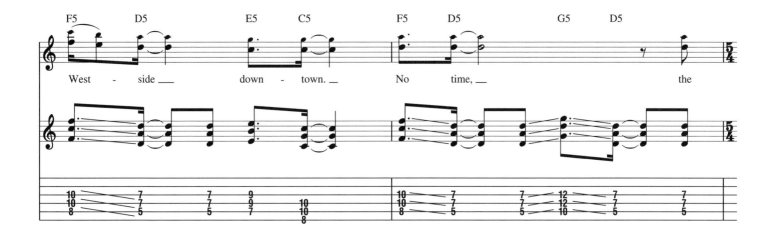

West - side \_\_ down - town. No time, \_\_ the

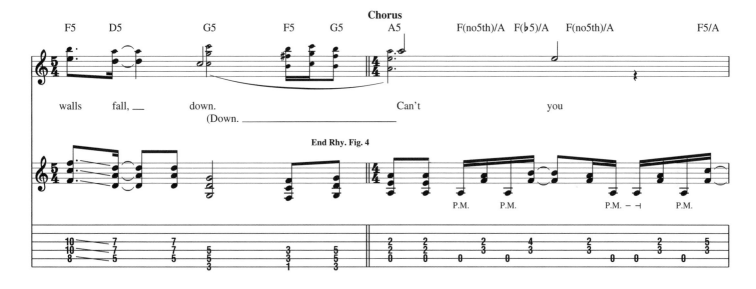

**Chorus**

walls fall, \_\_ down. Can't you
(Down. _____ )

**End Rhy. Fig. 4**

P.M. P.M. P.M. P.M.

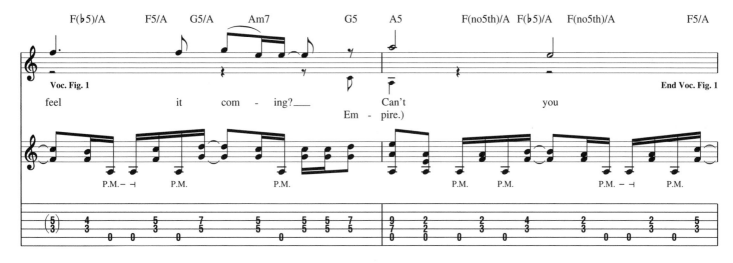

**Voc. Fig. 1** **End Voc. Fig. 1**

feel it com - ing?\_\_ Can't you you
Em - pire.)

P.M. P.M. P.M. P.M. P.M. P.M.

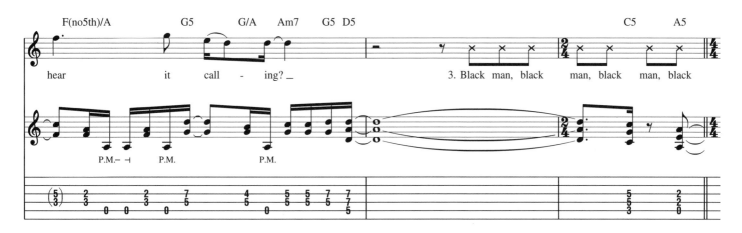

hear it call - ing? \_ 3. Black man, black man, black man, black

P.M. P.M. P.M.

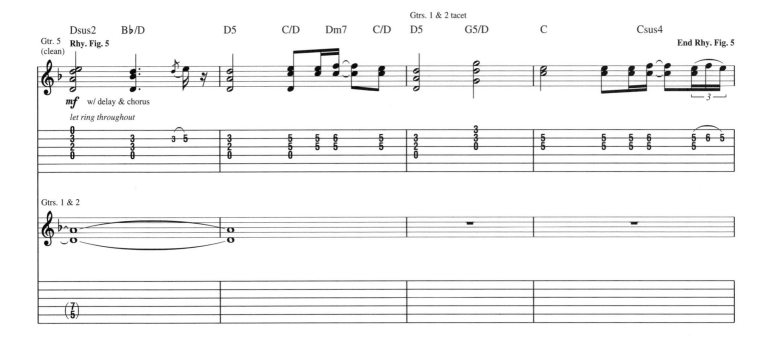

*Spoken: In fiscal year 1986 to '87 the local, state, and federal governments spent a combined total of 60.6 million dollars on law enforcement.*

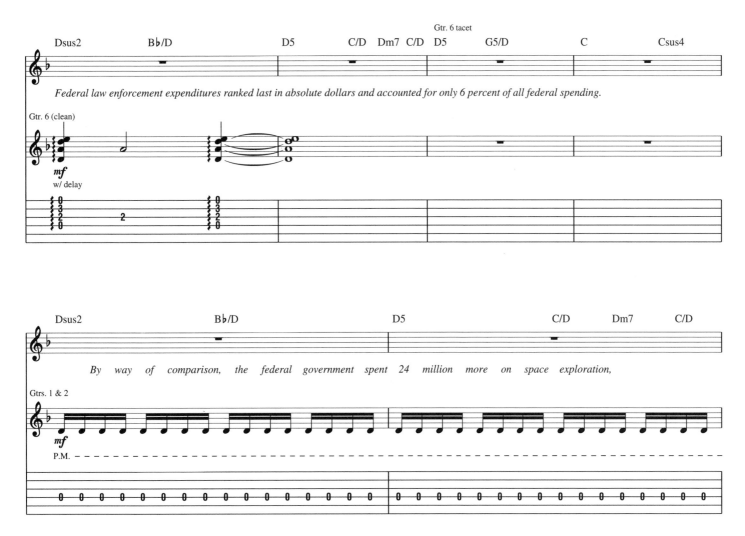

*Federal law enforcement expenditures ranked last in absolute dollars and accounted for only 6 percent of all federal spending.*

*By way of comparison, the federal government spent 24 million more on space exploration,*

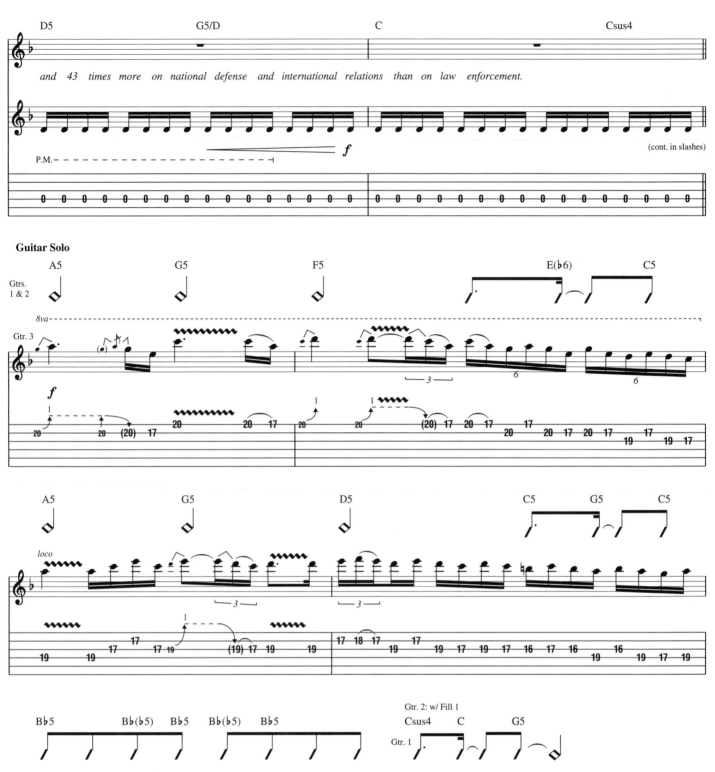

and 43 times more on national defense and international relations than on law enforcement.

**Guitar Solo**

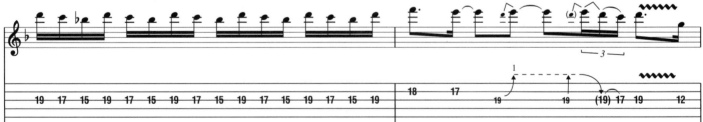

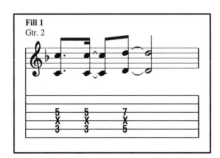

**Fill 1**
Gtr. 2

**Outro**
Bkgd. Voc.: w/ Voc. Fig. 2 (last meas.)
Gtrs. 1 & 2: w/ Rhy. Fig. 2 (4 times)
Gtr. 3: w/ Riff A (2 times)

# Eyes of a Stranger

**Words and Music by Chris DeGarmo and Geoff Tate**

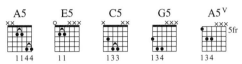

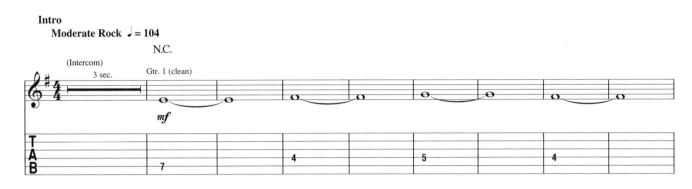

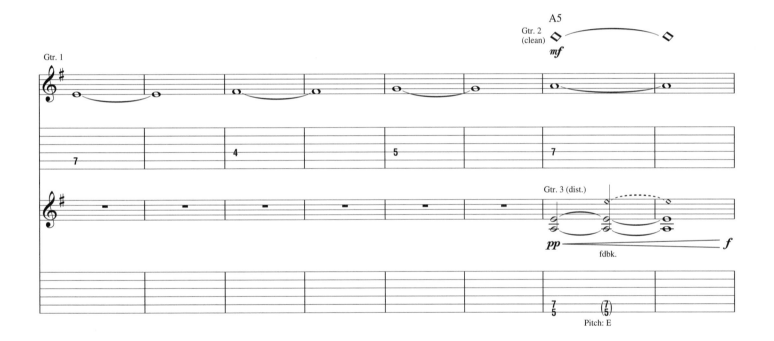

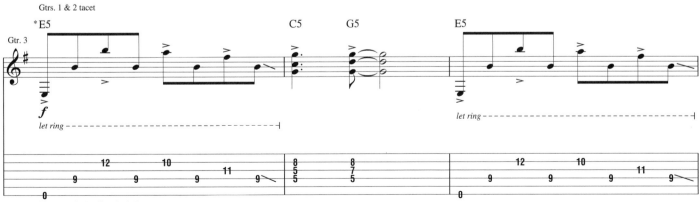

*Chord symbols reflect basic harmony.

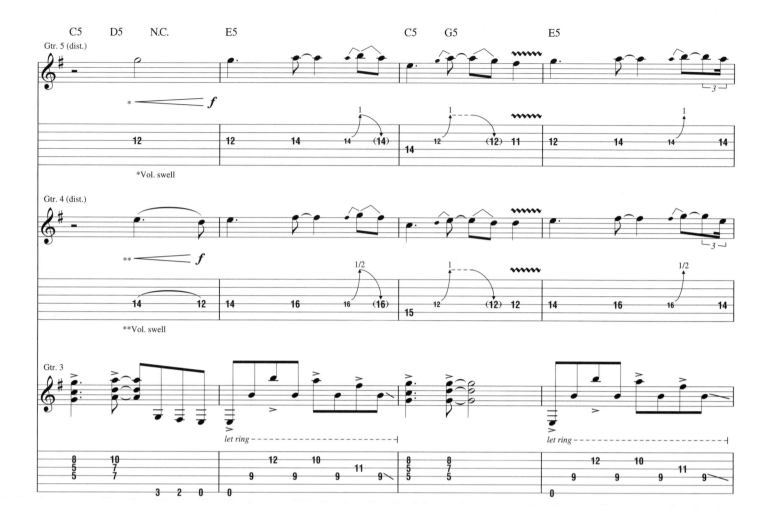

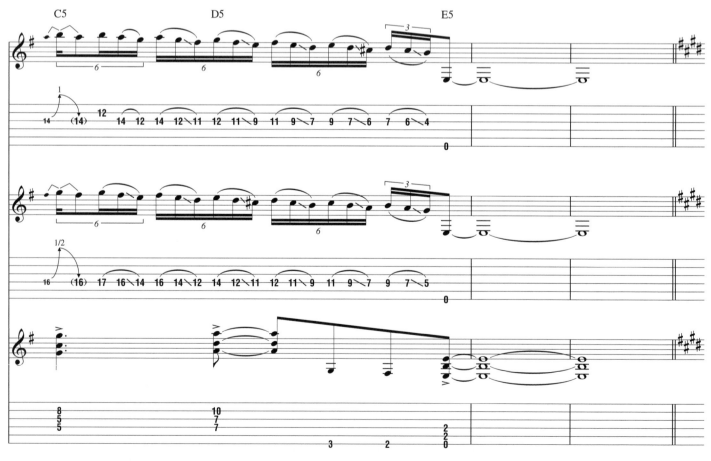

**Verse**

Gtrs. 3, 4 & 5 tacet

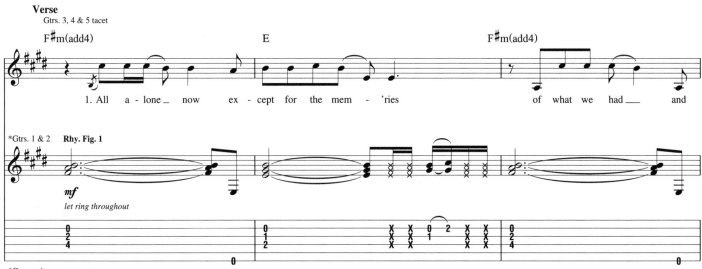

1. All a - lone now ex - cept for the mem - 'ries of what we had and

*Composite arrangement

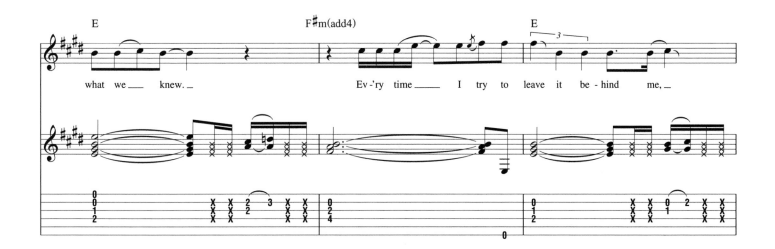

what we knew. Ev - 'ry time I try to leave it be - hind me,

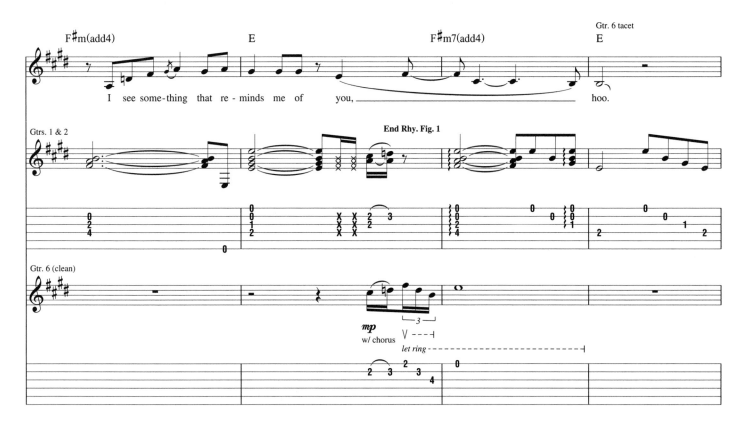

I see some-thing that re - minds me of you, hoo.

Ev-'ry night ___ the dreams re-turn to haunt me, ___ your ros-a-ry ___ wrapped a-round your throat. ___ I lie a-wake ___ and sweat, a-fraid ___ to fall a-sleep. ___ I see your face ___ look-ing back ___ at me. ___

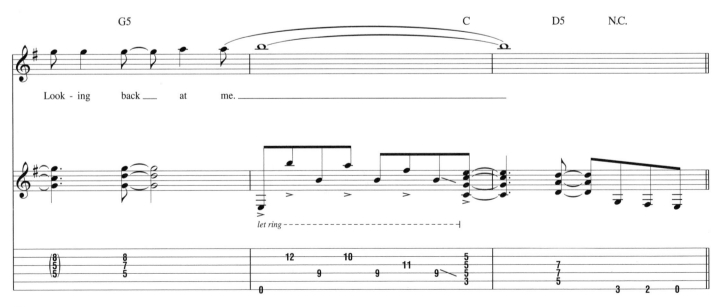

Look-ing back ___ at me. ___

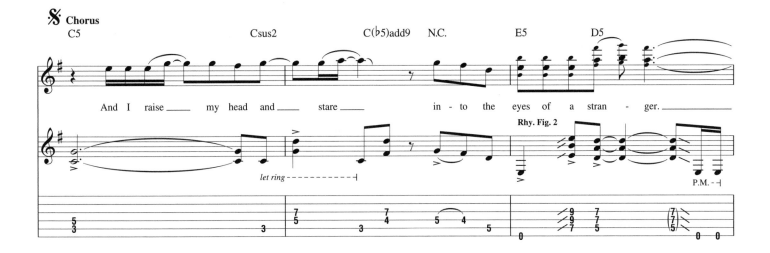

And I raise ___ my head and ___ stare ___ in - to the eyes of a stran - ger. ___

I've al - ways known ___ that the mir - ror nev - er lies. ___

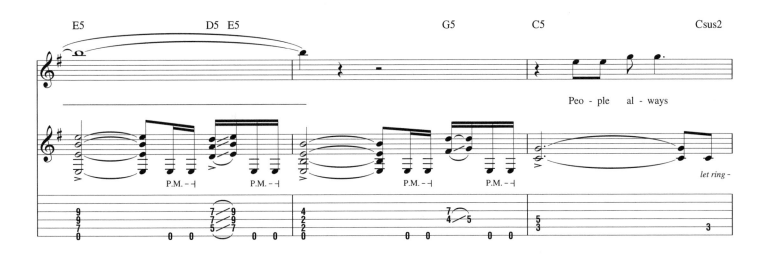

Peo - ple al - ways

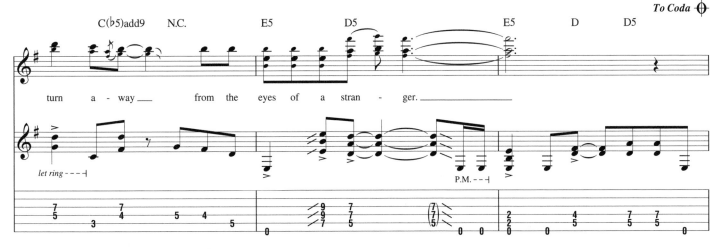

turn a - way ___ from the eyes of a stran - ger. ___

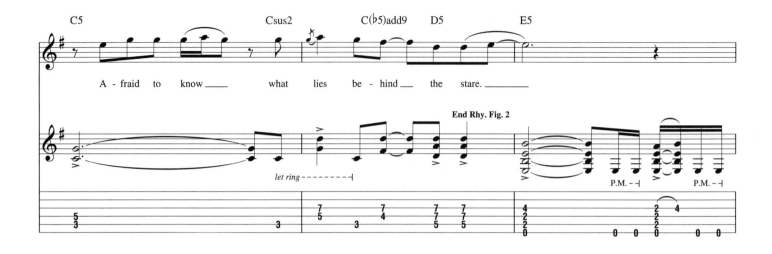

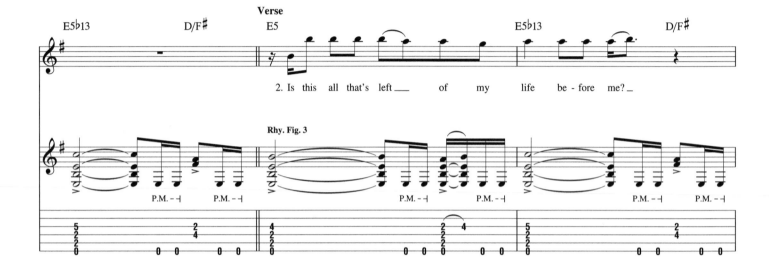

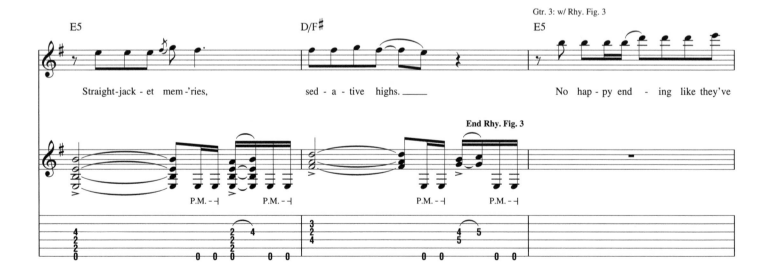

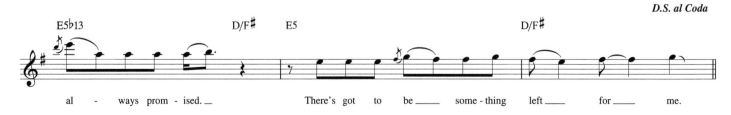

## ⊕ Coda

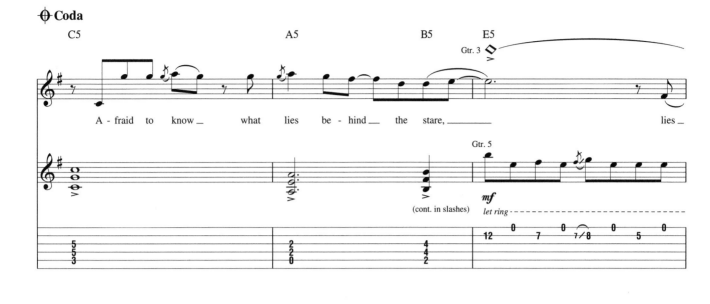

A - fraid to know___ what lies be - hind___ the stare,_____ lies_

### Guitar Solo

Gtrs. 3 & 5 tacet

___ be - hind my stare.

*Chord symbols reflect implied harmony.

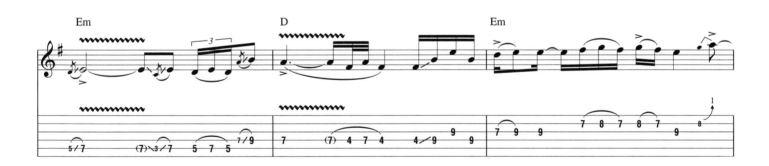

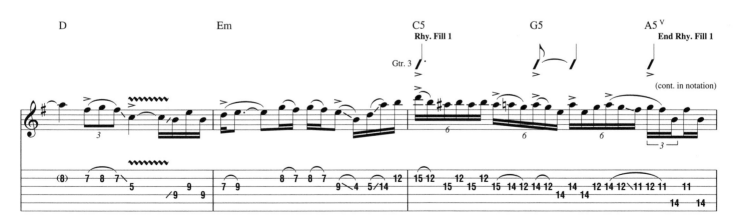

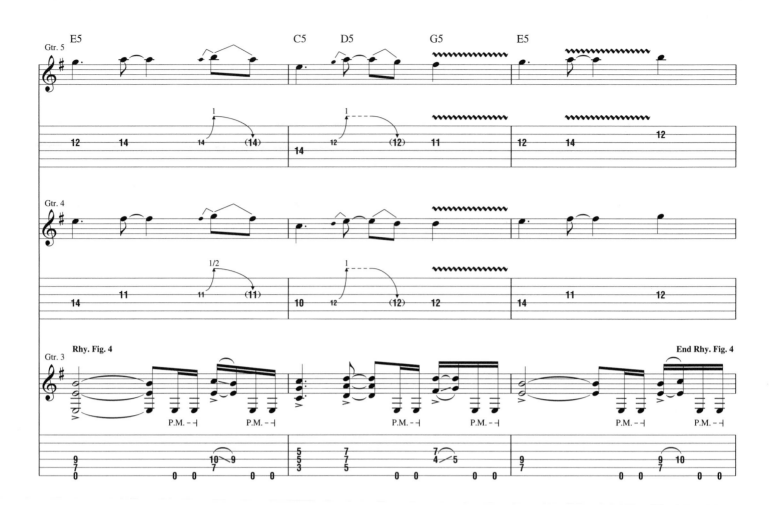

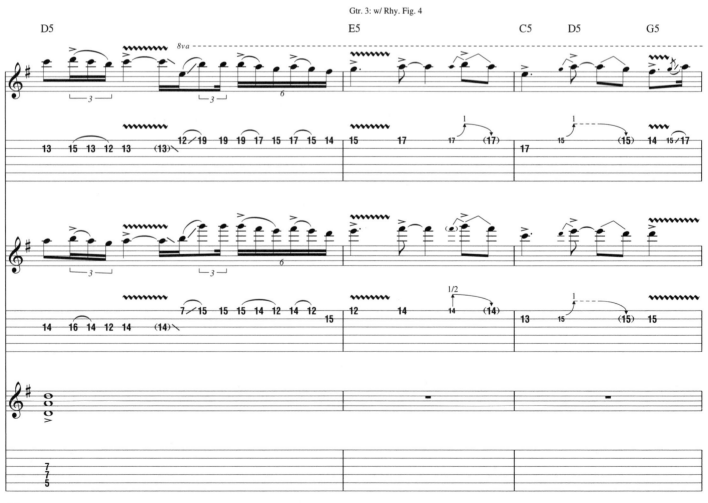

Gtr. 3: w/ Rhy. Fill 1

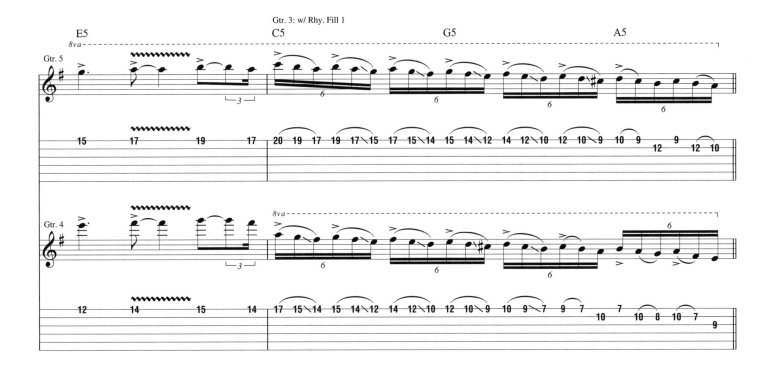

**Bridge**

Gtrs. 4 & 5 tacet

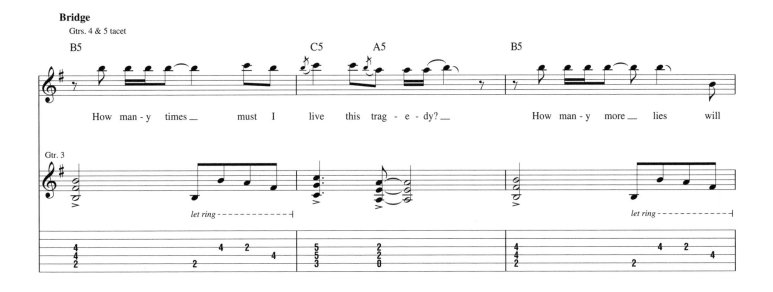

How man - y times __ must I live this trag - e - dy? __ How man - y more __ lies will

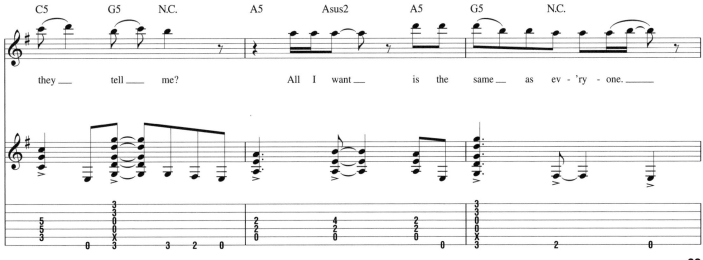

they __ tell __ me? All I want __ is the same __ as ev - 'ry - one. __

**Chorus**

Why am I here, and for __ how __ long? And I raise __ my head and __ stare in - to the

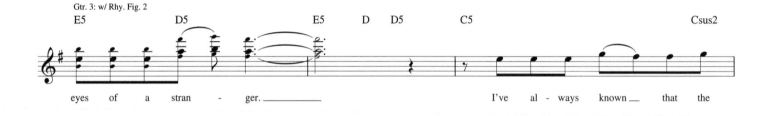

Gtr. 3: w/ Rhy. Fig. 2

eyes of a stran - ger. __ I've al - ways known __ that the

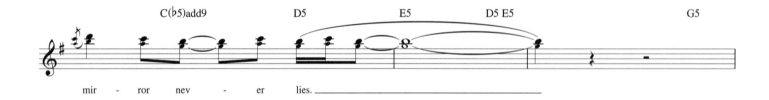

mir - ror nev - er lies. __

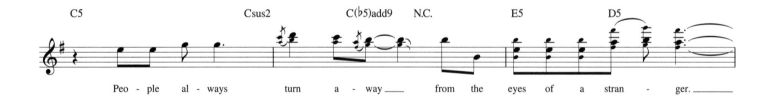

Peo - ple al - ways turn a - way __ from the eyes of a stran - ger. __

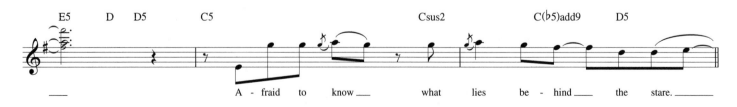

__ A - fraid to know __ what lies be - hind __ the stare. __

64

**Outro**

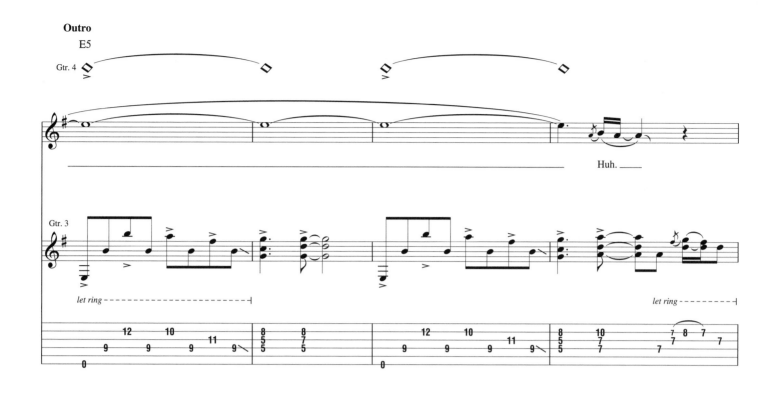

Huh. ____

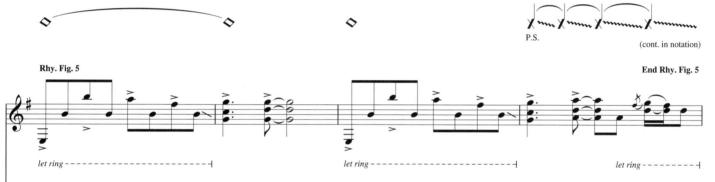

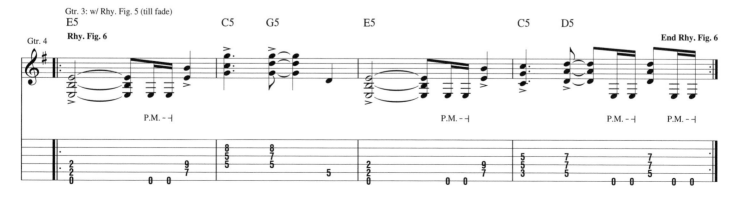

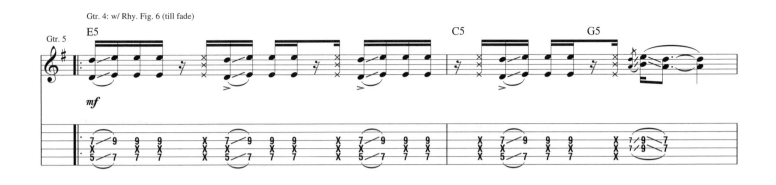

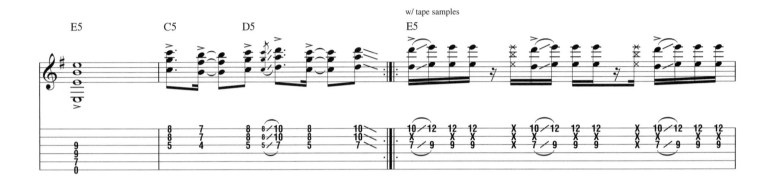

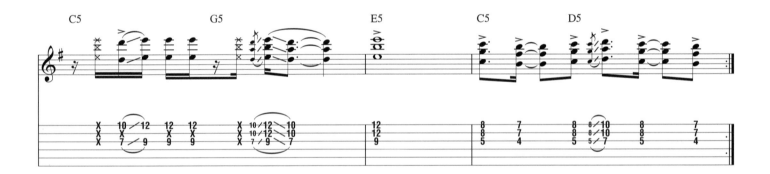

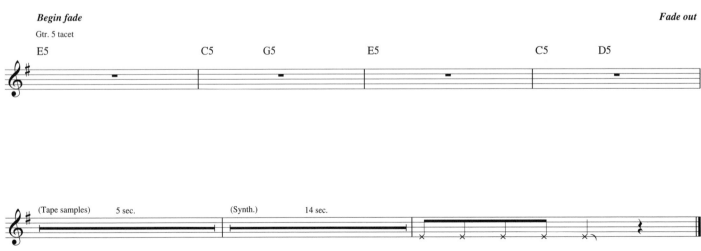

**66**

from Emerson, Lake & Palmer – *Trilogy*

# From the Beginning

### Words and Music by Greg Lake

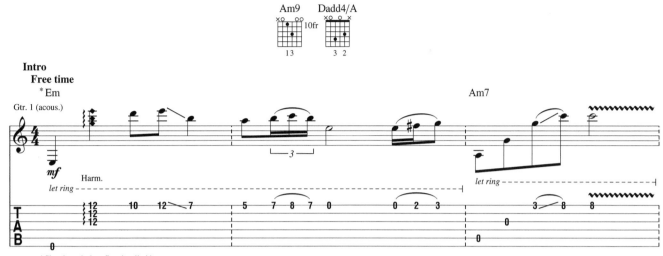

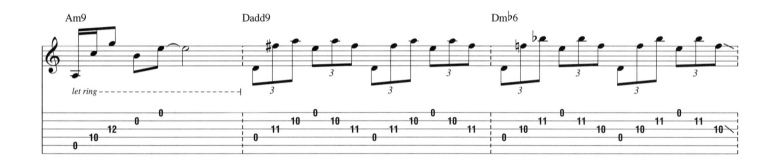

*Chord symbols reflect implied harmony.

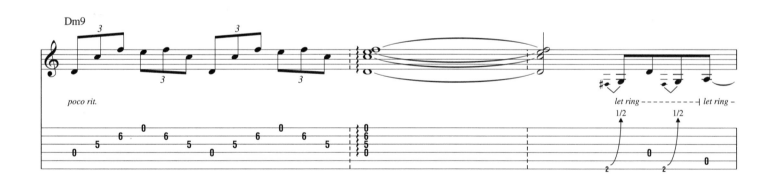

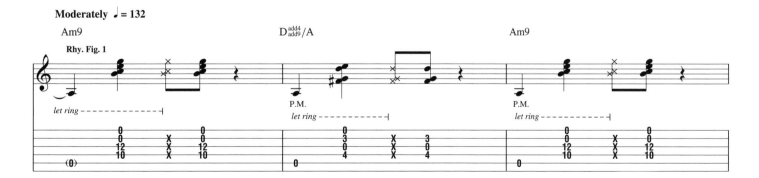

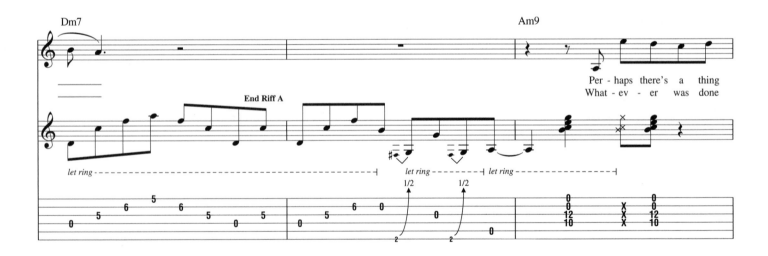

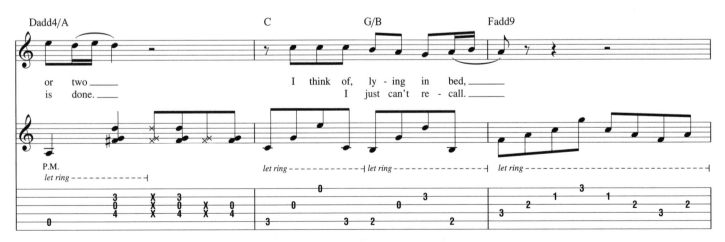

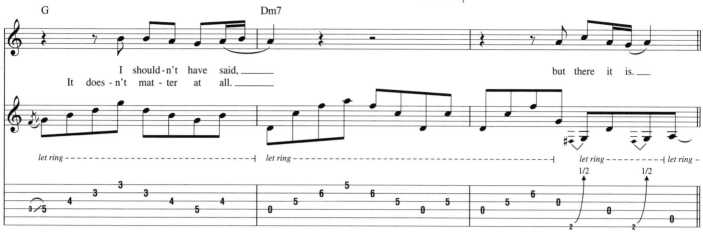

Interlude

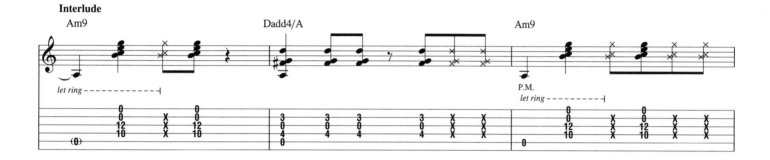

Chorus

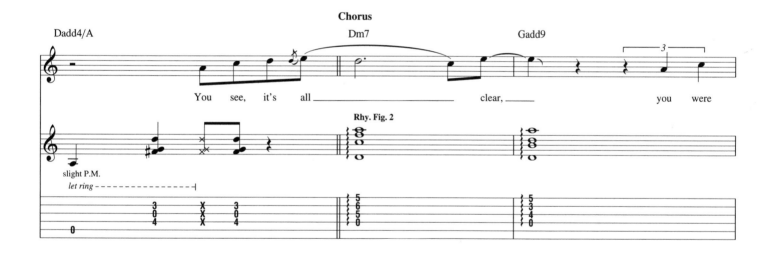

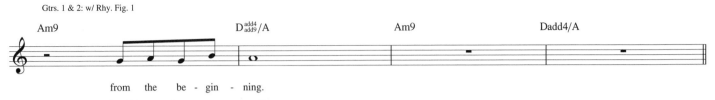

Gtrs. 1 & 2: w/ Rhy. Fig. 1

from the be - gin - ning.

**Coda**

**Interlude**

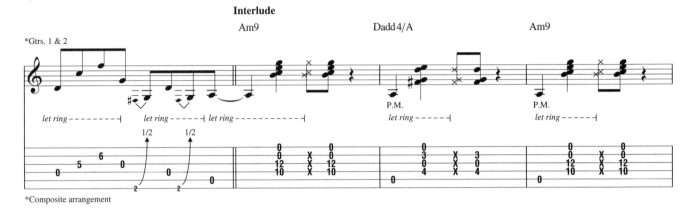

*Composite arrangement

**Chorus**

Gtr. 2: w/ Rhy. Fig. 2

You see, it's all _____ clear, you were meant to be __ here __

**A tempo**

Gtr. 1: w/ Rhy. Fig. 1 (1st 2 meas.)

from the be - gin - ning.

70

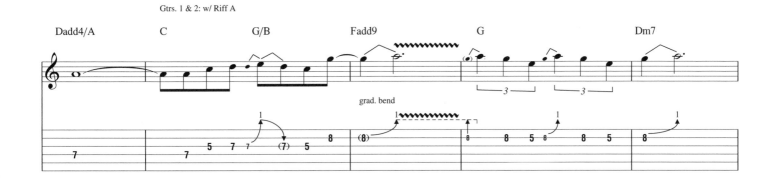

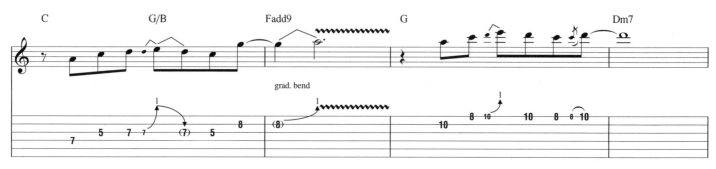

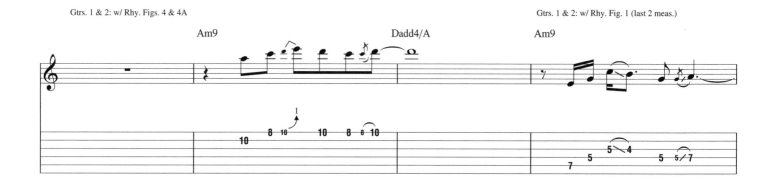

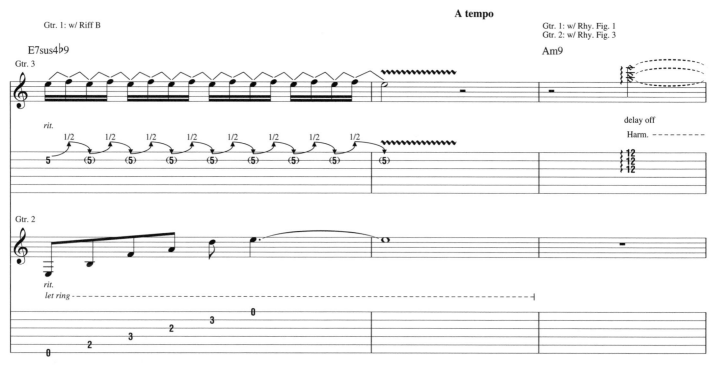

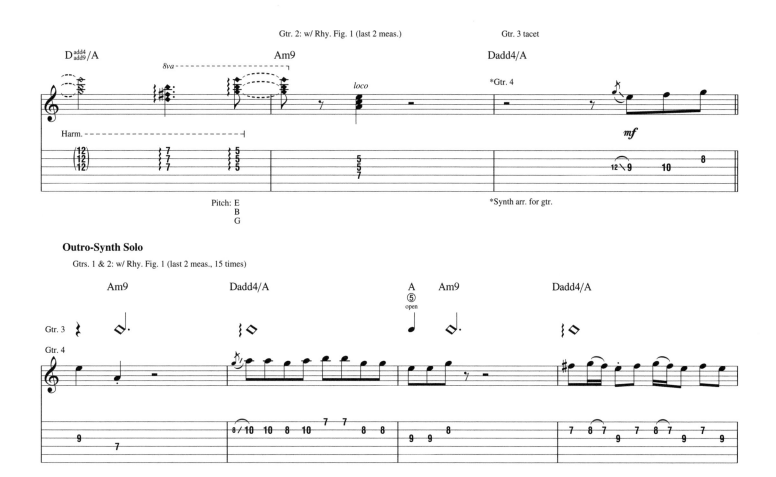

**Outro-Synth Solo**

Gtrs. 1 & 2: w/ Rhy. Fig. 1 (last 2 meas., 15 times)

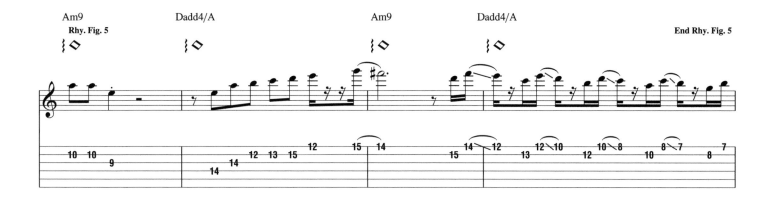

Gtr. 3: w/ Rhy. Fig. 5 (3 1/4 times)

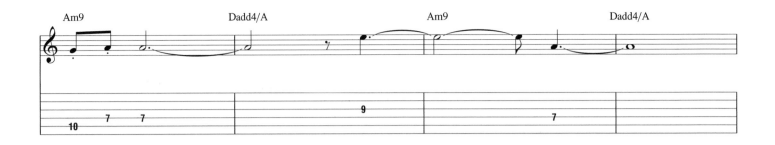

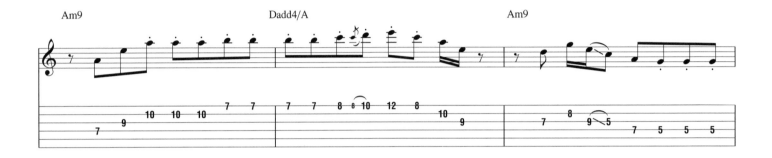

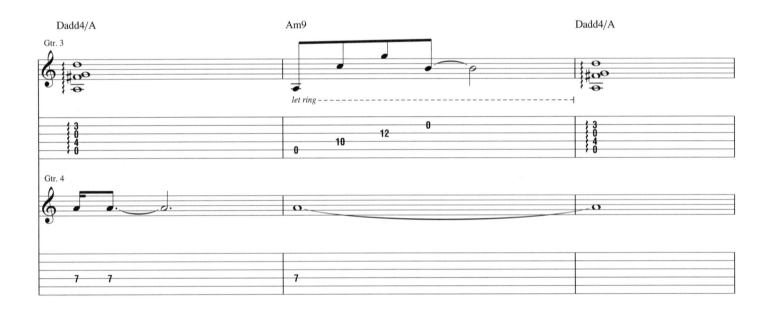

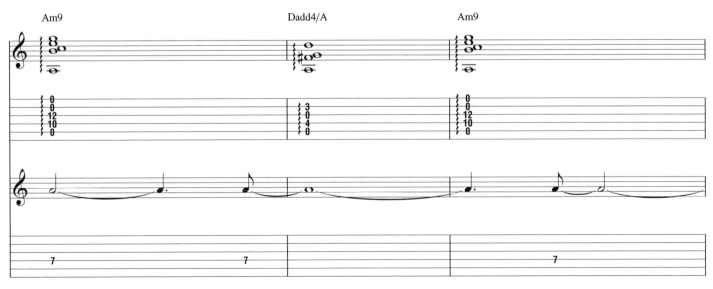

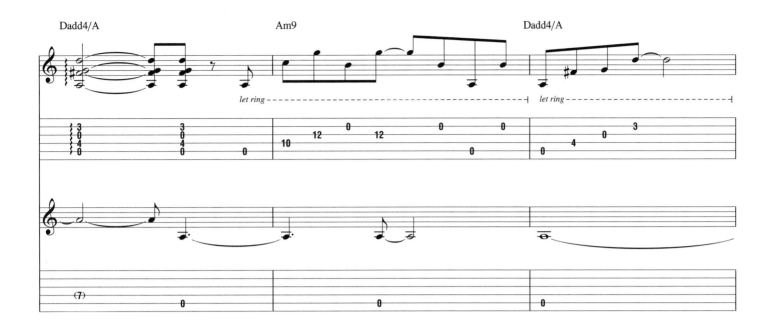

# Ghost of Karelia

### Words and Music by Brann Dailor, William Hinds, William Kelliher and Troy Sanders

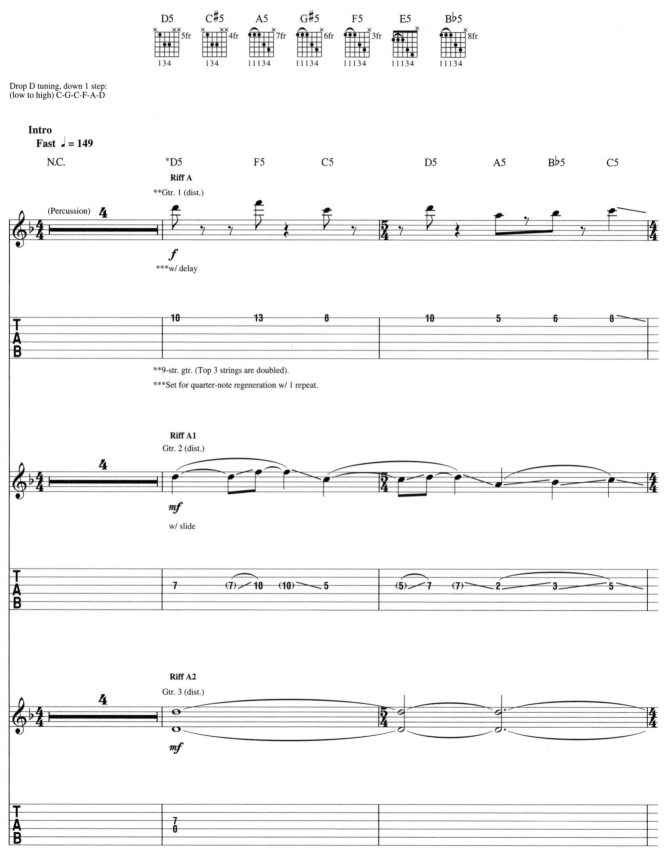

*Chord symbols reflect implied harmony.

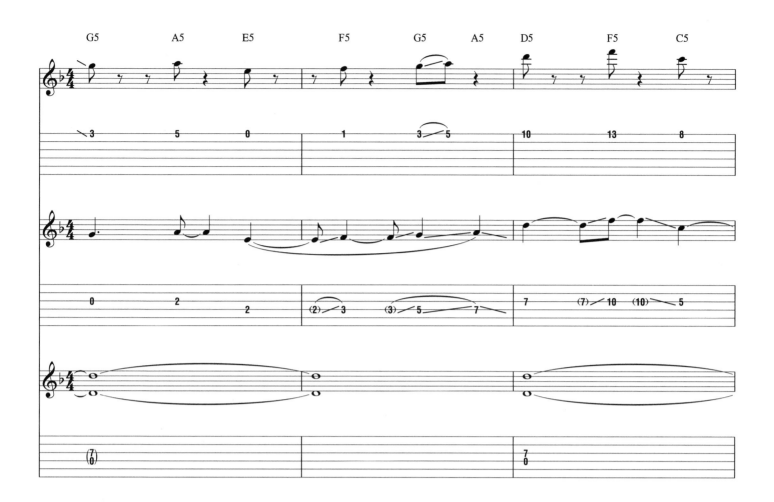

**Interlude**

Gtrs. 1, 2 & 3 tacet

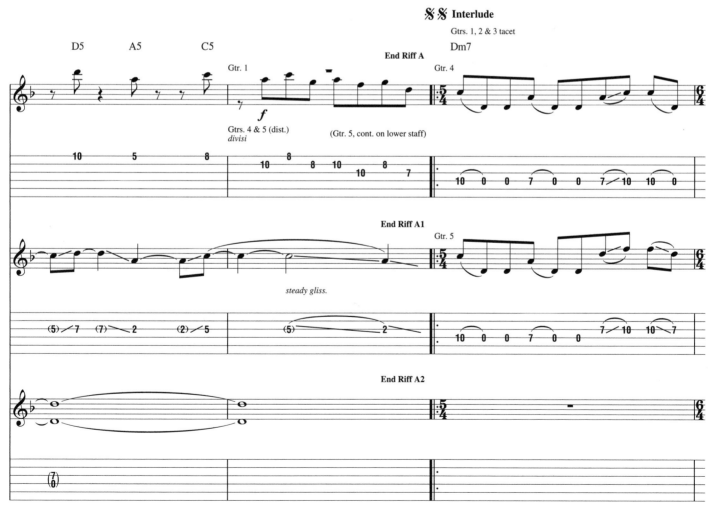

## Verse

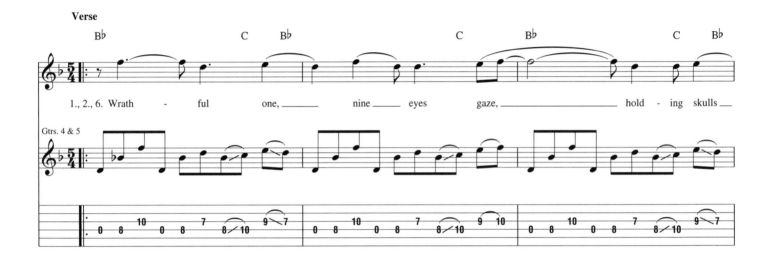

1., 2., 6. Wrath - ful one, ___ nine ___ eyes gaze, ___ hold - ing skulls ___

*Gtrs. 4 & 5*

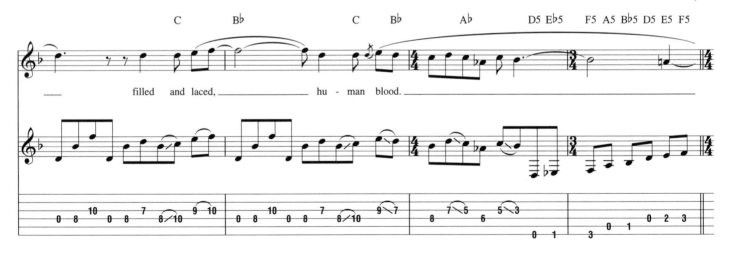

___ filled and laced, ___ hu - man blood. ___

*To Coda 2*

## Interlude

1st time, Gtrs. 1, 2 & 3: w/ Riffs A, A1 & A2
Gtrs. 4 & 5 tacet
2nd time, Gtrs. 1, 2 & 3: w/ Riffs A, A1 & A2 (1st 6 meas.)

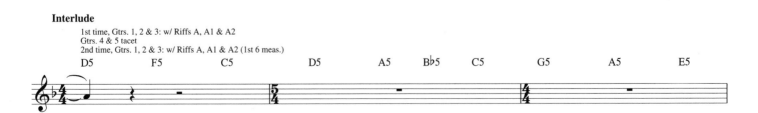

**Chorus**

Gtrs. 2 & 3 tacet

Shades of _____ dark - ened ____

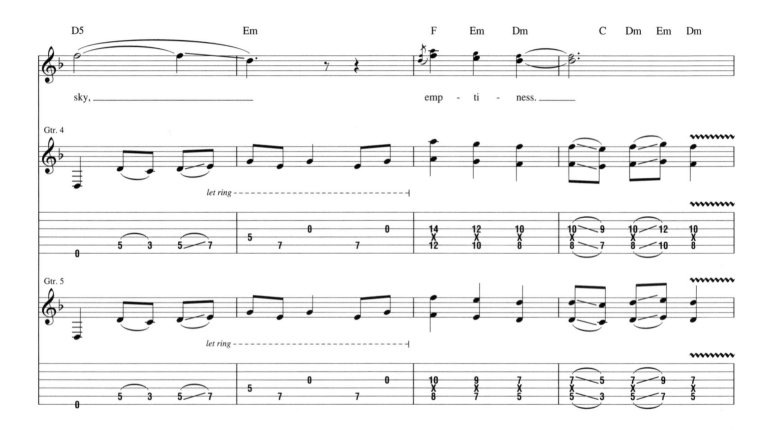

sky, _____ emp - ti - ness. ____

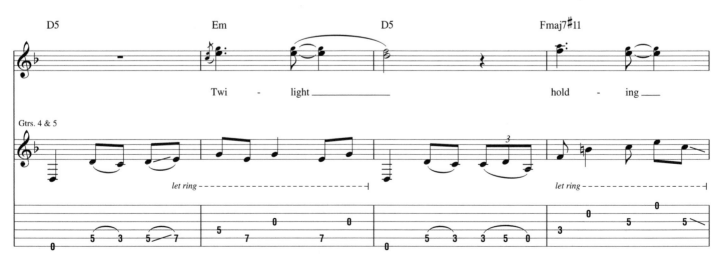

Twi - light _____ hold - ing ____

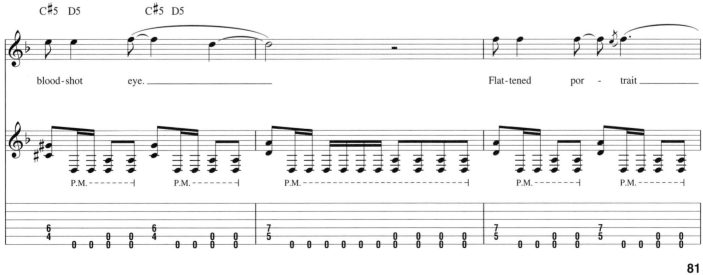

Gtrs. 4 & 5: w/ Rhy. Fig. 3 (2 times)
Gtrs. 6 & 7: w/ Riff B (2 times)

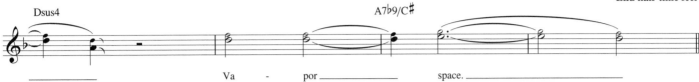

Hear dirt _____ waves _____ wad - ing forth. _____

*To Coda 1* $\oplus$
**End half-time feel**

Va - por _____ space. _____

**Bridge**

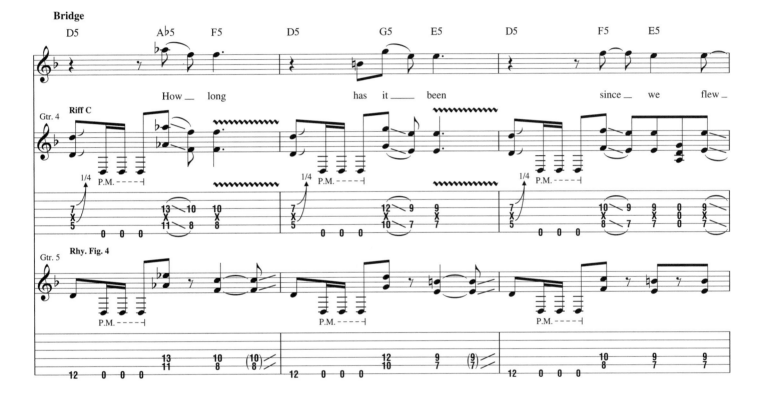

How _____ long has it _____ been since _____ we flew _____

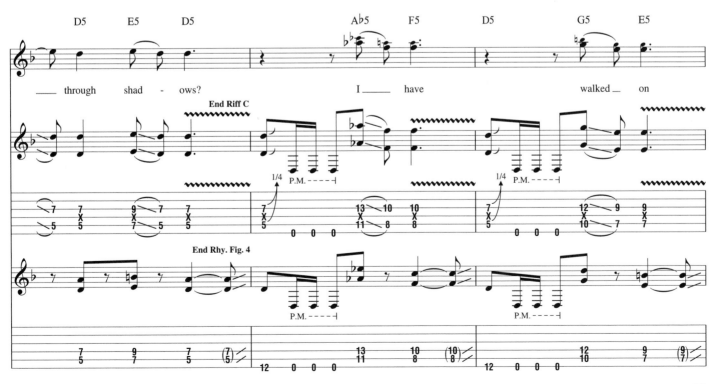

_____ through shad - ows? I _____ have walked _____ on

man - y oth - er plan - ets.

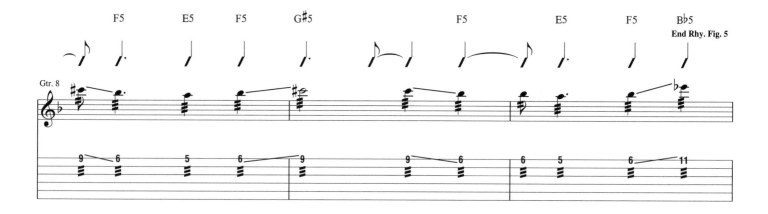

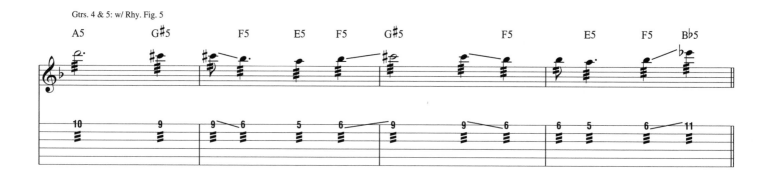

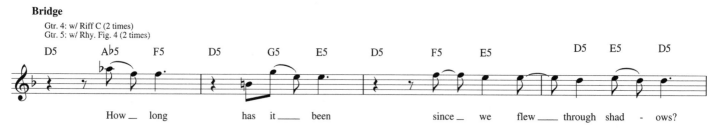

How __ long     has it __ been     since __ we  flew __ through shad - ows?

I ___ have walked ___ on man - y oth - er plan - ets.

*D.S. al Coda 1*
*(Half-time feel)*

**Interlude**

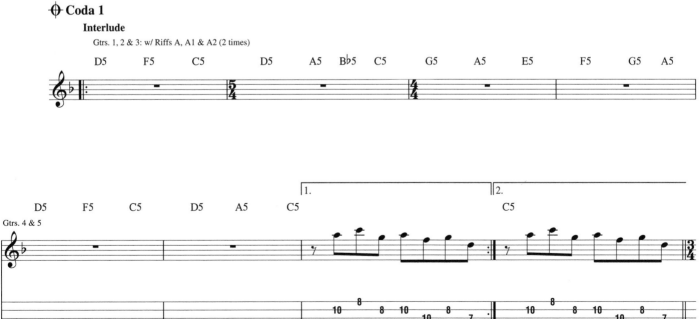

⊕ **Coda 1**

**Interlude**
Gtrs. 1, 2 & 3: w/ Riffs A, A1 & A2 (2 times)

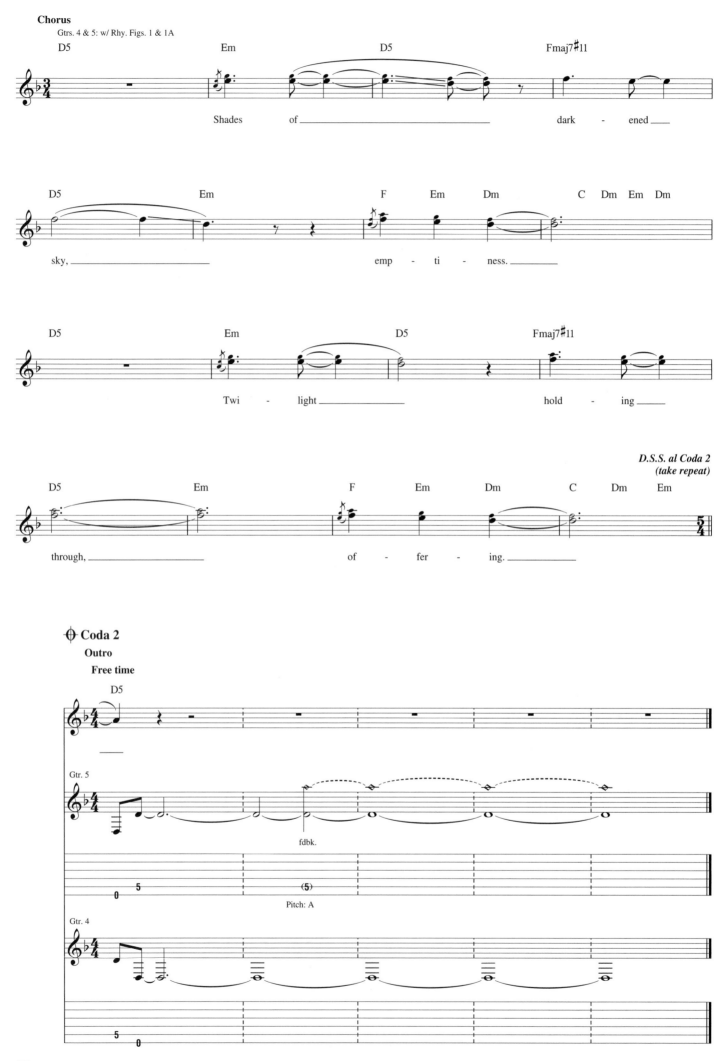

**Chorus**

Shades of _____ dark - ened _____

sky, _____ emp - ti - ness. _____

Twi - light _____ hold - ing _____

through, _____ of - fer - ing. _____

*D.S.S. al Coda 2*
*(take repeat)*

**Coda 2**

**Outro**

**Free time**

Gtr. 5

fdbk.

Pitch: A

Gtr. 4

# Ice Cakes

## Music by Steve Morse

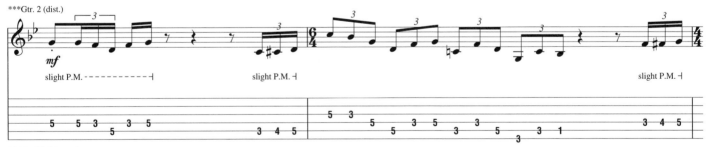

*\*\*\*Doubled throughout*

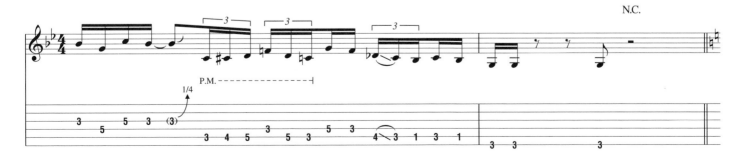

**B**

***C/G   D/G   E♭/G   F/G

*Gtr. 3

*Violin arr. for gtr.

Gtr. 2

**Gtr. 4

**Synth. arr. for gtr.

***Bass plays G pedal (next 4 meas.).

B♭   E♭   F   C   F   G   D   G   A   Gm7   F/G

8va

steady gliss.

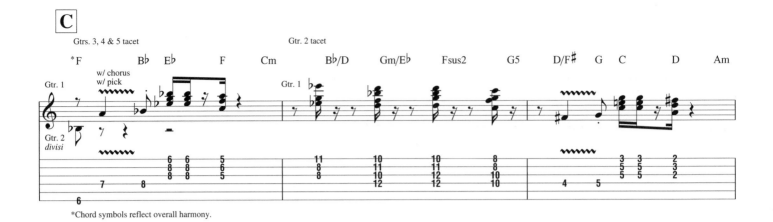

*Chord symbols reflect overall harmony.

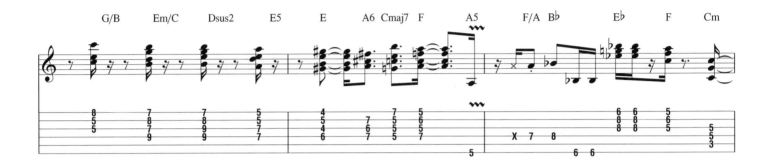

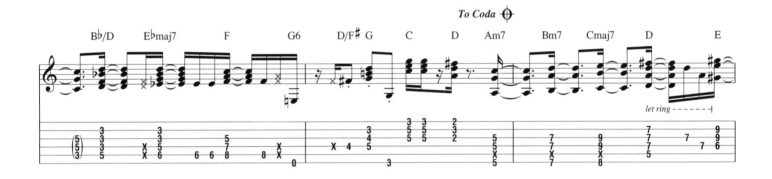

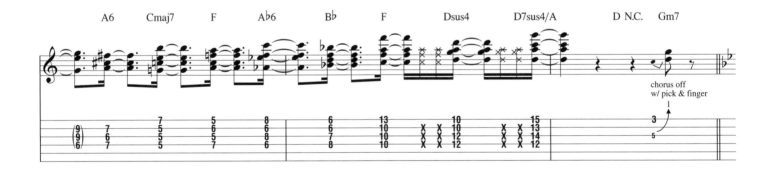

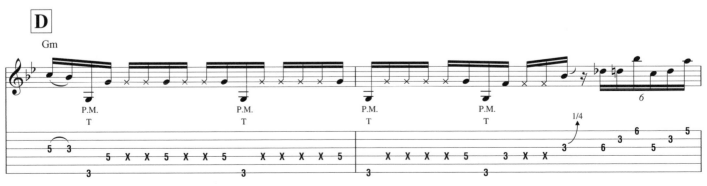

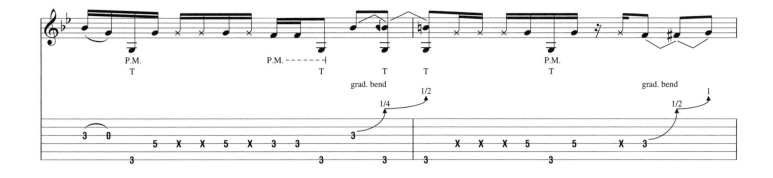

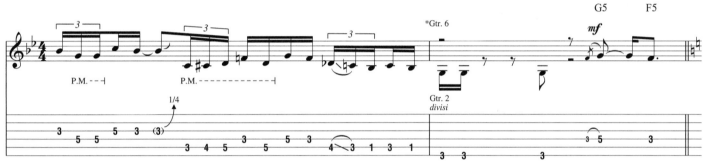

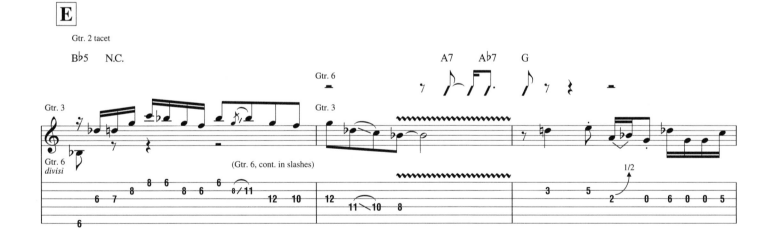

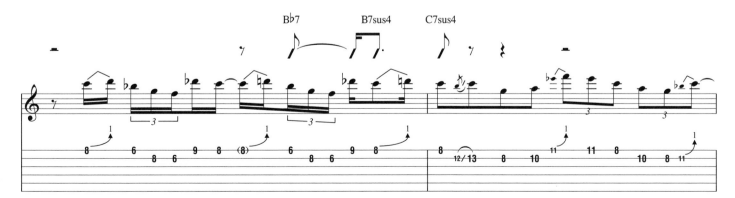

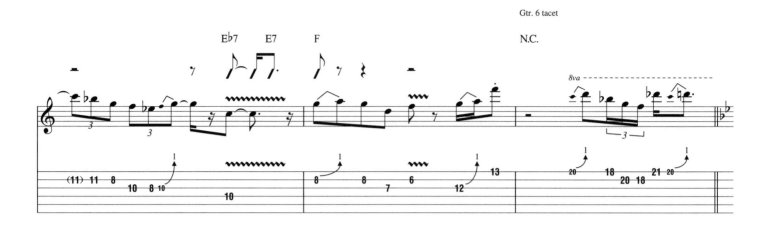

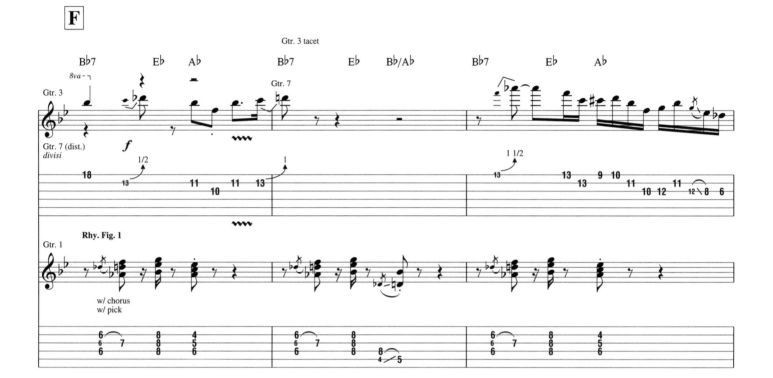

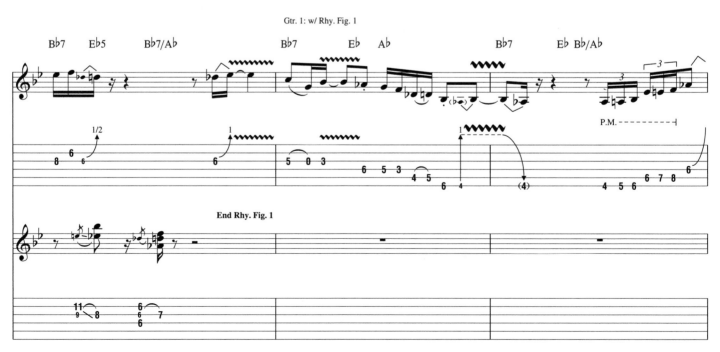

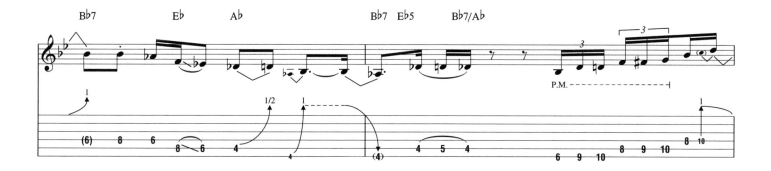

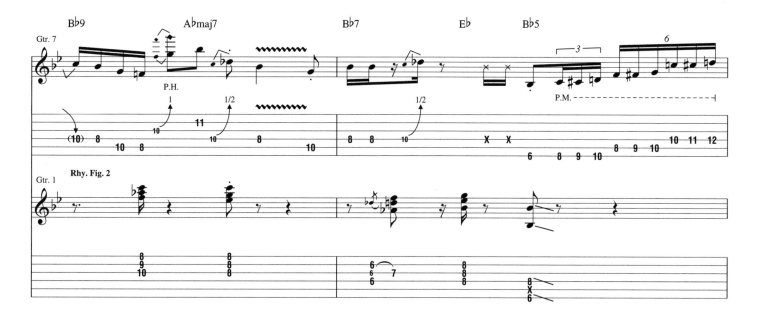

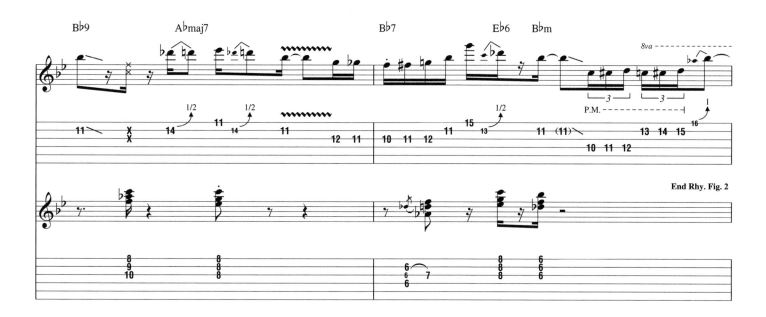

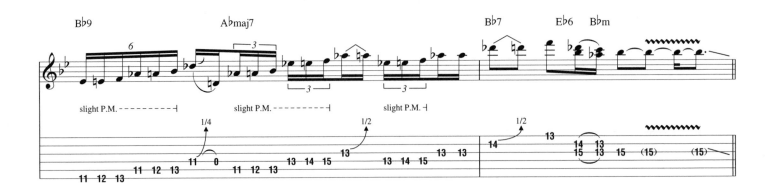

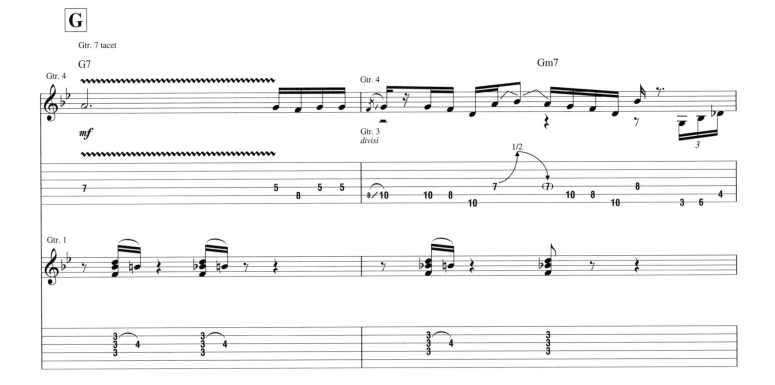

G

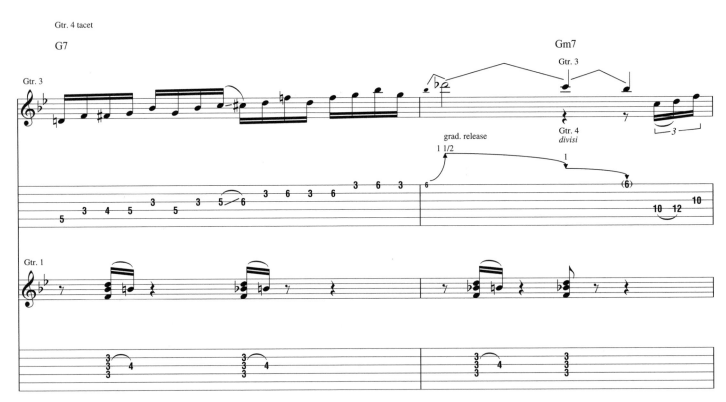

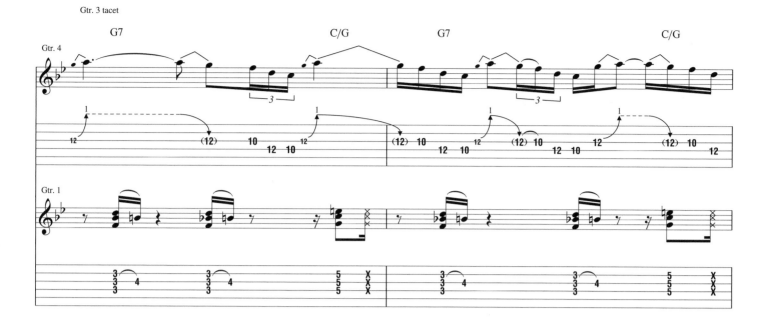

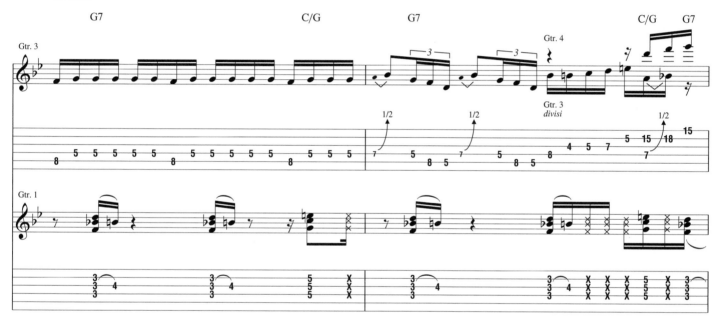

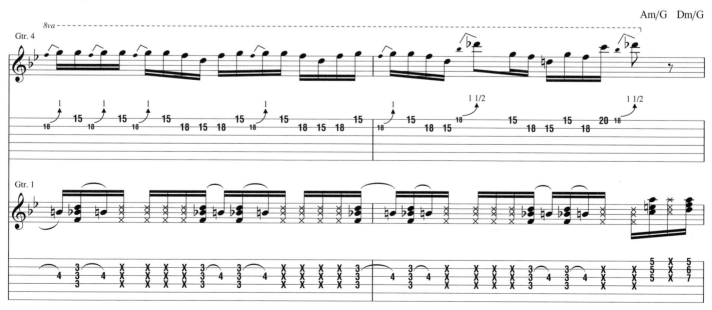

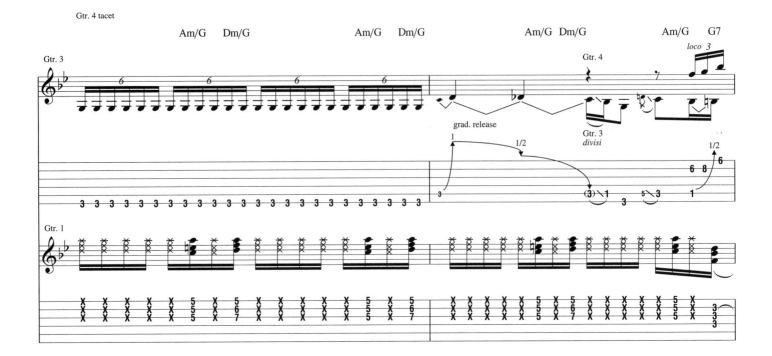

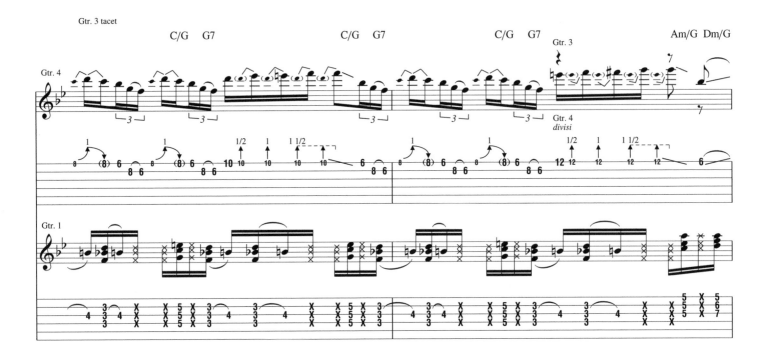

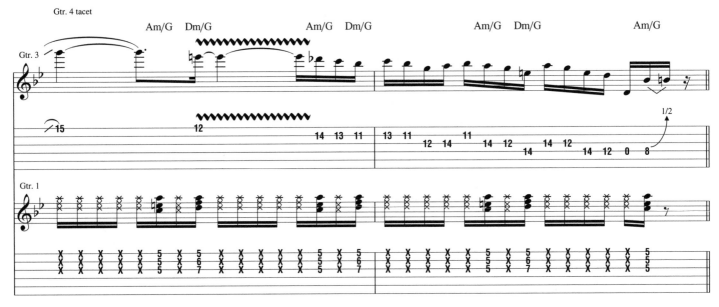

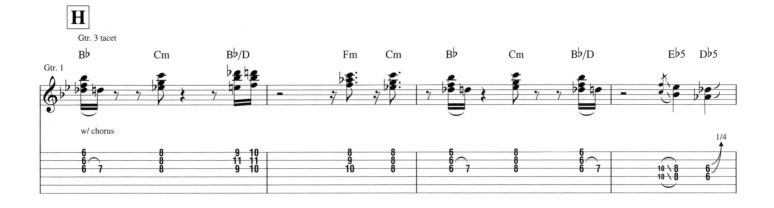

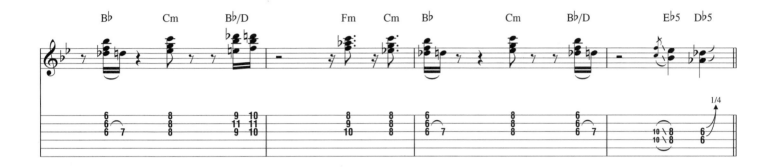

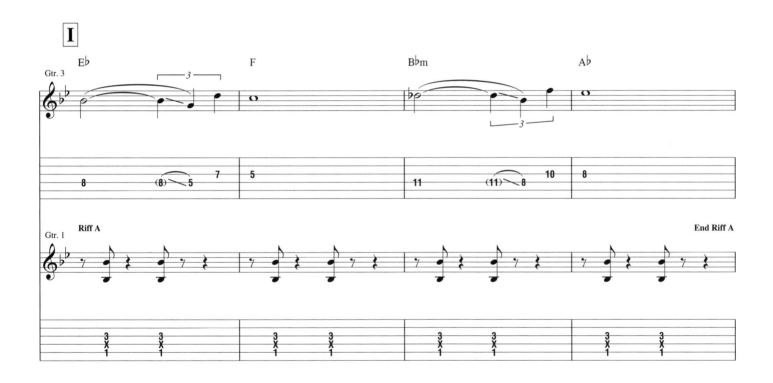

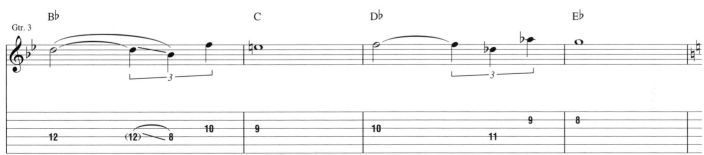

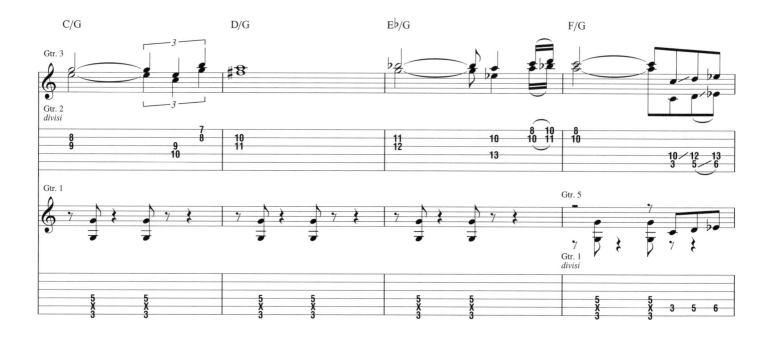

D.S. al Coda

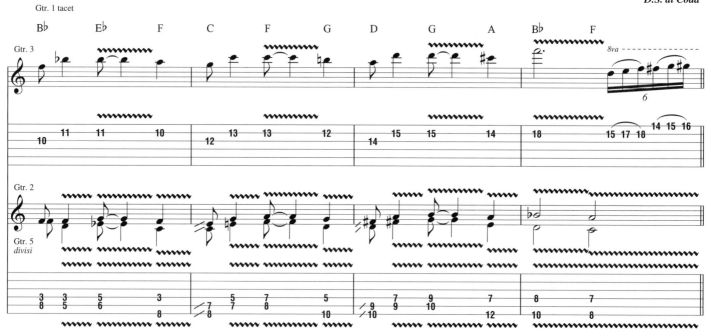

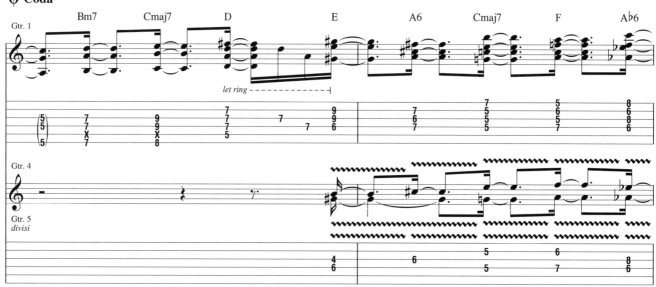

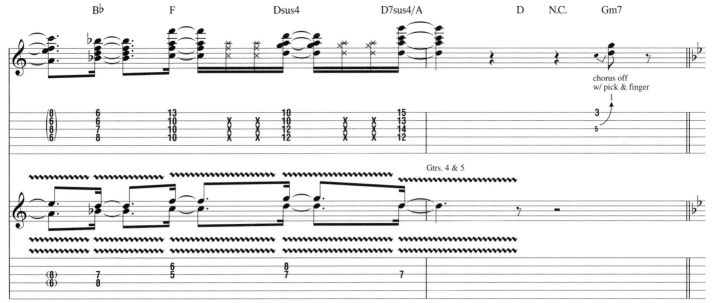

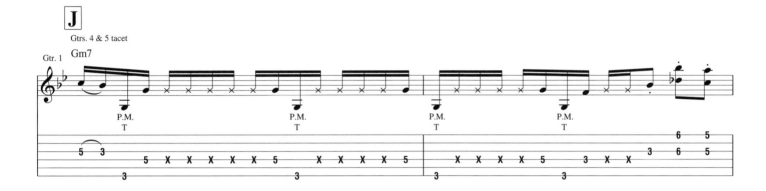

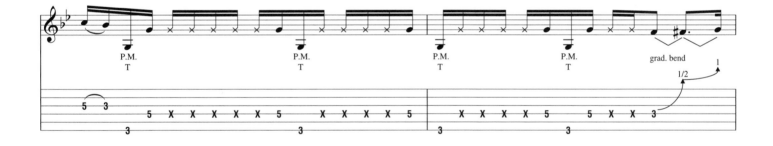

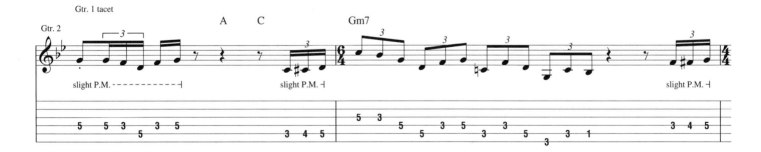

# It Can Happen

**Words and Music by John Anderson, Trevor Rabin and Chris Squire**

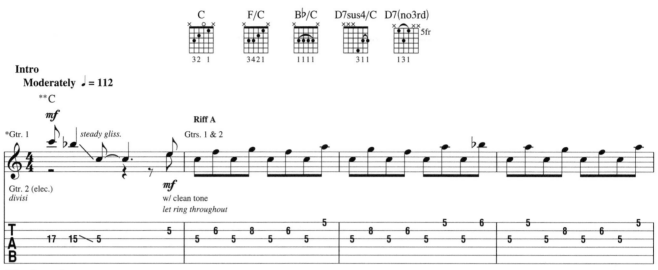

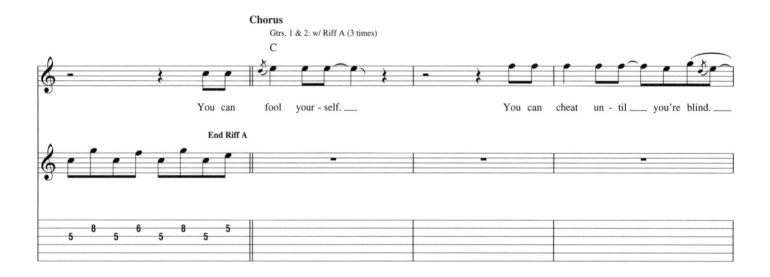

\*Elec. sitar arr. for gtr.

\*\*Chord symbols reflect implied harmony.

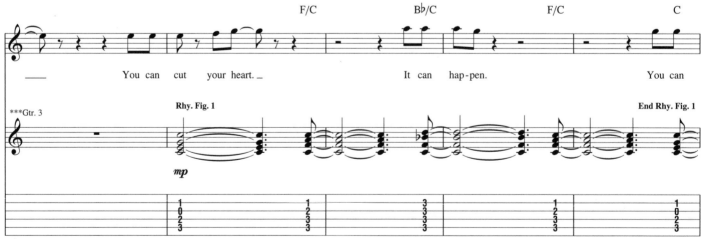

\*\*\*Synth. arr. for gtr.

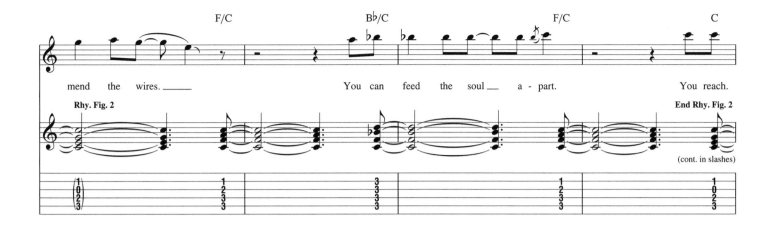

mend the wires. ___  You can feed the soul ___ a - part.  You reach.

Rhy. Fig. 2

End Rhy. Fig. 2

(cont. in slashes)

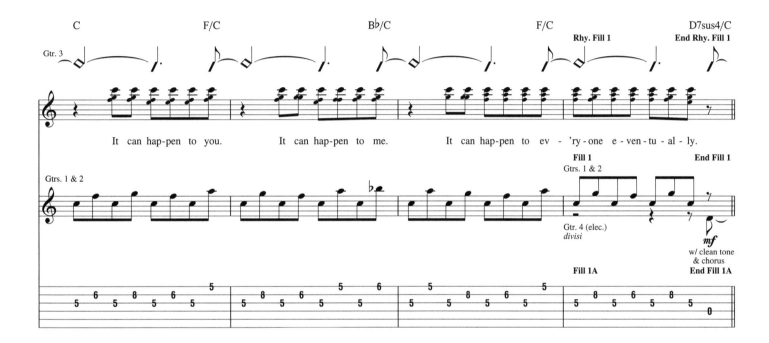

Gtr. 3

It can hap-pen to you.  It can hap-pen to me.  It can hap-pen to ev - 'ry-one e - ven-tu- al - ly.

Rhy. Fill 1   End Rhy. Fill 1

Fill 1   End Fill 1

Gtrs. 1 & 2

Gtrs. 1 & 2

Gtr. 4 (elec.)
divisi

Fill 1A   End Fill 1A

mf
w/ clean tone
& chorus

**Interlude**

Gtrs. 1 & 2 tacet

Gtr. 4

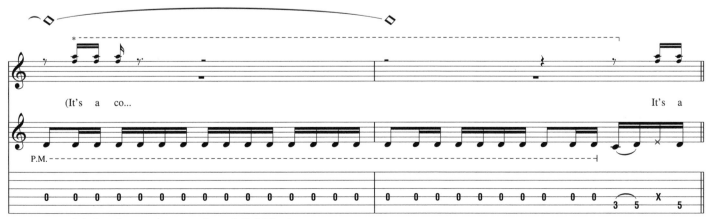

P.M.

(It's a co...)

It's a

P.M.

*w/ echo set for quarter-note regeneration; gradually fade in echo repeats.

**Verse**

D7sus4/C

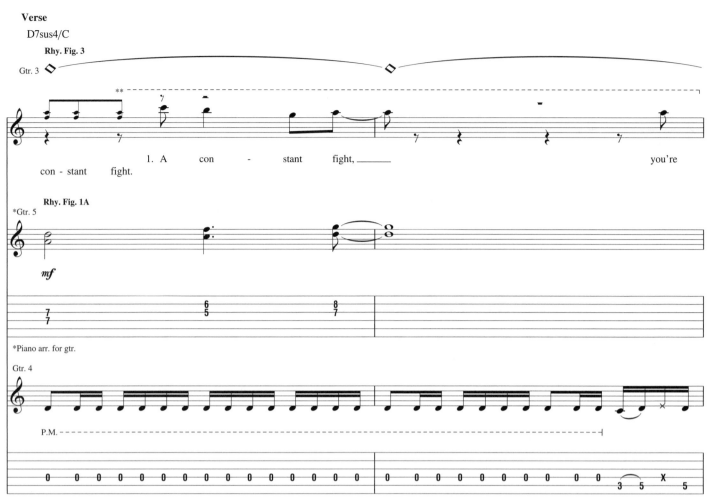

**Rhy. Fig. 3**
Gtr. 3

1. A con - stant fight, _____ you're
con - stant fight.

**Rhy. Fig. 1A**
*Gtr. 5

*mf*

*Piano arr. for gtr.

Gtr. 4

P.M. - - - - - - - - - - - - - - - - - - - - - - - - - - - - - - - - - - - - - - - -

**w/ echo set for quarter-note regeneration; gradually fade out echo repeats.

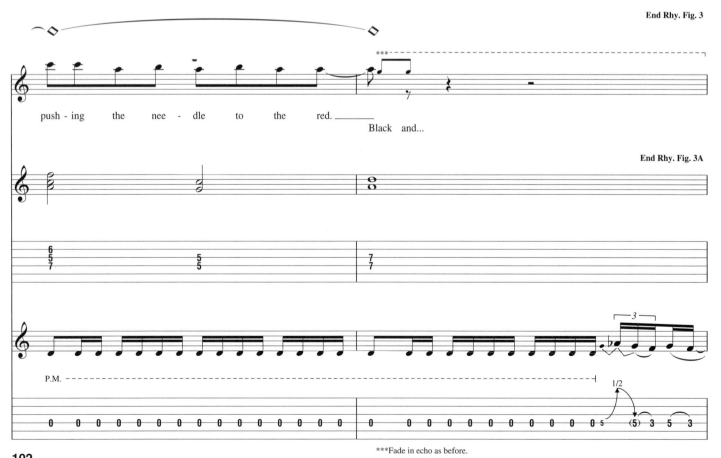

**End Rhy. Fig. 3**

***

push - ing the nee - dle to the red. _____
Black and...

**End Rhy. Fig. 3A**

P.M. - - - - - - - - - - - - - - - - - - - - - - - - - - - - - - - - - - - - - - - -

1/2

***Fade in echo as before.

**Pre-Chorus**

look down, ___ look out, look a - round.

Look up, look down. ___ There's a cra -

**Chorus**

- zy world ___ out - side, we're not a - bout ___ to lose ___ our pride. It can hap - pen to you.

*Synth. arr. for gtr.
**Gtr. 7 to left of slash in tab.
***Gtr. 8 (elec.) w/ dist., played *mf*.

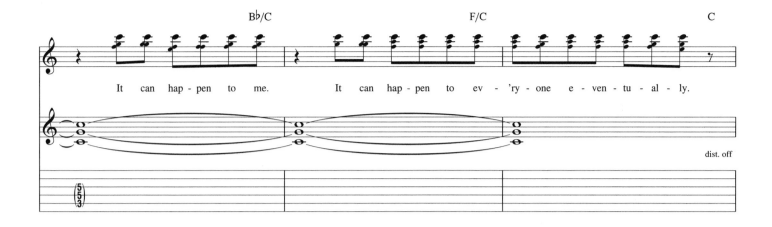

It can hap-pen to me. It can hap-pen to ev-'ry-one e-ven-tu-al-ly.

dist. off

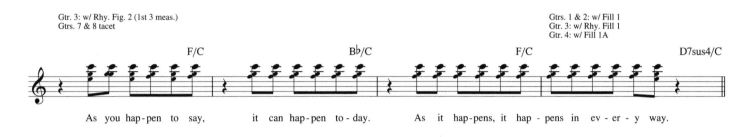

Gtr. 3: w/ Rhy. Fig. 2 (1st 3 meas.)
Gtrs. 7 & 8 tacet

Gtrs. 1 & 2: w/ Fill 1
Gtr. 3: w/ Rhy. Fill 1
Gtr. 4: w/ Fill 1A

As you hap-pen to say, it can hap-pen to-day. As it hap-pens, it hap-pens in ev-er-y way.

**Interlude**

Gtrs. 3 & 5: w/ Rhy. Figs. 3 & 3A

D7sus4/C

Gtr. 4

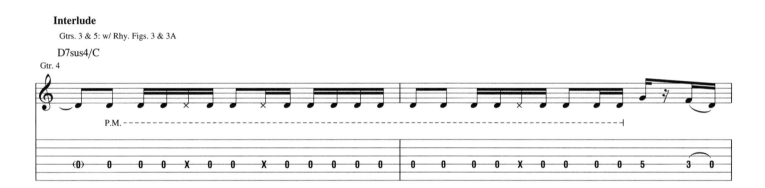

**Verse**

Gtr. 3: w/ Rhy. Fig. 3 (2 3/4 times)

D7sus4/C

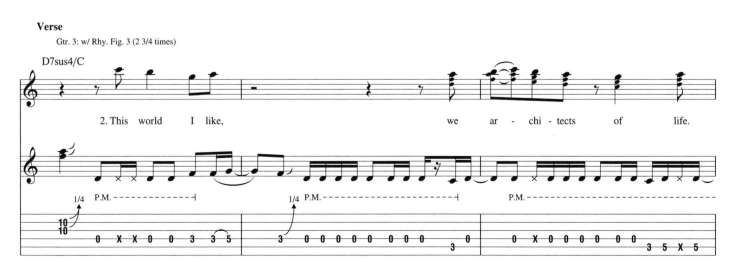

2. This world I like, we ar-chi-tects of life.

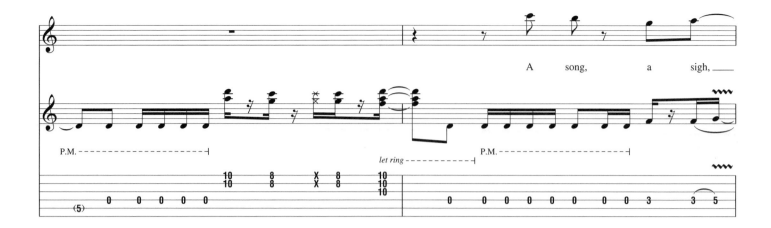

A song, a sigh, _____

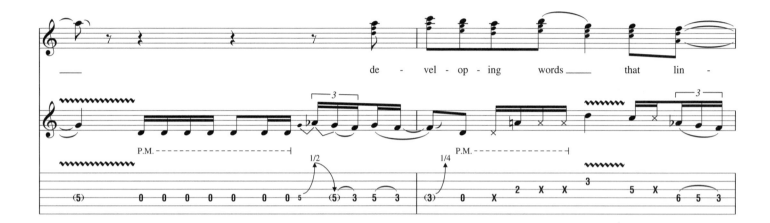

_____ de - vel - op - ing words _____ that lin -

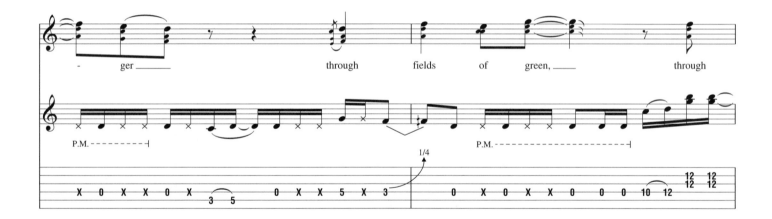

- ger _____ through fields of green, _____ through

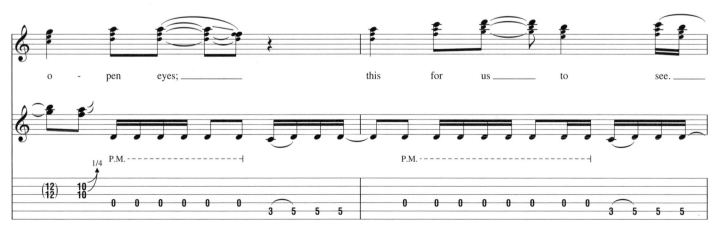

o - pen eyes; _____ this for us _____ to see. _____

**Pre-Chorus**

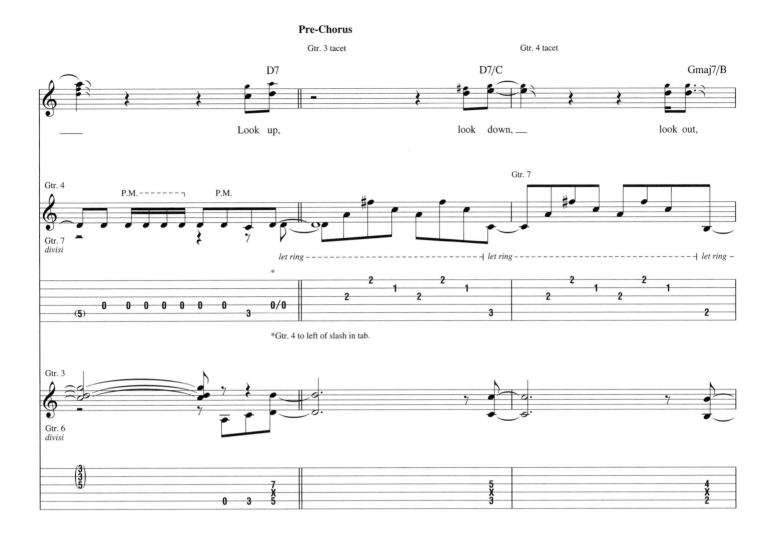

There's a cra - zy world out - side, we're not a - bout to lose our pride.

**Chorus**

It can hap-pen to you. It can hap-pen to me. It can hap-pen to ev - 'ry-one e - ven-tu - al - ly.

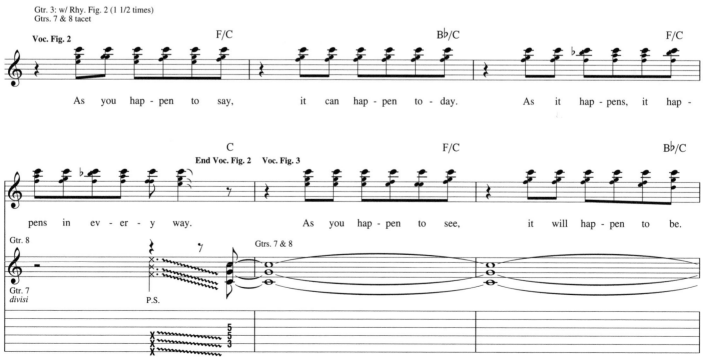

As you hap - pen to say, it can hap - pen to - day. As it hap - pens, it hap -

pens in ev - er - y way. As you hap - pen to see, it will hap - pen to be.

**Guitar Solo**

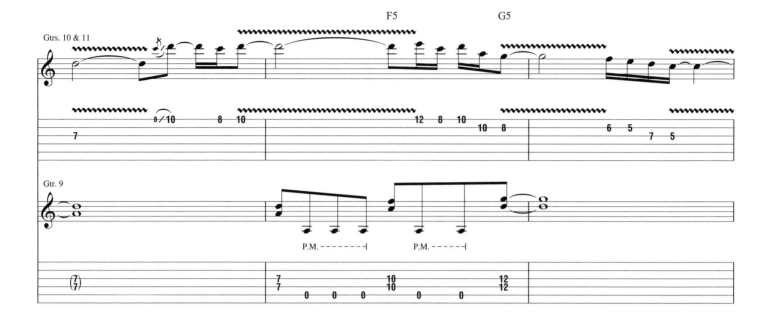

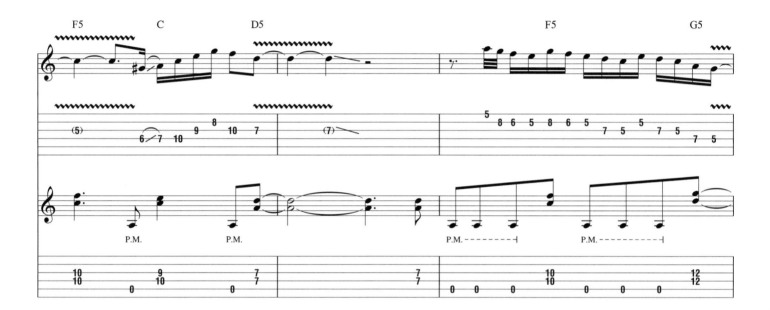

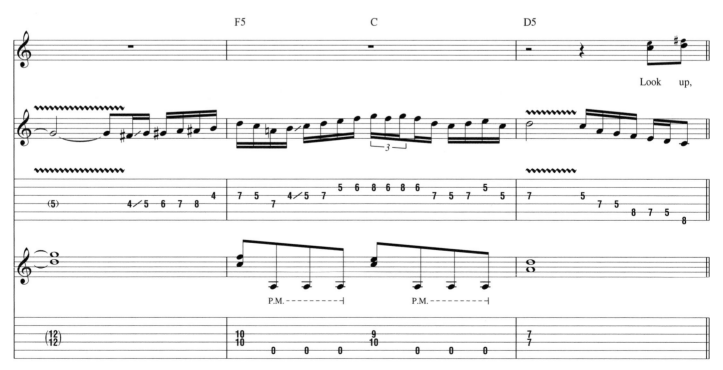

Look up,

## Pre-Chorus

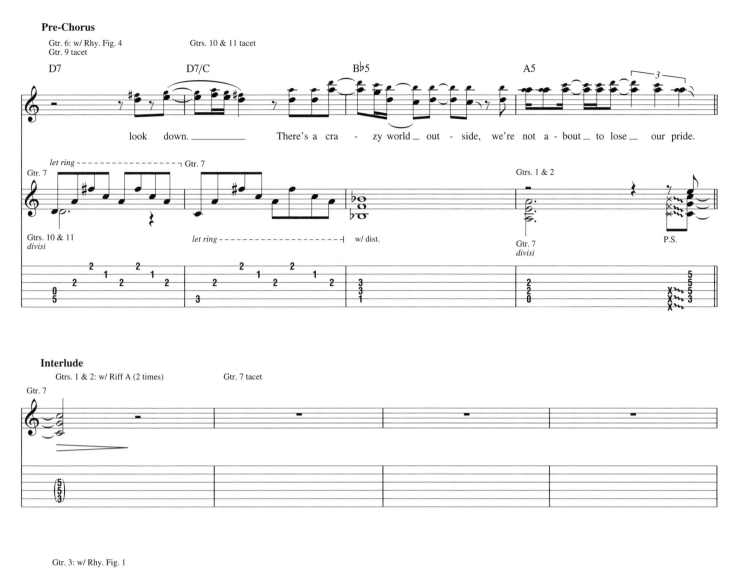

look down._____ There's a cra - zy world__ out - side, we're not a - bout__ to lose__ our pride.

## Interlude

It can

## Chorus

hap - pen to you, it can hap - pen to me. It can hap - pen to you, it can

(It can hap - pen to you, it can hap - pen to me, it can hap - pen to ev -

hap - pen to me. It can hap - pen to you, it can hap - pen to me. It can

'ry - one e - ven - tu - al - ly. As you hap - pen to see, it will hap - pen to be,

**Interlude**

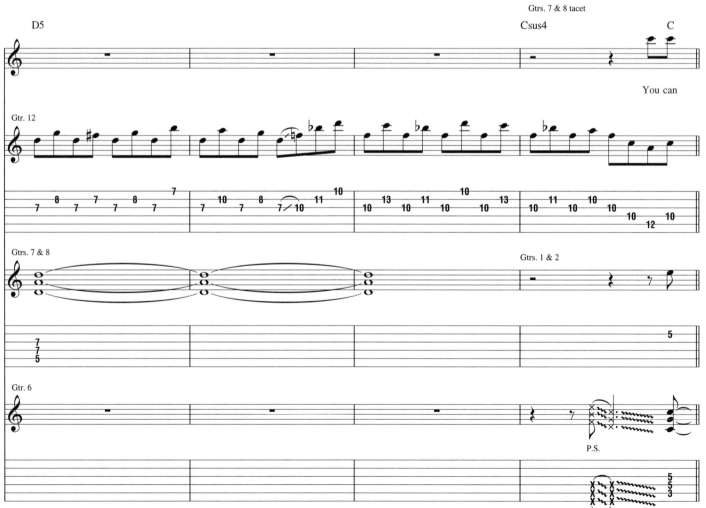

## Outro-Chorus

Bkgd. Voc.: w/ Voc. Fig. 1
Gtrs. 1 & 2: w/ Riff A (till fade)
Gtr. 3: w/ Rhy. Fig. 1
Gtr. 12 tacet

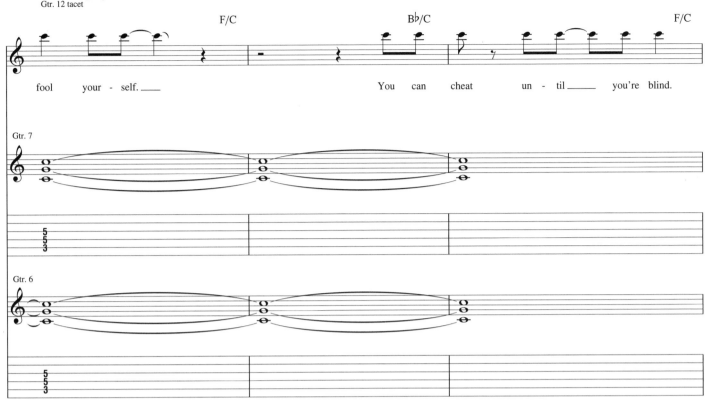

fool your - self. \_\_\_\_ You can cheat un - til \_\_\_\_ you're blind.

Gtrs. 6 & 7 tacet

Bkgd. Voc.: w/ Voc. Fig. 2
Gtr. 3: w/ Rhy. Fig. 2 (till fade)

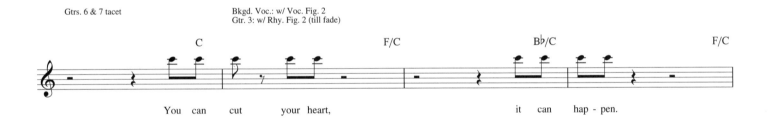

You can cut your heart, it can hap - pen.

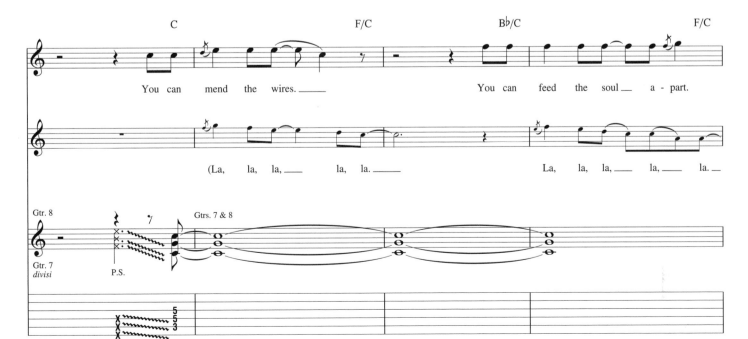

You can mend the wires. \_\_\_\_ You can feed the soul \_\_\_ a - part.

(La, la, la, \_\_\_\_ la, la. \_\_\_\_ La, la, la, \_\_\_\_ la, \_\_\_\_ la. \_\_\_\_

# Lavender

**Words and Music by Derek Dick, Mark Kelly, Ian Mosley, Peter Trewavas and Steve Rothery**

Gtr. 3: Capo II

*Piano arr. for gtr.

**Chord symbols reflect implied harmony.

***Steve Rothery          †Vol. swells

**Chorus**

Gtr. 1: w/ Riff A (4 times)

*Symbols in parentheses represent chord names respective to capoed guitar.
Symbols above reflect actual sounding chords. Capoed fret is "0" in tab.

When I ___ am ___ King, ___ dil - ly, dil - ly, you will ___ be ___ Queen. A pen - ny for your

**End Riff C**

Gtr. 3: w/ Riff C (3 times)

thoughts, my _____ dear, a pen - ny for your thoughts, my ___ dear. ___ I. O.

U. for your love. I. O. U. for your love.

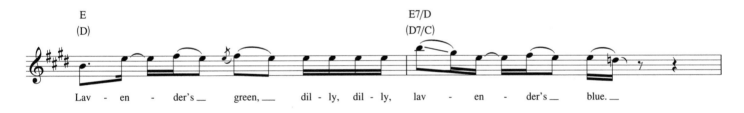

Lav - en - der's ___ green, ___ dil - ly, dil - ly, lav - en - der's ___ blue. ___

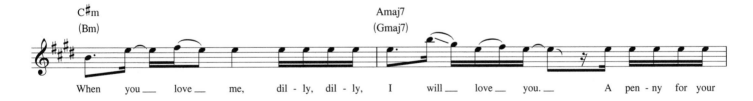

When you ___ love ___ me, dil - ly, dil - ly, I will ___ love ___ you. ___ A pen - ny for your

thoughts, my ___ dear, a pen - ny for your thoughts, my ___ dear. I. O.

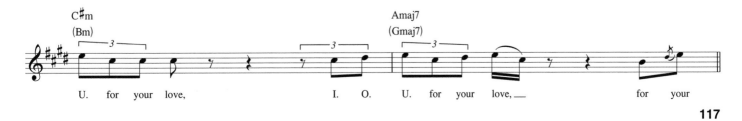

U. for your love, I. O. U. for your love, ___ for your

## Outro-Guitar Solo

Gtr. 1: w/ Riff A (1 3/4 times)

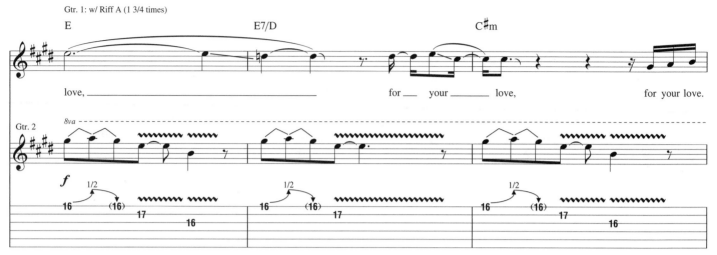

love, _____   for ___ your _____ love,                              for your love.

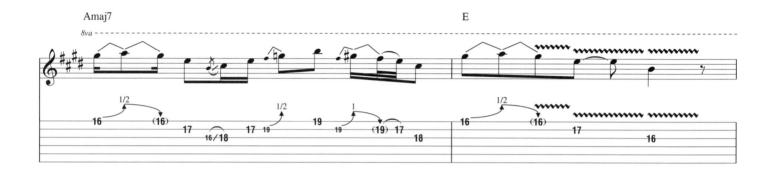

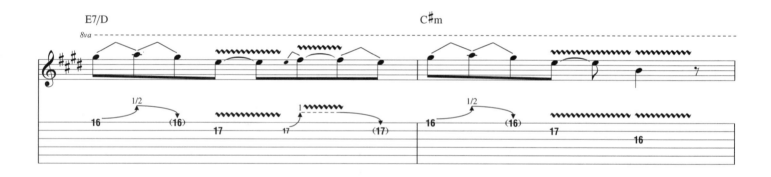

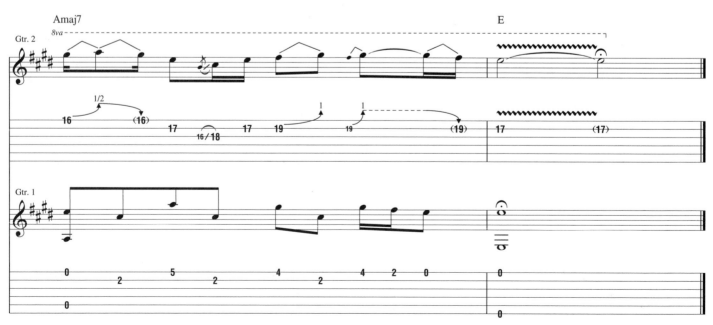

# Lucky Man

**Words and Music by Greg Lake**

*Chord symbols reflect overall harmony.   **T = Thumb on 6th string

**Verse**

Gtr. 1: w/ Riff A (2 times)
Gtr. 2: w/ Riff A1 (4 times)

1. He _____ had white hors-es and la-dies _____ by the score,

all _____ dressed in sat-in and wait-ing _____ by ___ the door. ___

Gtr. 1

(cont. in slashes)

**Chorus**

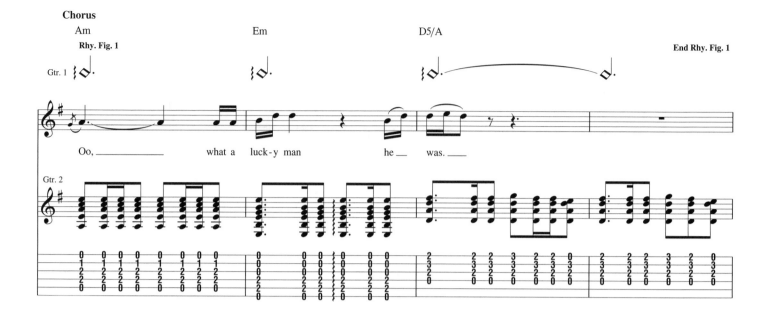

Oo, _____ what a luck-y man he _____ was. _____

Gtr. 1: w/ Rhy. Fig. 1

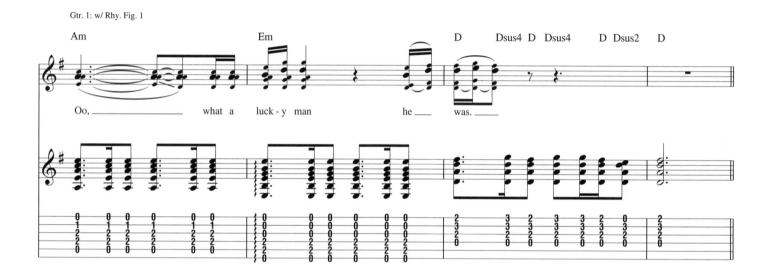

Oo, _____ what a luck-y man he _____ was. _____

**Verse**

Gtr. 1: w/ Riff A (2 times)
Gtr. 2: w/ Riff A1 (3 times)

2. White lace and feath-ers, they made up _____ his ____ bed: ____ a

Gtr. 2: w/ Riff B

gold _____ cov-ered mat-tress on which he was ___ laid. ____

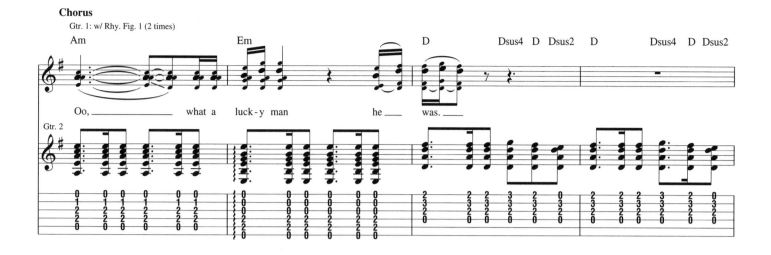

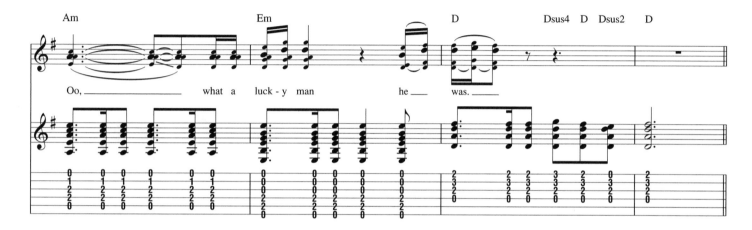

**Guitar Solo**

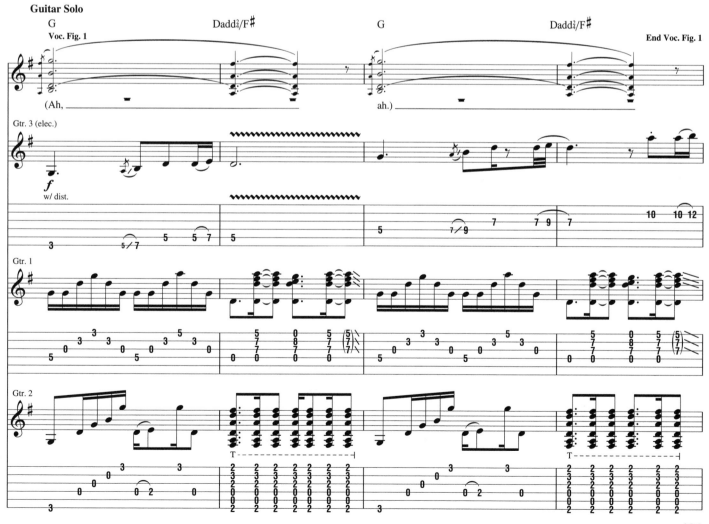

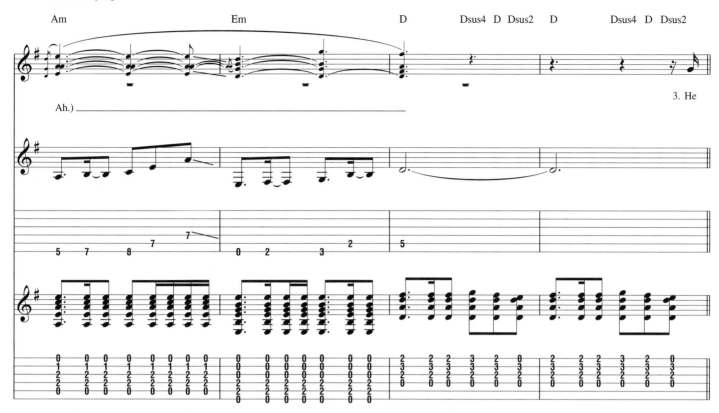

**Verse**

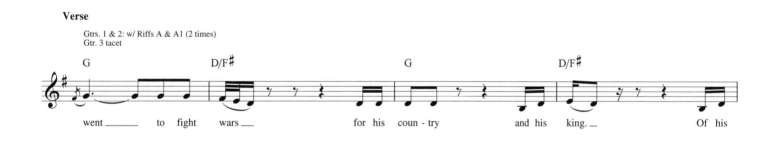

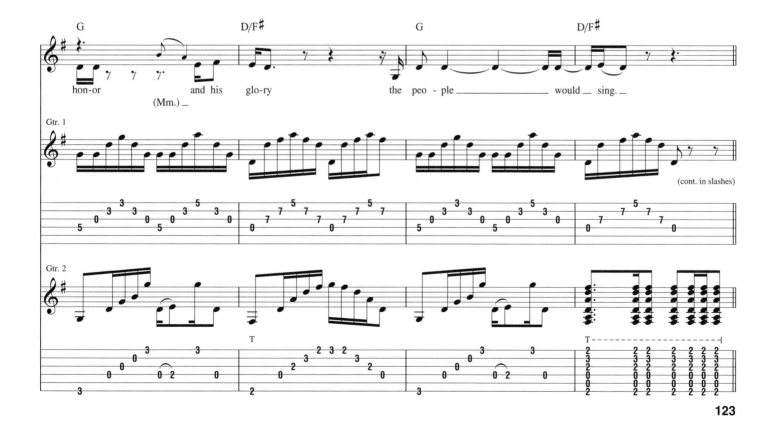

**Chorus**

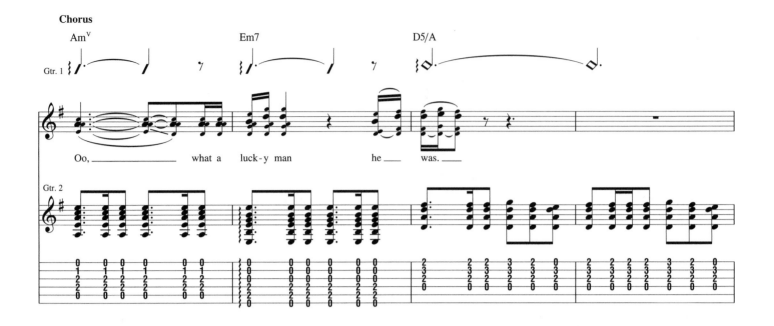

Oo, _____ what a luck-y man he _____ was. _____

Gtr. 1: w/ Rhy. Fig. 1

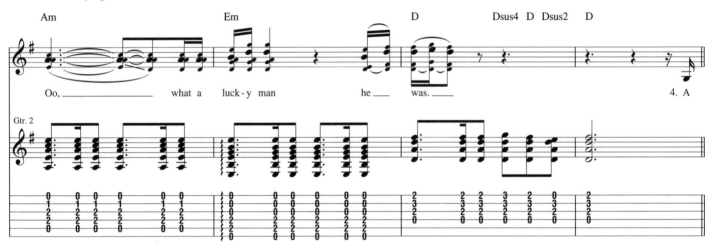

Oo, _____ what a luck-y man he _____ was. _____

4. A

**Verse**

Gtr. 2: w/ Riff A1 (4 times)

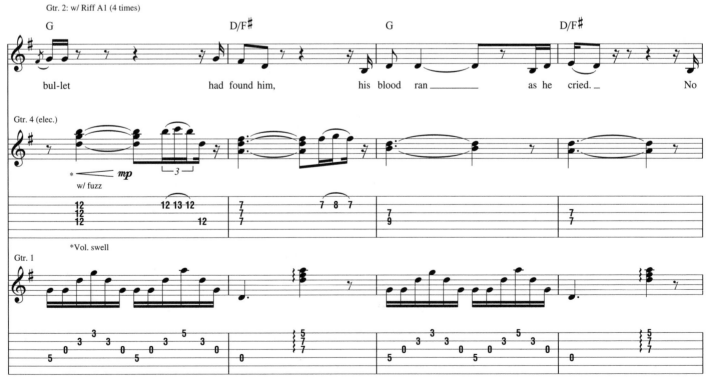

bul-let     had found him,     his blood ran _____ as he cried. ___     No

*w/ fuzz

*Vol. swell

124

mon-ey could save him, so he laid down and he died.

(cont. in slashes)

**Chorus**

Gtr. 4 tacet

Oo, what a luck-y man he was.

Gtr. 2

*Gtr. 5

*Synth. arr. for gtr.       **Vol. swell

Gtr. 1: w/ Rhy. Fig. 1

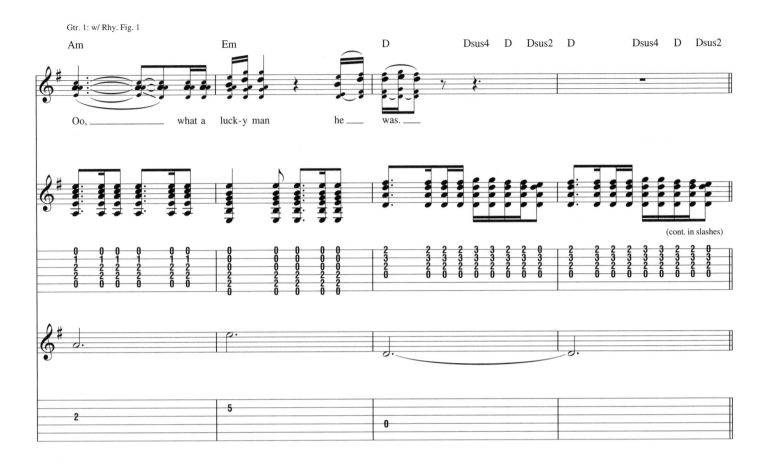

Oo, _____ what a luck-y man he ____ was. ____

## Outro-Synth Solo

Bkgd. Voc.: w/ Voc. Fig. 2 (5 times)

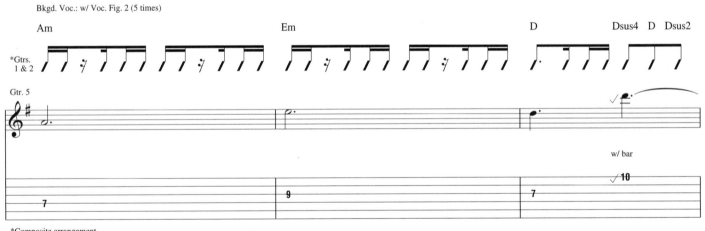

*Composite arrangement

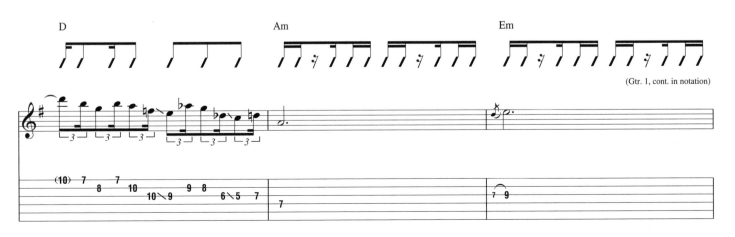

(Gtr. 1, cont. in notation)

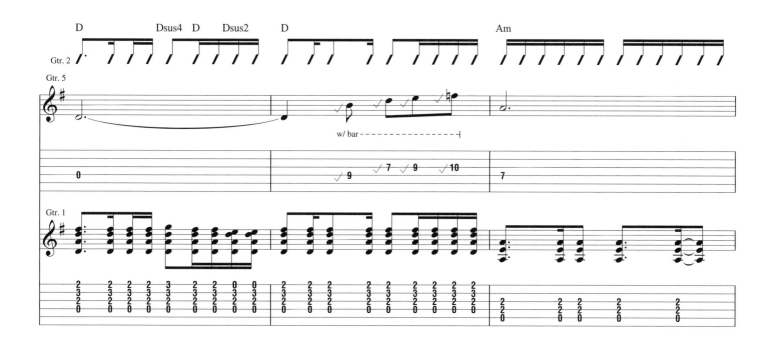

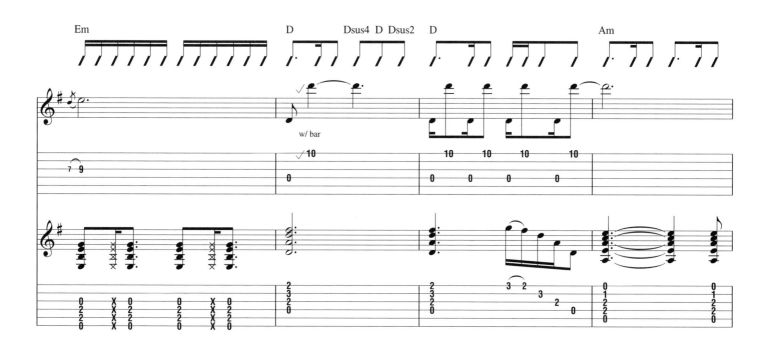

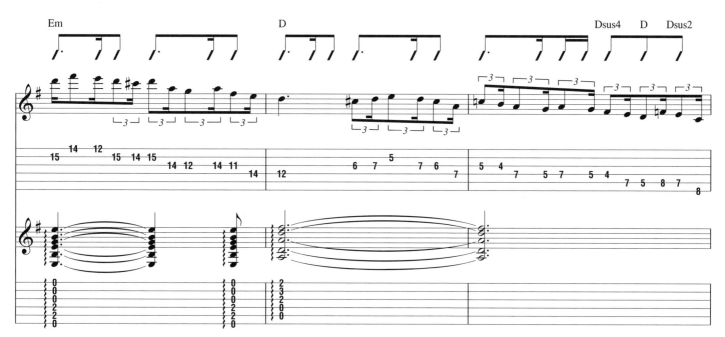

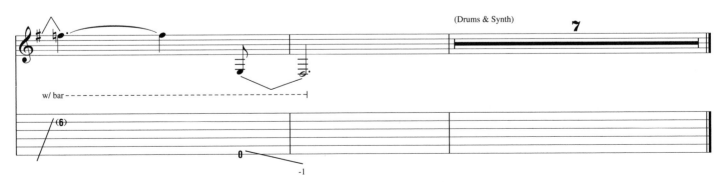

# Money

**Words and Music by Roger Waters**

New car, cav - i - ar, four star day - dream. Think I'll buy me a foot - ball ____

_____ team.

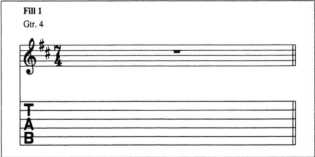

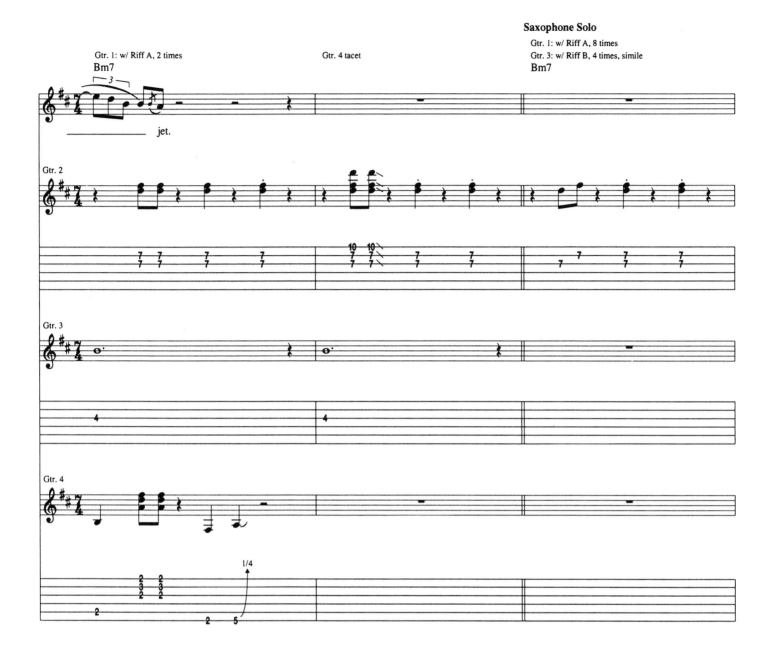

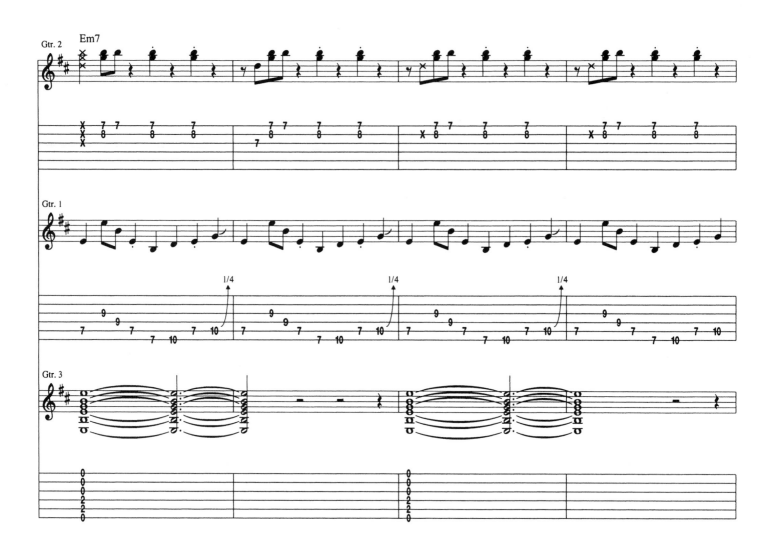

Gtr. 1: w/ Riff A, 4 times
Gtr. 3: w/ Riff B, 2 times, simile

Gtr. 3: w/ Rhy. Fig. 2
Gtr. 2 tacet

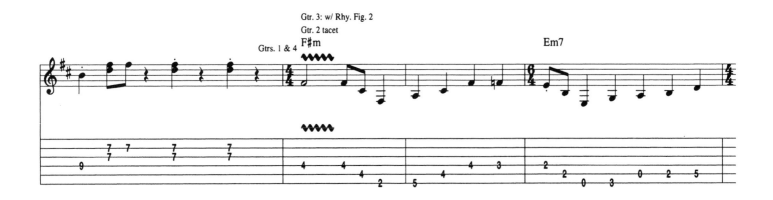

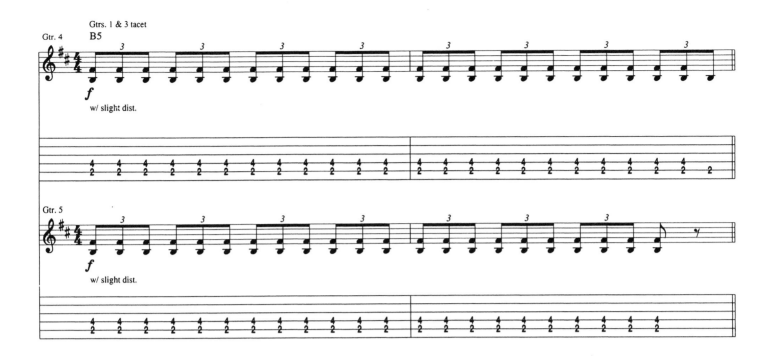

**Guitar Solo**

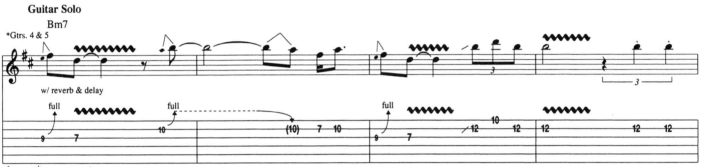

*composite arrangement

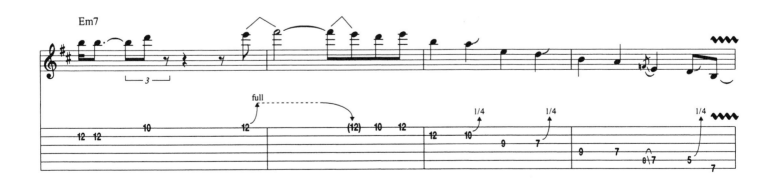

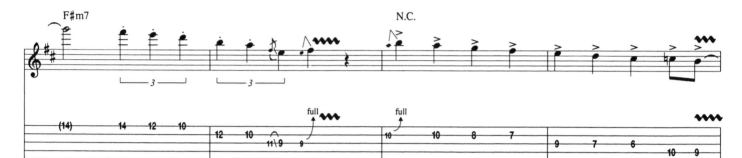

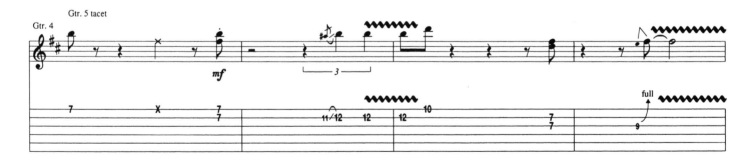

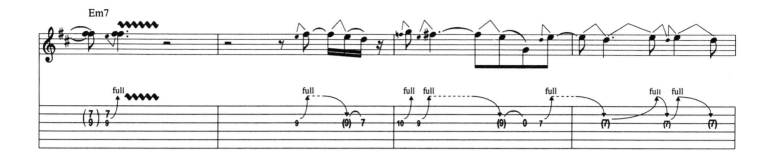

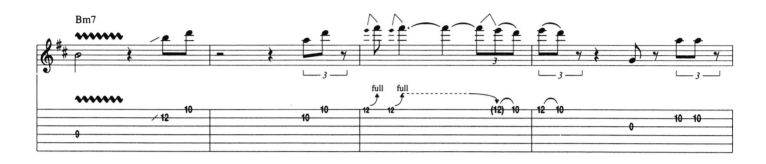

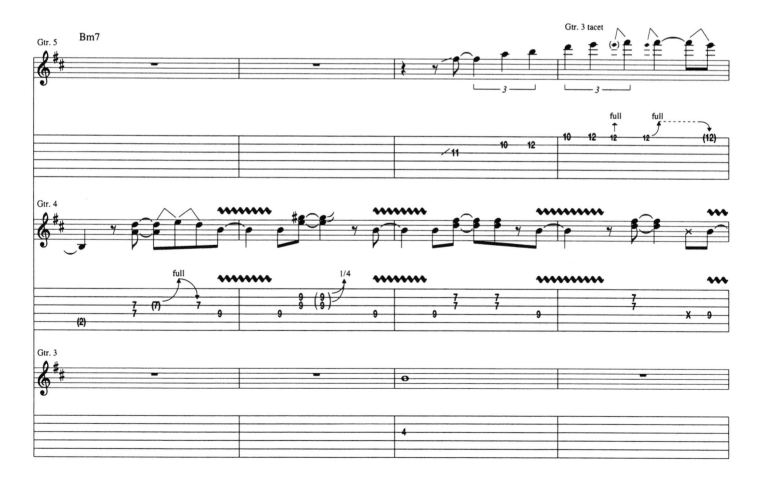

138

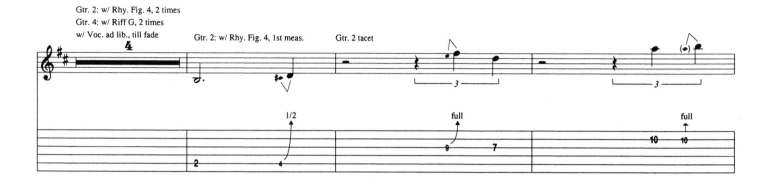

Gtr. 2: w/ Rhy. Fig. 4, 2 times
Gtr. 4: w/ Riff G, 2 times
w/ Voc. ad lib., till fade

Gtr. 2: w/ Rhy. Fig. 4, 1st meas.

Gtr. 2 tacet

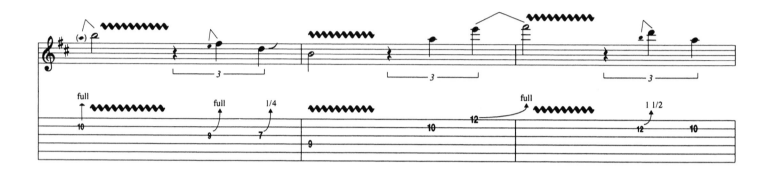

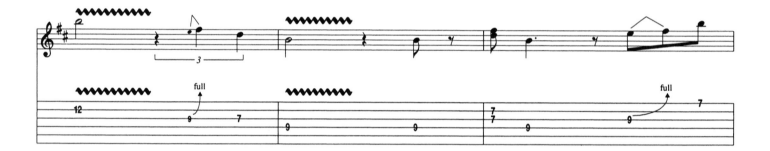

*Fade Out*

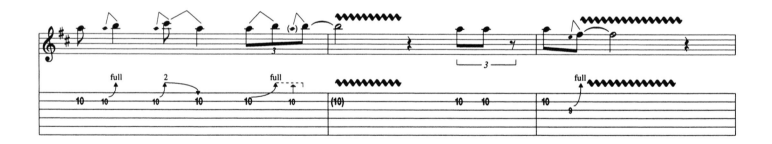

142

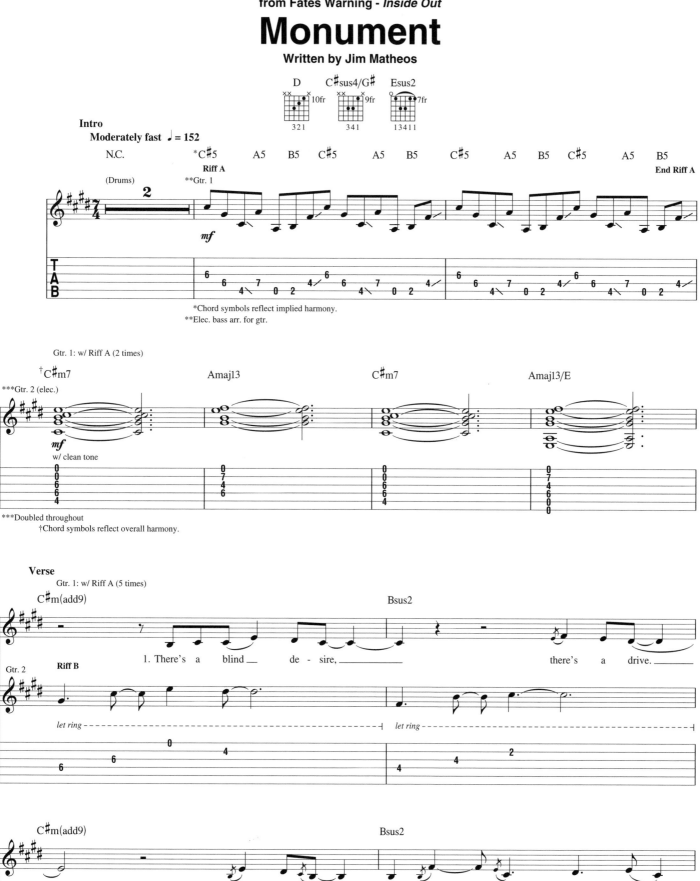

from Fates Warning - *Inside Out*

# Monument

**Written by Jim Matheos**

*Chord symbols reflect implied harmony.
**Elec. bass arr. for gtr.

***Doubled throughout
†Chord symbols reflect overall harmony.

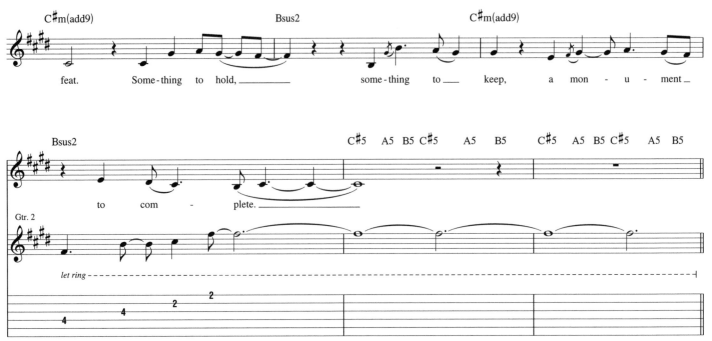

feat.   Some-thing to hold, _____   some-thing to ___ keep,   a mon - u - ment

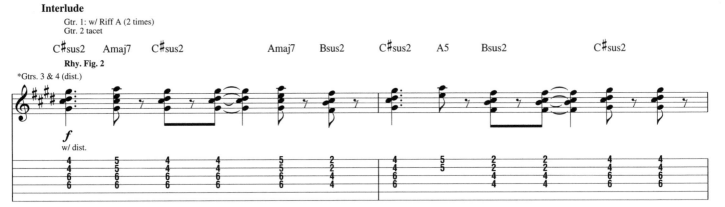

to com - plete. _____

Interlude

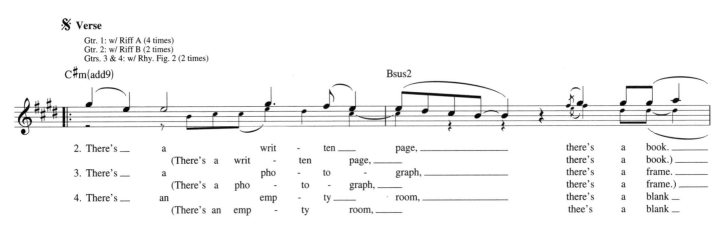

144

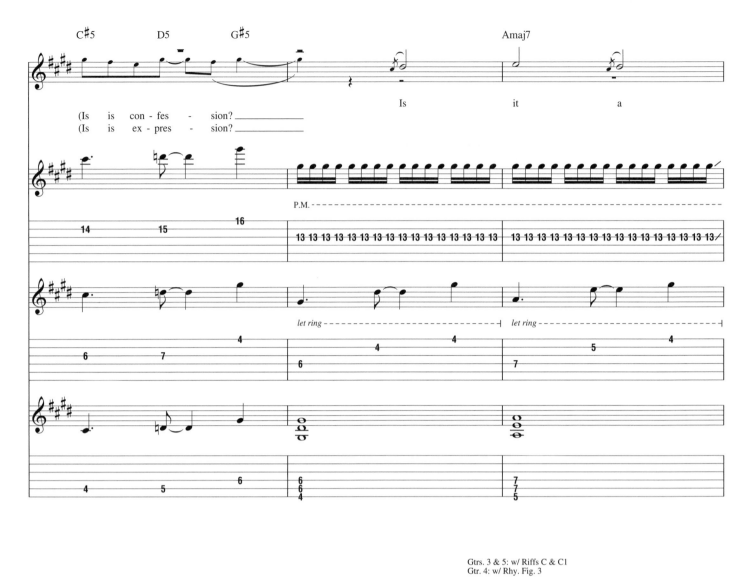

Gtrs. 3 & 5: w/ Riffs C & C1
Gtr. 4: w/ Rhy. Fig. 3

form - ance? \_\_

tion? \_\_\_\_\_

Is it ex - pres - sion? _____

Is is con - fes - sion? _____

Is it a pas - sion,... \_

...or

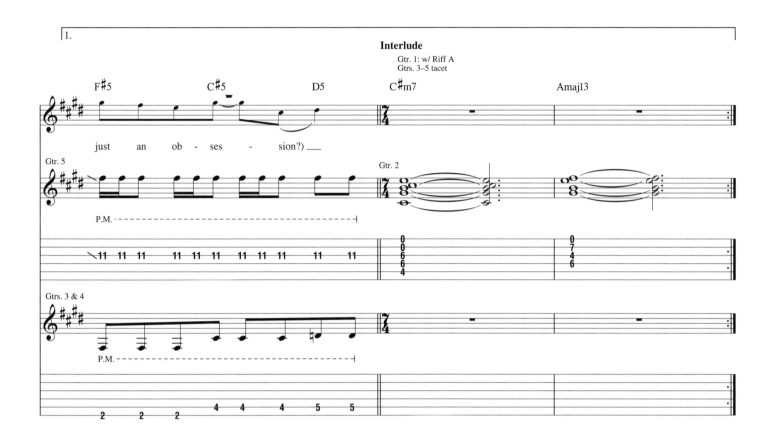

**Interlude**

Gtr. 1: w/ Riff A
Gtrs. 3–5 tacet

just an ob - ses - sion?) \_\_\_

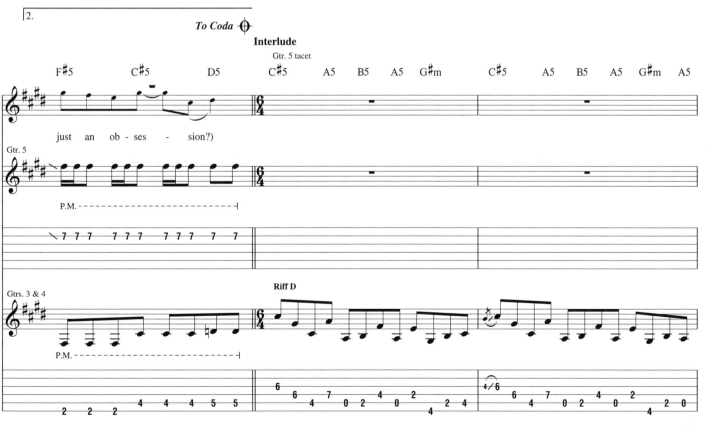

*To Coda*

**Interlude**

Gtr. 5 tacet

just an ob - ses - sion?)

**Riff D**

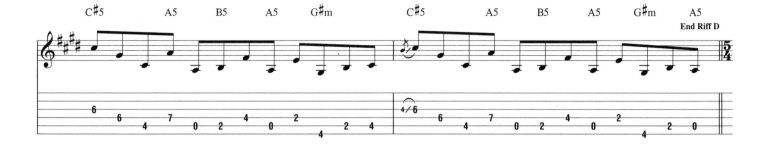

**Guitar Solo**

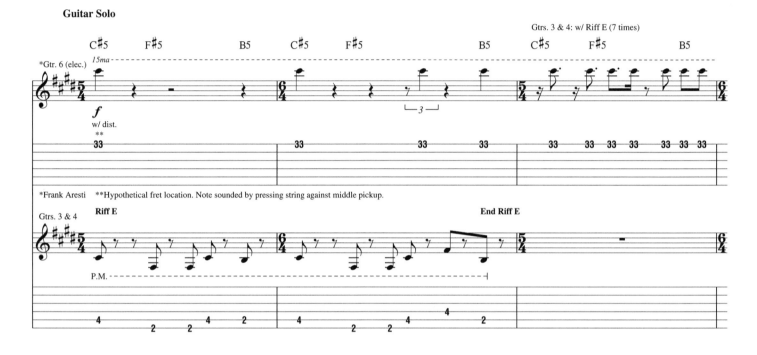

*Frank Aresti    **Hypothetical fret location. Note sounded by pressing string against middle pickup.

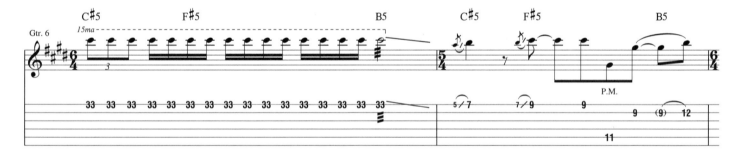

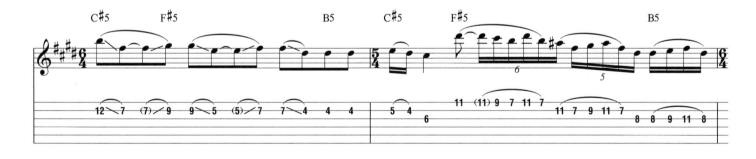

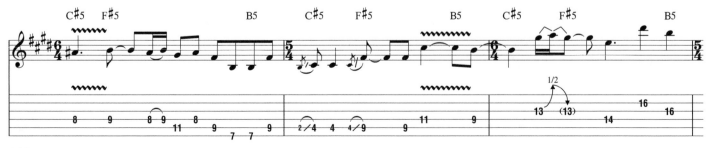

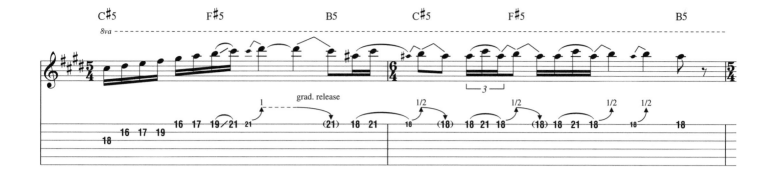

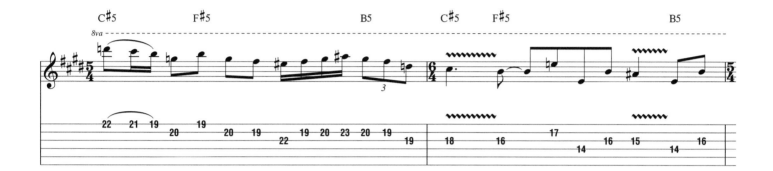

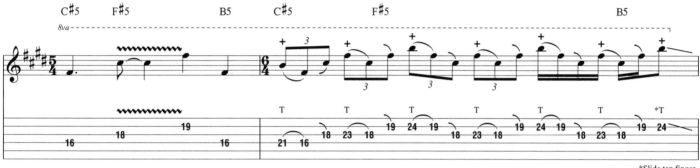

*Slide tap finger.

149

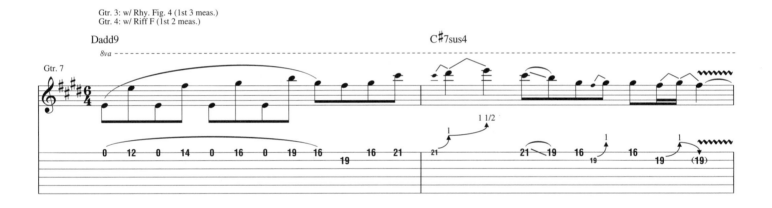

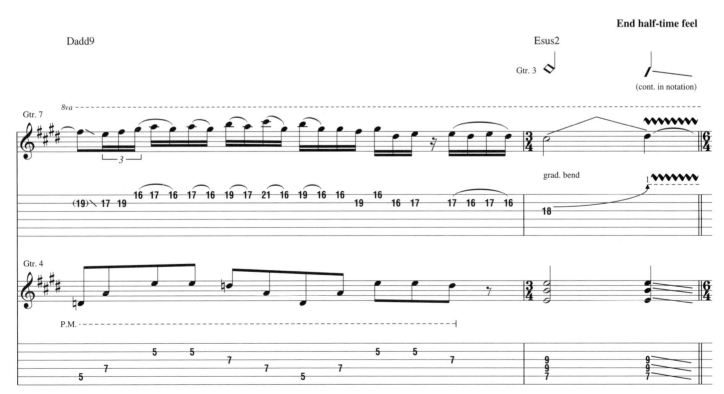

## Guitar Solo

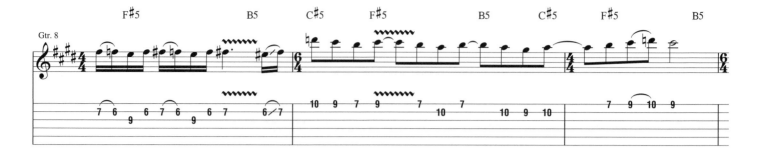

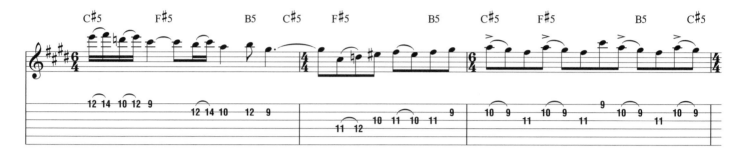

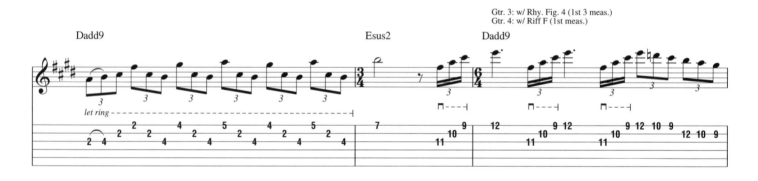

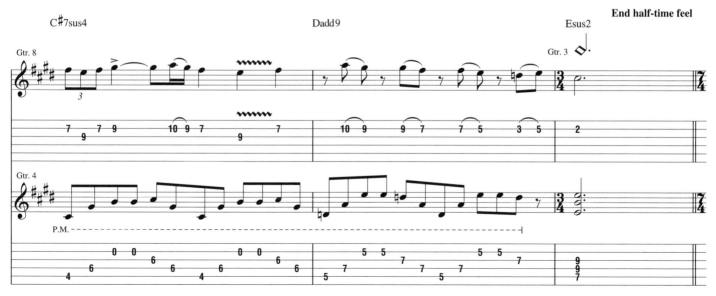

152

**Interlude**

Gtr. 1: w/ Riff A (1 1/2 times)
Gtr. 2: w/ Rhy. Fig. 1
Gtrs. 3, 4 & 8 tacet

C#m7                    Amaj13                    C#m7                    Amaj13/E

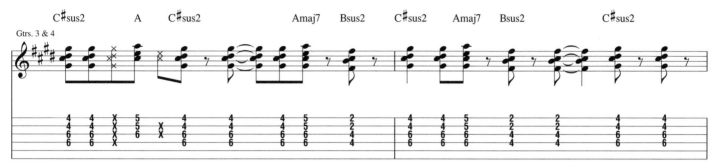

Gtr. 1: w/ Riff A (2 times)

C#sus2      A      C#sus2            Amaj7   Bsus2   C#sus2   Amaj7   Bsus2        C#sus2

Gtrs. 3 & 4

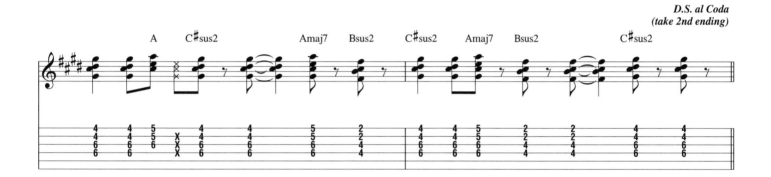

*D.S. al Coda*
*(take 2nd ending)*

A      C#sus2            Amaj7   Bsus2   C#sus2   Amaj7   Bsus2        C#sus2

⊕ **Coda**

**Outro**

Gtr. 3: w/ Riff D
Gtr. 5 tacet

Gtr. 4

C#5   A5   B5   A5   G#m   A5   C#5   A5   B5   A5   G#m   A5   C#5   A5   B5   A5   G#m   A5

*Fade out*

Gtr. 4 tacet

C#5        A5        B5        A5        G#m        A5        C#m7

Gtr. 2

**153**

from Mastodon - *Crack the Skye*

# Oblivion

**Words and Music by Brann Dailor, William Hinds, William Kelliher and Troy Sanders**

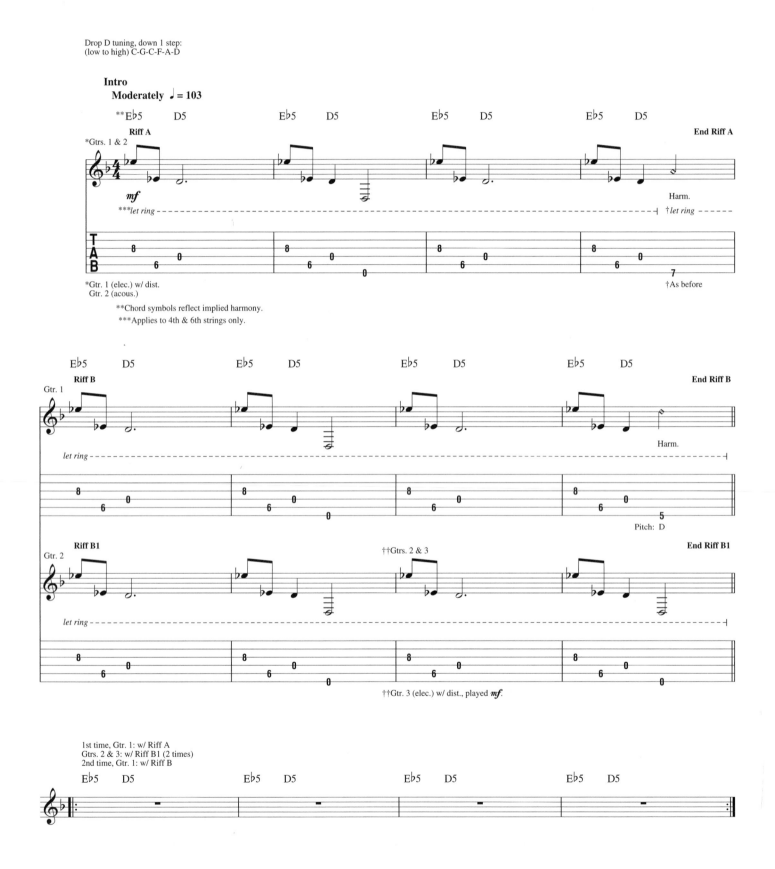

**Guitar Solo**

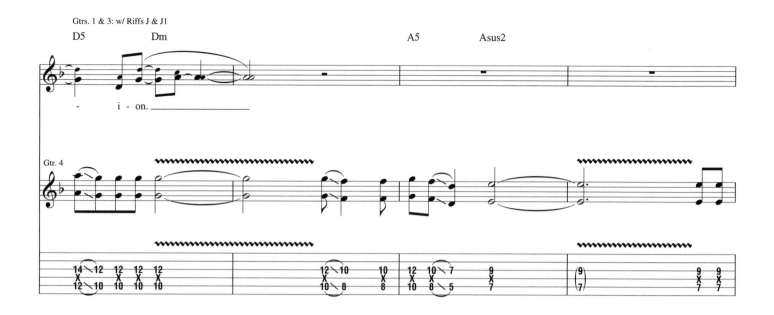

# Portrait (He Knew)

**Words and Music by Kerry Livgren and Steve Walsh**

**Verse**

1. He had an-oth-er i-de-a, you might have heard his name,___

**Rhy. Fig. 1**
*Gtrs. 1 & 2 (dist.)

**slight P.M. throughout

*composite arrangement
**next 8 meas.

he lived a-lone with a vi-sion, not look-ing for for-tune and fame.

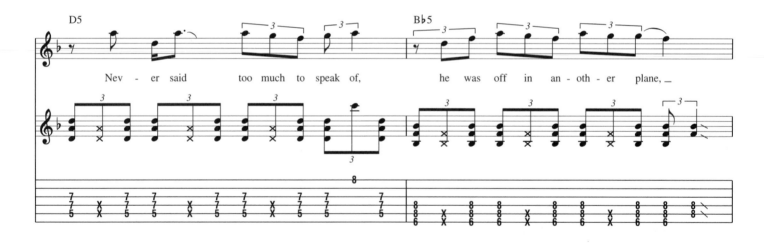

Nev-er said too much to speak of, he was off in an-oth-er plane,___

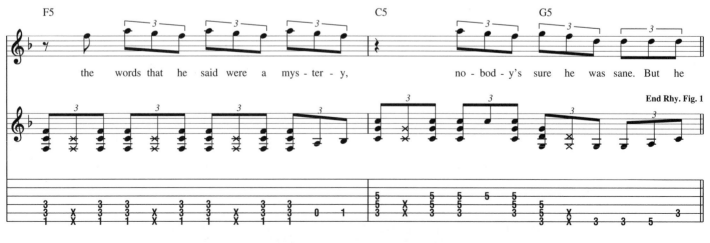

the words that he said were a mys-ter-y, no-bod-y's sure he was sane. But he

**End Rhy. Fig. 1**

166

*Played slightly ahead of the beat.

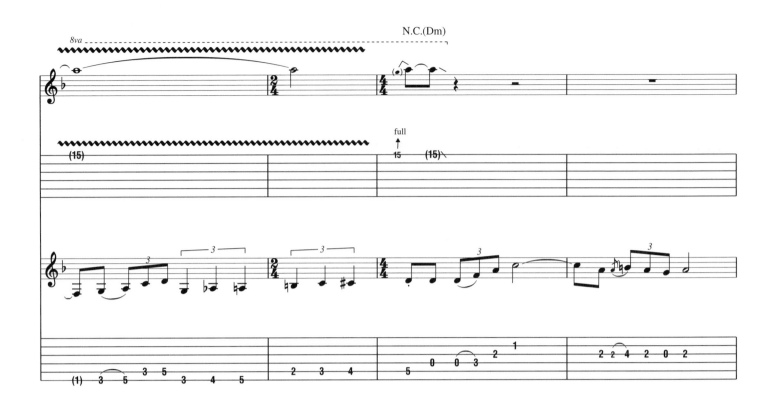

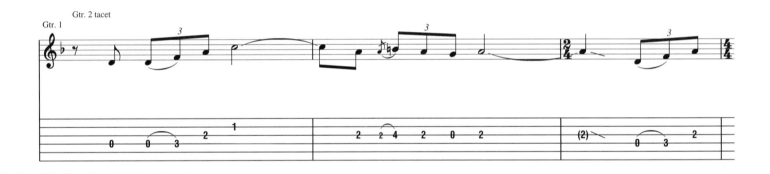

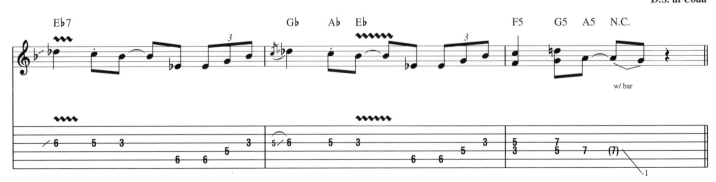

170

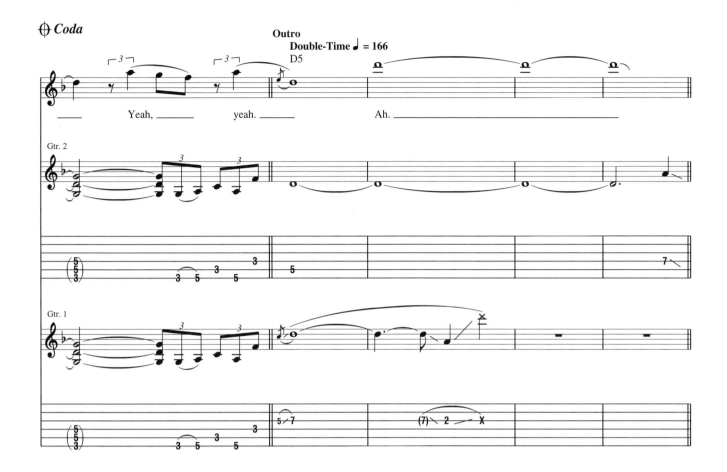

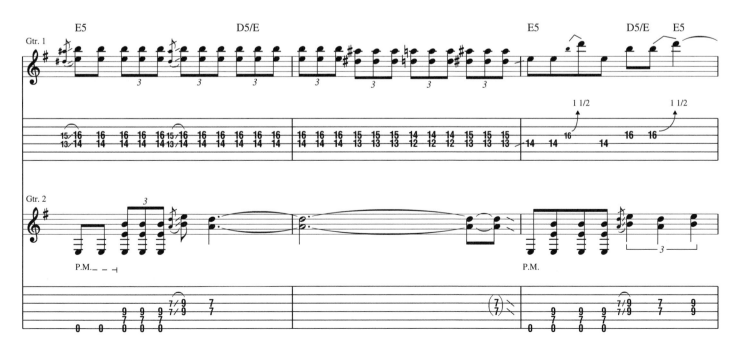

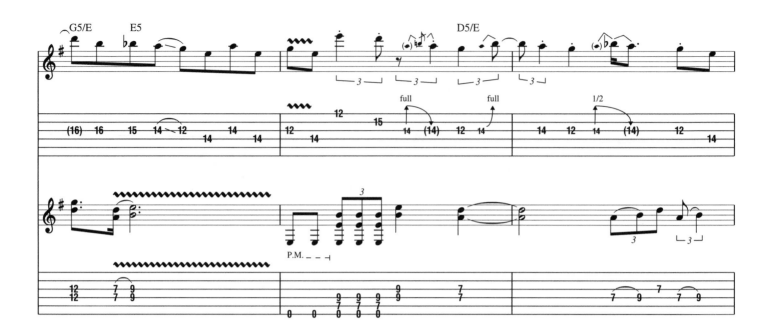

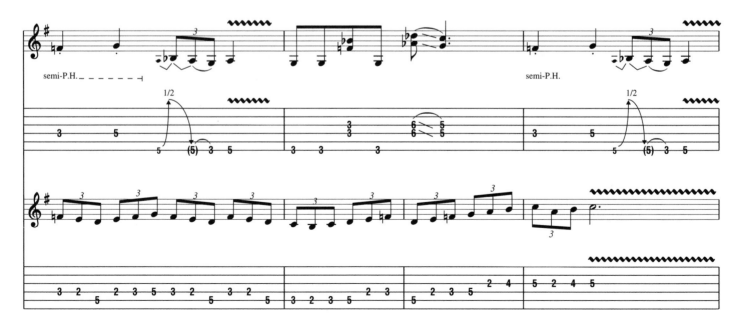

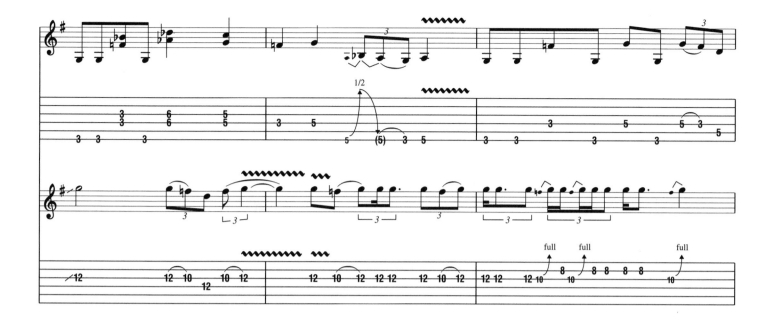

E5

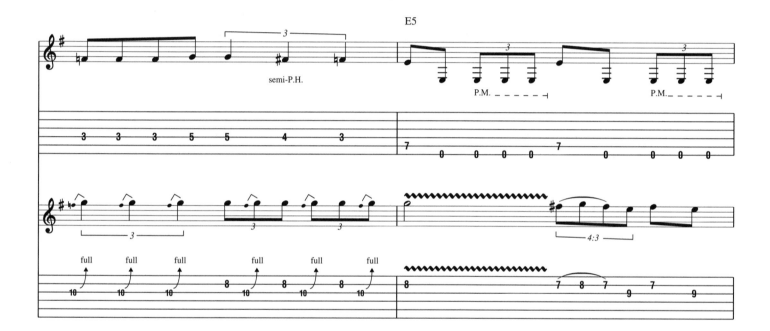

G7

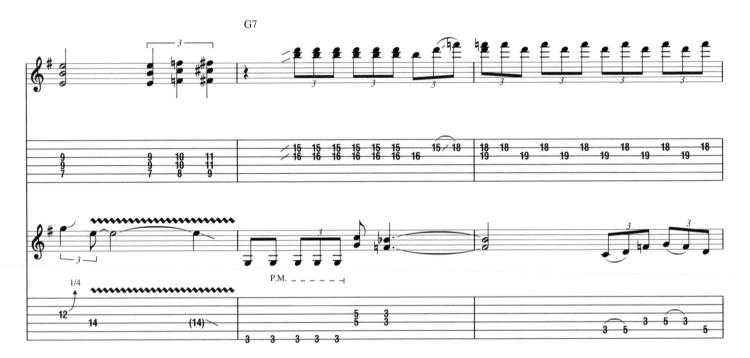

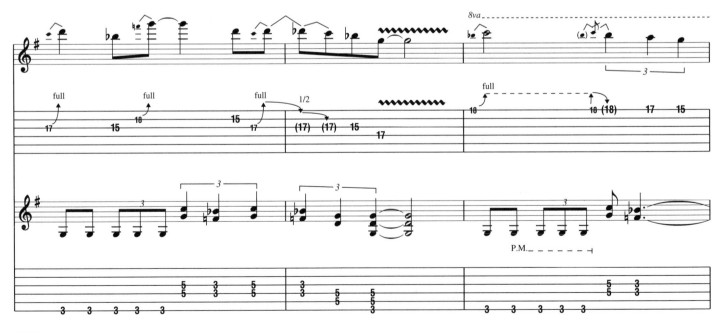

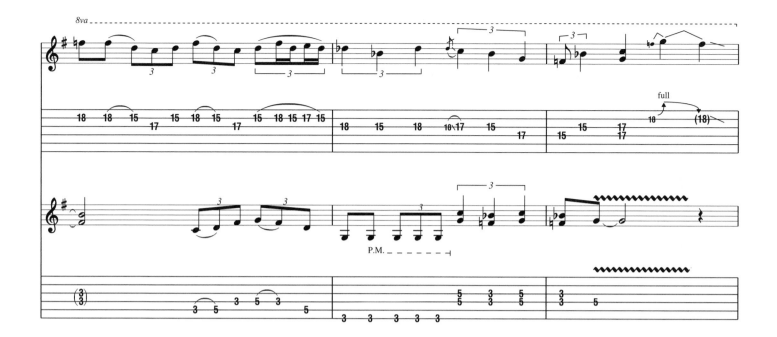

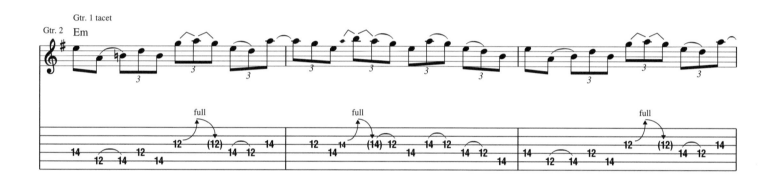

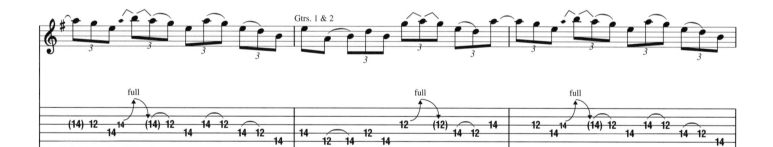

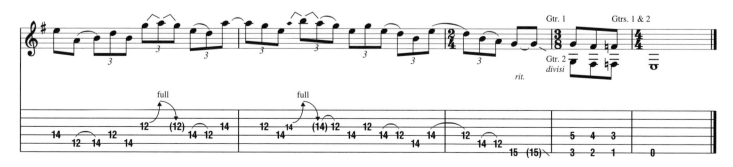

from Yes – *Big Generator*

# Rhythm of Love

**Words and Music by John Anderson, Trevor Rabin, Chris Squire, Tony Kaye and Alan White**

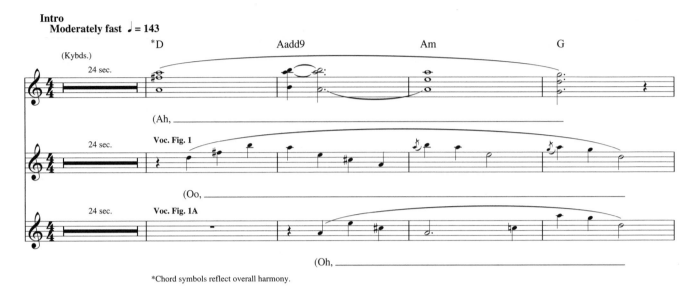

*Chord symbols reflect overall harmony.

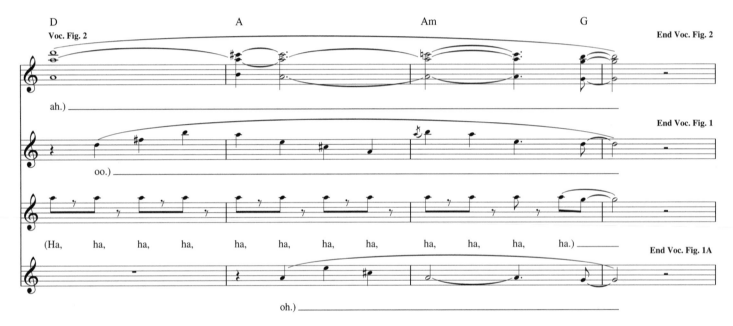

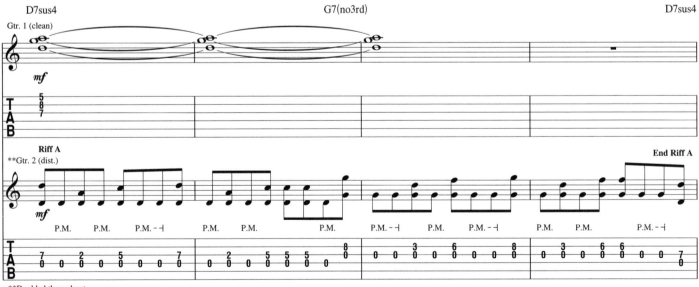

**Doubled throughout

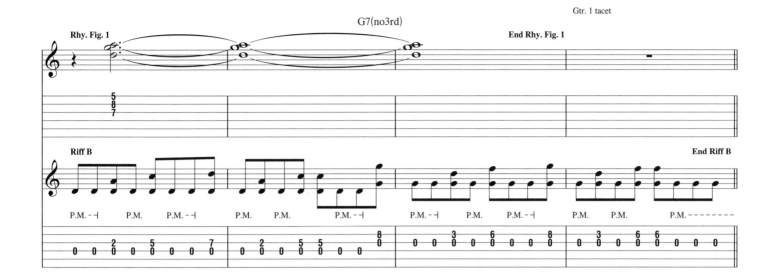

**Verse**

1. In - no - cence, __ no an - swer to __ your break - ing heart, __ if __
__ the sit - u - a - tion some - times falls __ a - part. __ Then in __

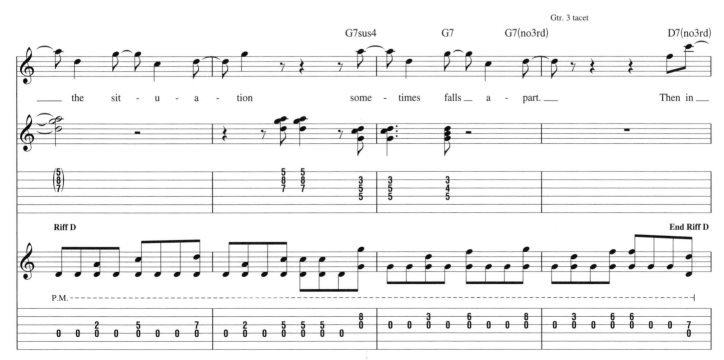

Gtrs. 4 & 5 tacet          Gtr. 1 tacet

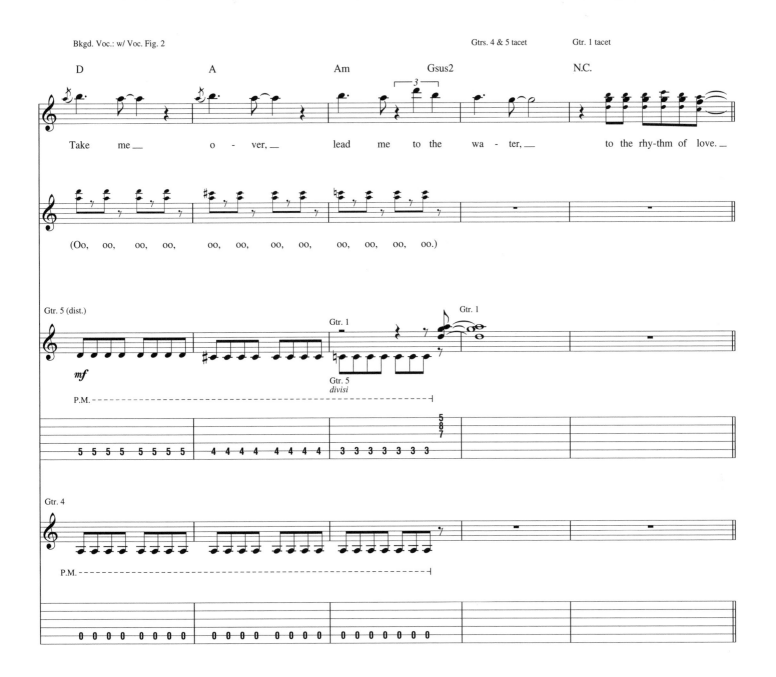

| D | A | Am | Gsus2 | N.C. |

Take  me ___  o - ver, ___  lead  me  to  the  wa - ter, ___  to  the  rhy-thm  of  love. ___

(Oo,   oo,   oo,   oo,    oo,   oo,   oo,   oo,    oo,   oo,   oo,   oo.)

Gtr. 5 (dist.)

Gtr. 1

Gtr. 1

*mf*

Gtr. 5
*divisi*

P.M. - - - - - - - - - - - - - - - - - - - - - - - - - - -

Gtr. 4

P.M. - - - - - - - - - - - - - - - - - - - - - - -

**Chorus**

Gtr. 2: w/ Riff A

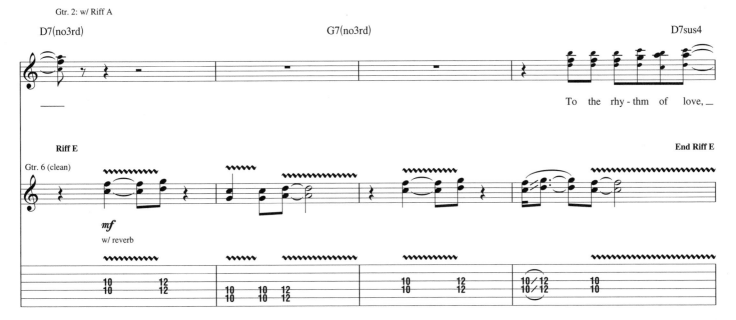

| D7(no3rd) | G7(no3rd) | D7sus4 |

___  To  the  rhy - thm  of  love, ___

**Riff E**                                        **End Riff E**

Gtr. 6 (clean)

*mf*
w/ reverb

Gtr. 1: w/ Rhy. Fig. 1
Gtr. 2: w/ Riff B
Gtr. 6: w/ Riff E

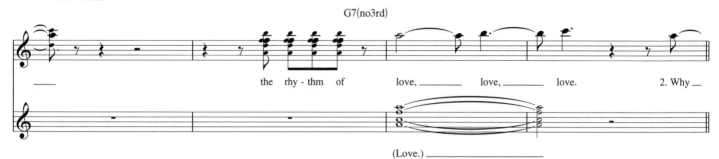

**Verse**

Gtr. 2: w/ Riff C                                          Gtr. 3 tacet

Gtr. 2: w/ Riff D

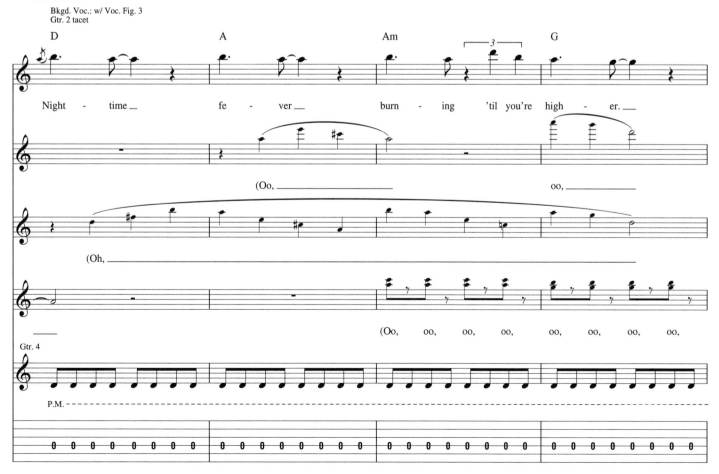

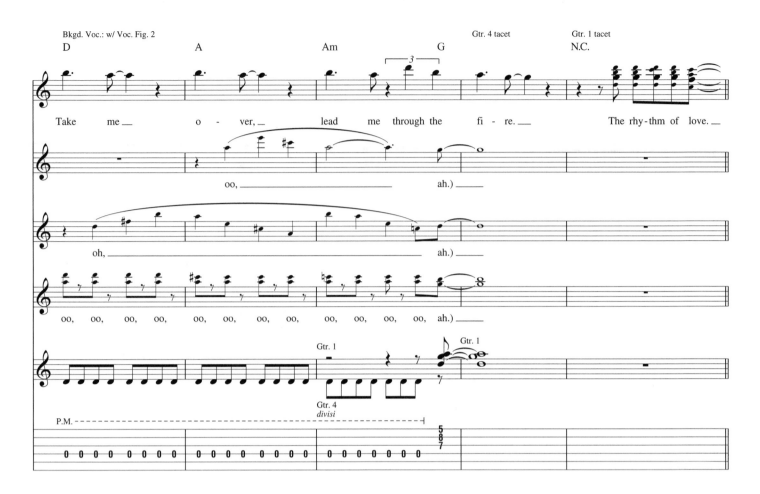

**Chorus**

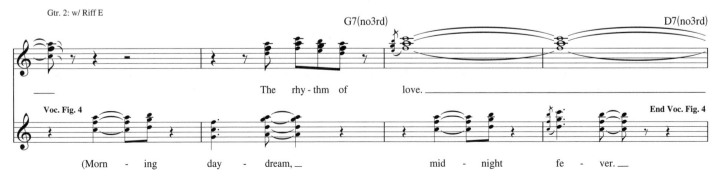

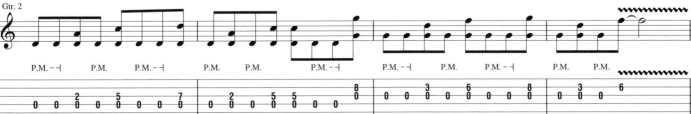

## Bridge

Gtrs. 2 & 8 tacet

In-hi-bi-tion keep ___ you from ___ your point ___ of view. ___

In-for-ma-tion need - ed ___ to ___ con - fuse ___

Rhy. Fig. 2

*Gtr. 9

End Rhy. Fig. 2

*Kybd. arr. for gtr.

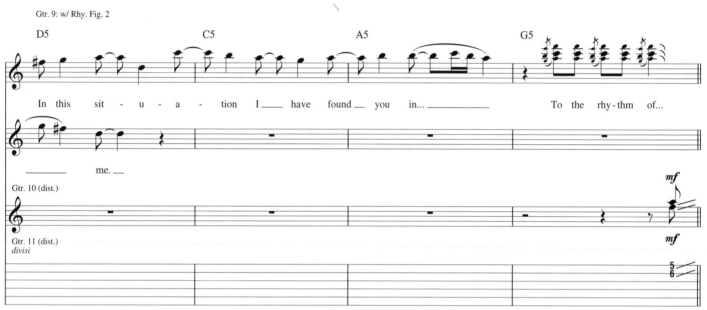

Gtr. 9: w/ Rhy. Fig. 2

In this sit - u - a - tion I ___ have found ___ you in... ___ To the rhy-thm of...

___ me. ___

Gtr. 10 (dist.)

Gtr. 11 (dist.)
*divisi*

## Guitar Solo

Gtr. 10

Gtr. 11

Gtr. 11 tacet

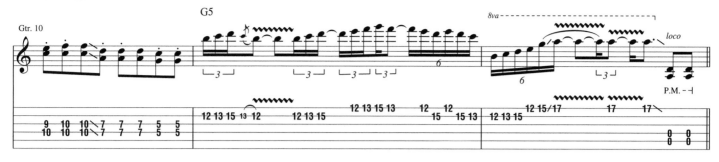

**Outro-Chorus**

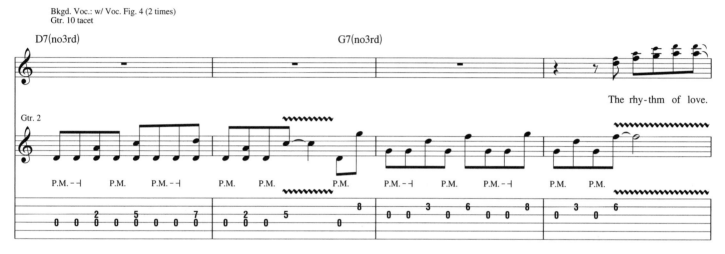

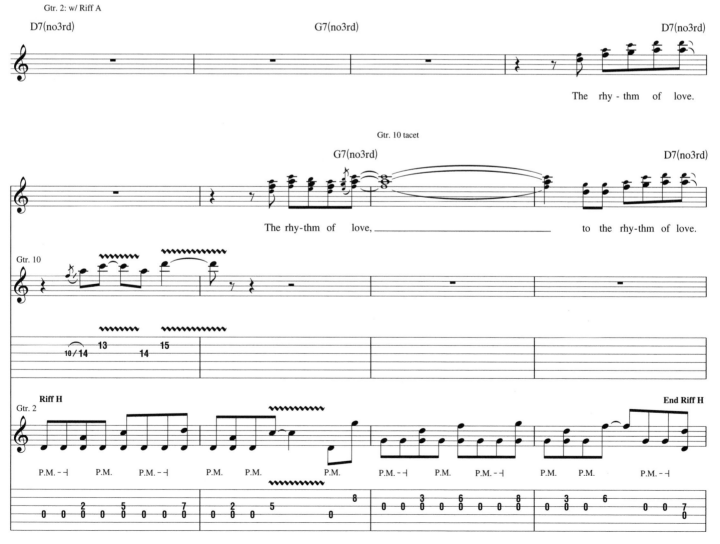

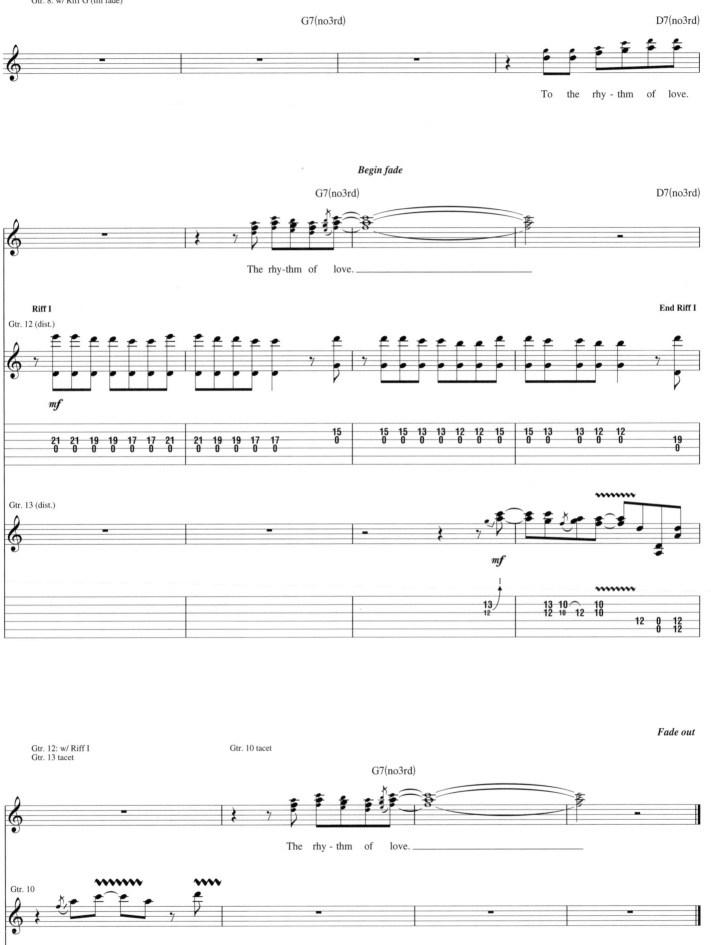

from The Moody Blues – *Every Good Boy Deserves Favour*

# The Story in Your Eyes

**Words and Music by Justin Hayward**

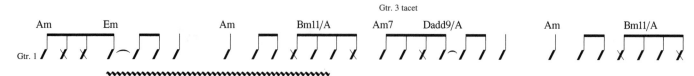

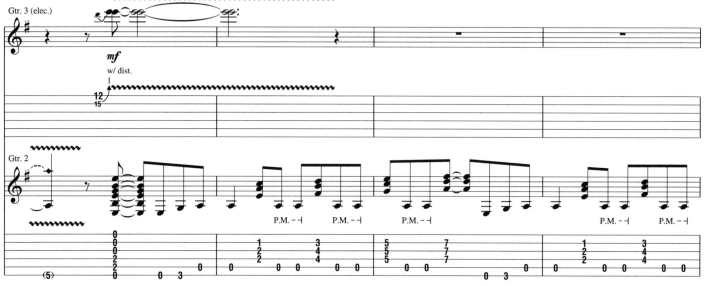

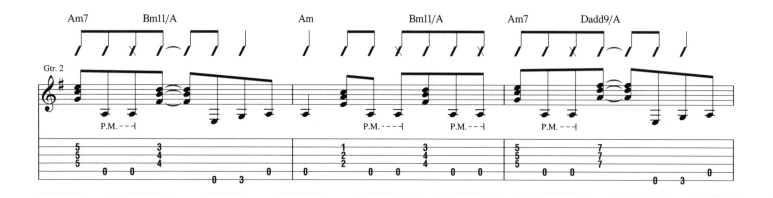

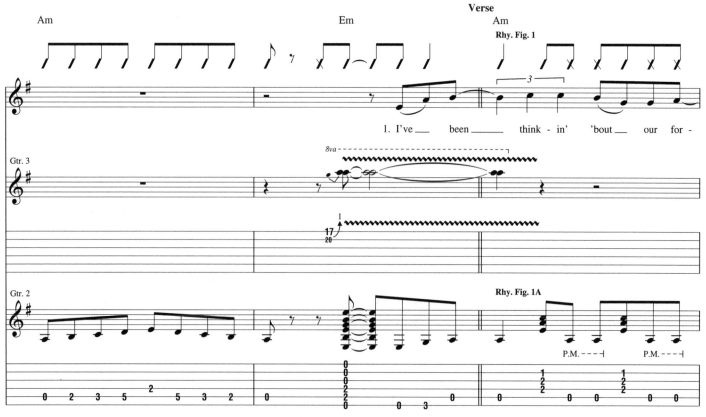

*Harm. performed by lightly touching 4th string while fretting note on 5th string.

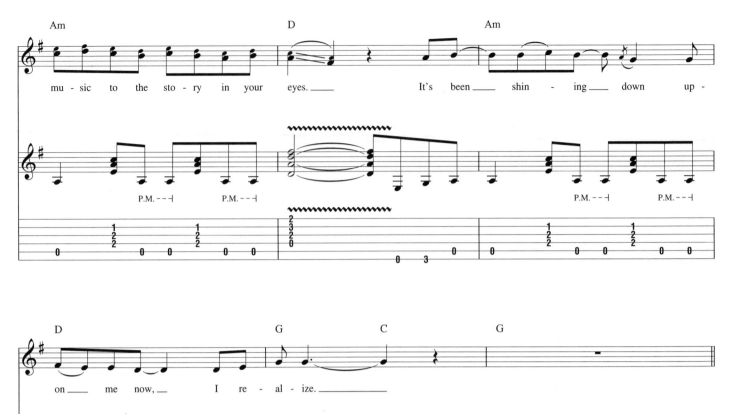

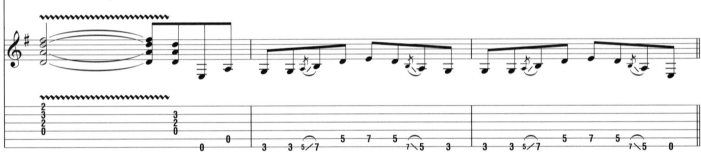

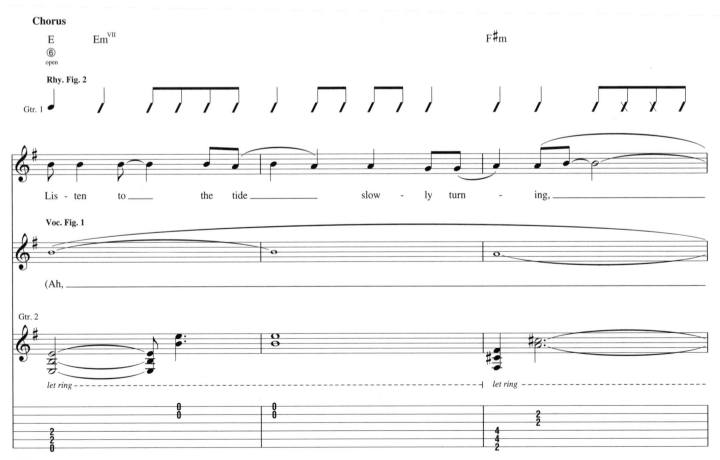

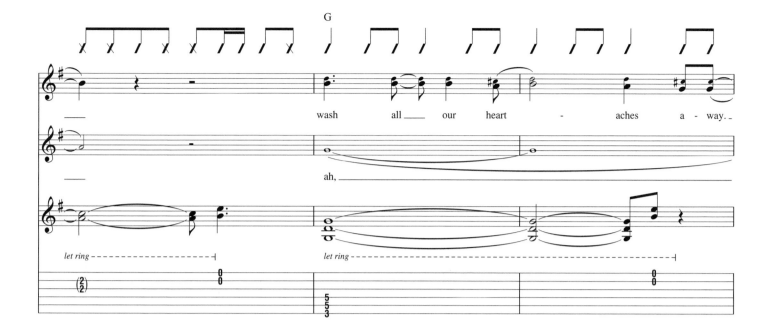

*Gtr. 5 (elec.) w/ dist., played *mf*. Composite arrangement

**Chorus**

Bkgd. Voc.: w/ Voc. Fig. 1
Gtr. 1: w/ Rhy. Fig. 2
Gtr. 4 tacet

Gtr. 5 tacet

Lis - ten to the tide slow - ly turn - ing,

*D.S. al Coda*

wash all our heart - aches a - way. We're part

**Verse**

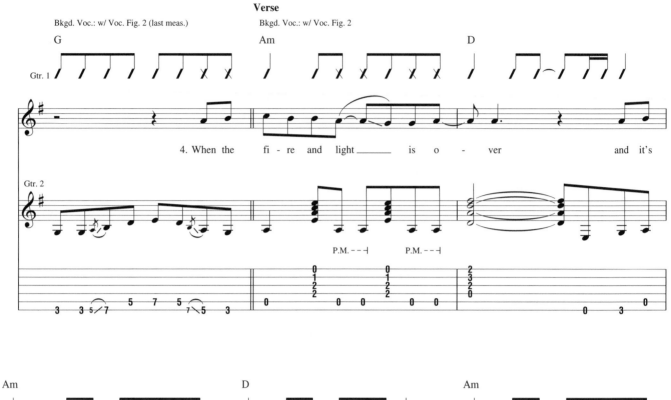

Bkgd. Voc.: w/ Voc. Fig. 2 (last meas.)  Bkgd. Voc.: w/ Voc. Fig. 2

4. When the fi - re and light ___ is o - ver ___ and it's

cer - tain that the cur - tain's ___ gon - na fall, ___ I can hide ___ in - side ___ your

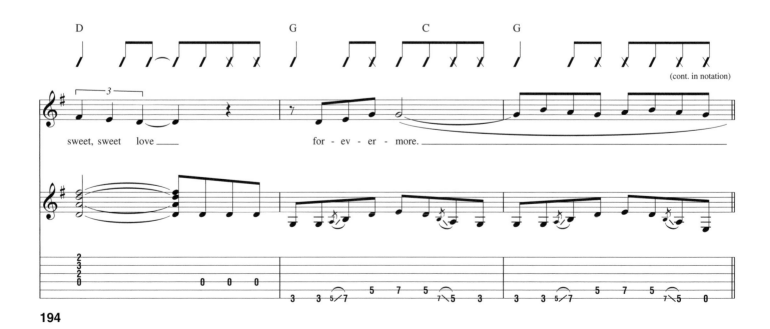

sweet, sweet love ___ for - ev - er - more. ___

(cont. in notation)

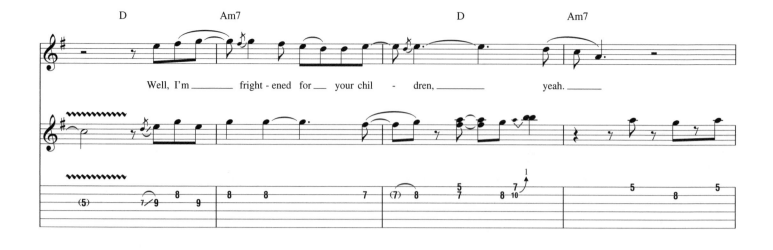

Well, I'm _____ fright-ened for ____ your chil - dren, _____ yeah. _____

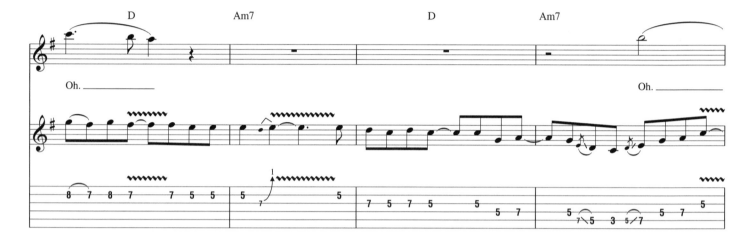

Oh. _____ Oh. _____

_____ Yes, I'm fright - ened for _____ your chil - dren.

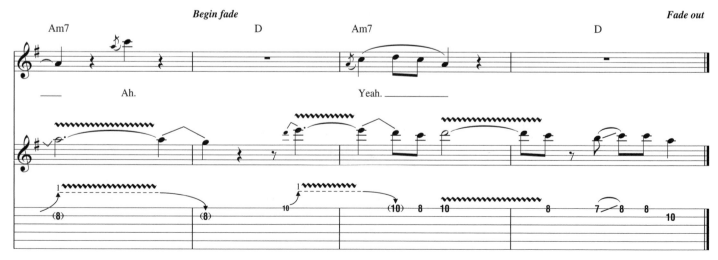

Ah. Yeah. _____

from Electric Light Orchestra - *Face the Music*

# Strange Magic

### Words and Music by Jeff Lynne

2nd time, Bkgd. Voc.: w/ Voc. Fill 1 (2 times)   Gtrs. 2 & 3 tacet

1. You're sail - ing soft - ly _ through the sun, _ in a bro - ken _ stone age dawn. _
2. You're walk - ing mead - ows _ in my mind. _ Mak - ing waves a - cross my time. _

**Gtr. 2

**2nd time tacet.

***Gtr. 3

***2nd time tacet.

Gtr. 4   **Riff B**

*let ring* - - - - - - - - - - - - - - - - - - - - - - - - - - - - - - -

Gtr. 1   **Rhy. Fig. 3**

*let ring* - - - - - - - - - - - - - - - - - - - - - - - - - - - - - - -

*Chord symbols reflect overall harmony.

**Voc. Fill 1**

(Ah, ah, _ ah, ah, ah.) _

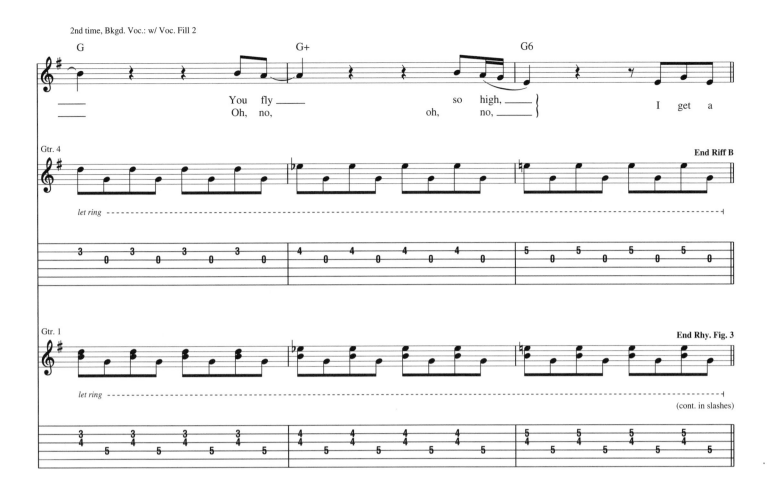

You fly _____ so high, _____
Oh, no, oh, no, _____
I get a

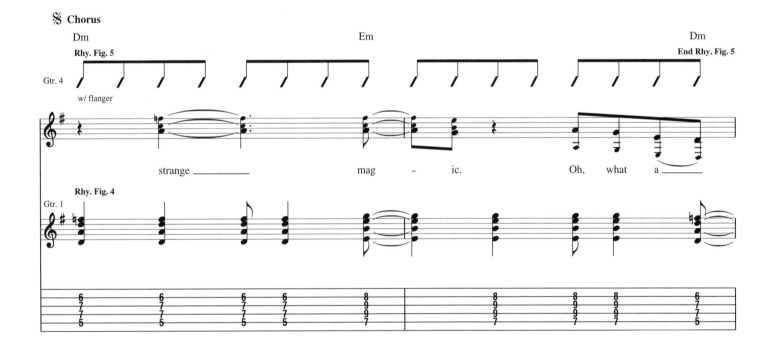

strange _____ mag - ic. Oh, what a _____

(Ah, ah, ___ Yo ah, ah, ah, ___ ah, ah, ___ ah, ah, ah, ___ ah, ah, ___ ah, ah.)

Gtr. 4: w/ Rhy. Fig. 5 (2 times)

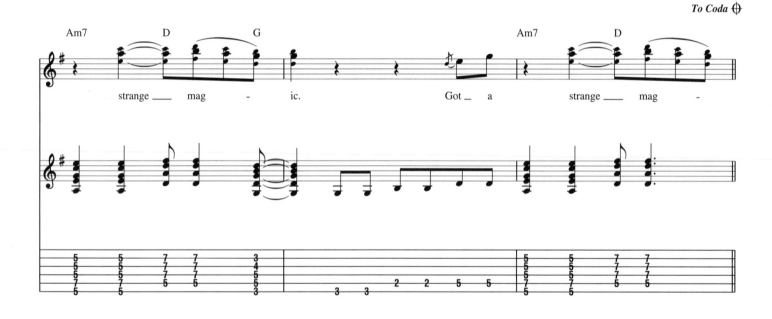

strange ___ mag - ic. Oh, it's a ___ strantge ___ mag - ic. Got ___ a

End Rhy. Fig. 4

*To Coda* ⊕

strange ___ mag - ic. Got ___ a strange ___ mag -

## Interlude

Gtrs. 1 & 4: w/ Rhy. Figs. 1 & 1A
Gtrs. 2 & 3: w/ Riffs A & A1

Gtrs. 1 & 4: w/ Rhy. Figs. 1 & 1A
Gtrs. 2 & 3: w/ Riffs A & A1

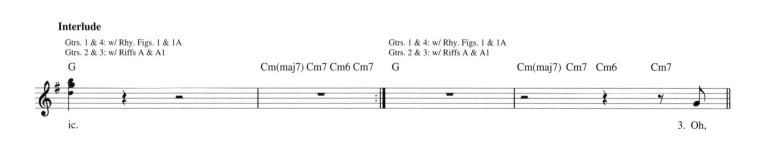

ic.

3. Oh,


200

**Verse**

Gtr. 1: w/ Rhy. Fig. 3
Gtr. 4: w/ Riff B

*Violins arr. for gtrs.

**Gtr. 7

**String ensemble arr. for gtr.

*D.S. al Coda*

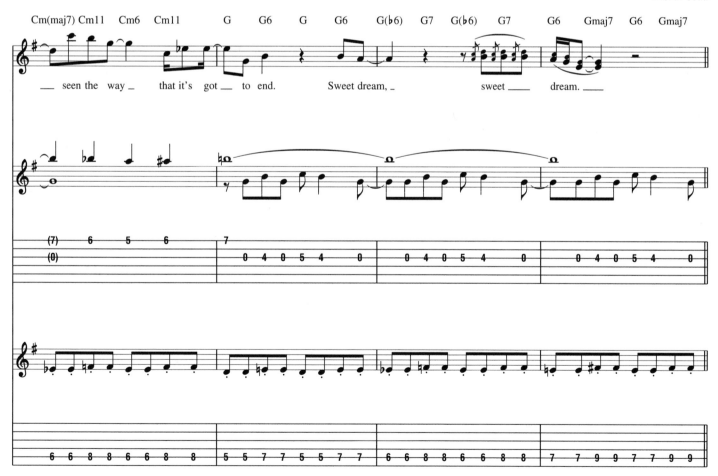

## ⊕ Coda

**Bridge**

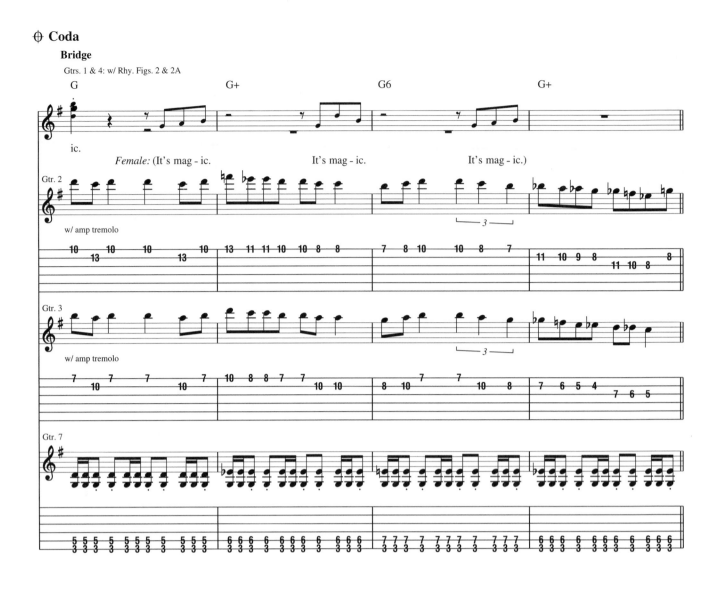

**Chorus**

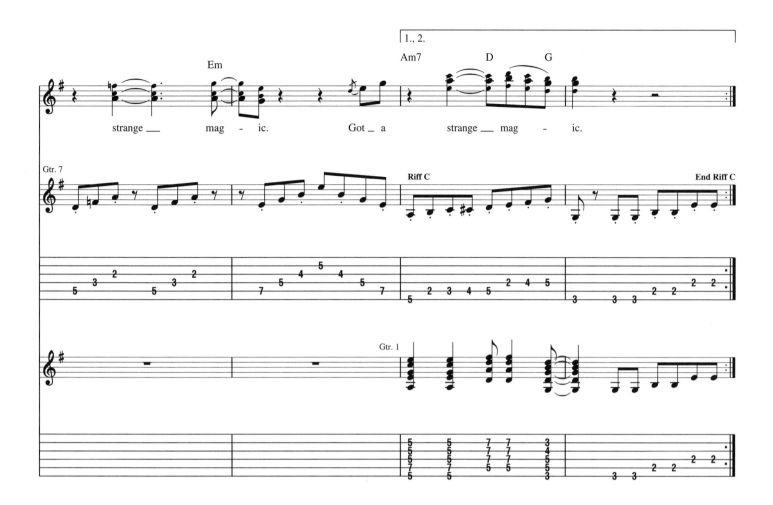

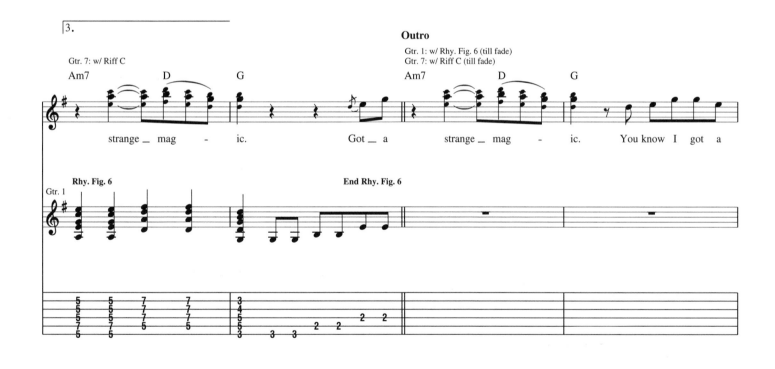

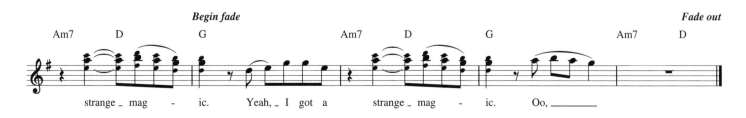

# Three of a Perfect Pair

### Words and Music by Adrian Belew, Robert Fripp, Tony Levin and Bill Bruford

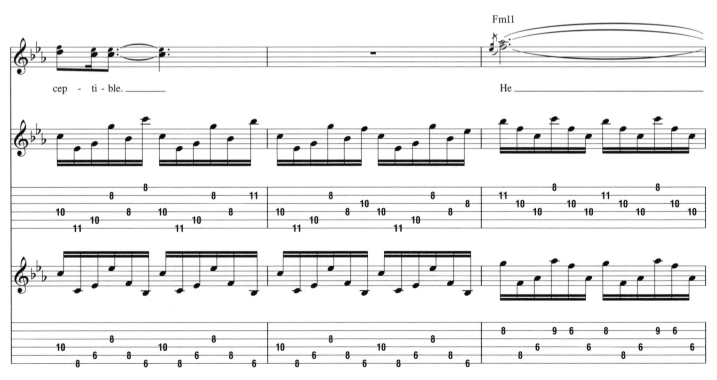

*Chord symbols reflect implied harmony.

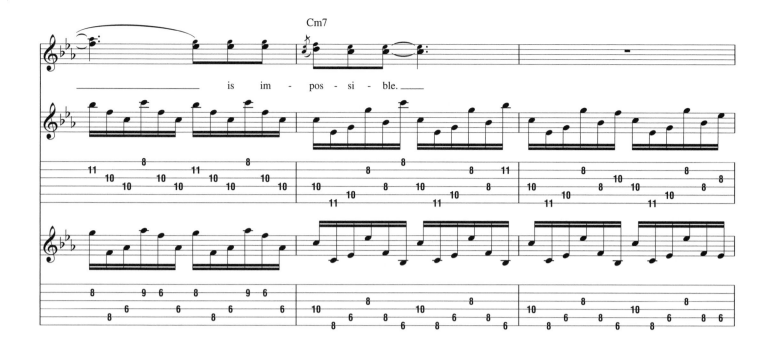

is im - pos - si - ble.____

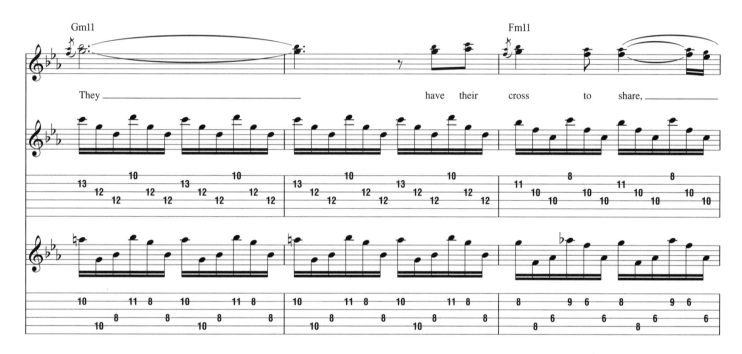

They _____ have their cross to share,____

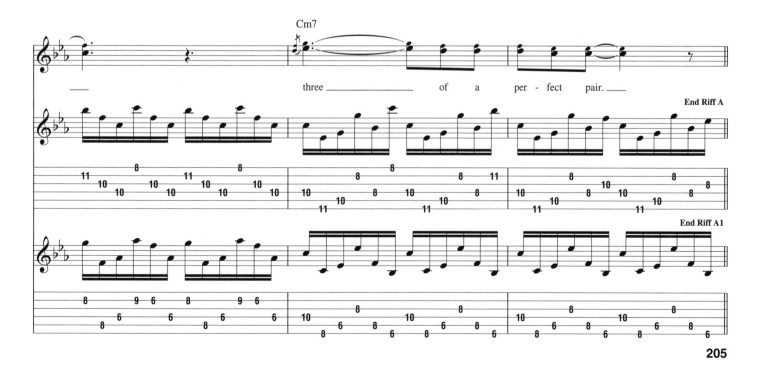

____ three _____ of a per - fect pair.____

**End Riff A**

**End Riff A1**

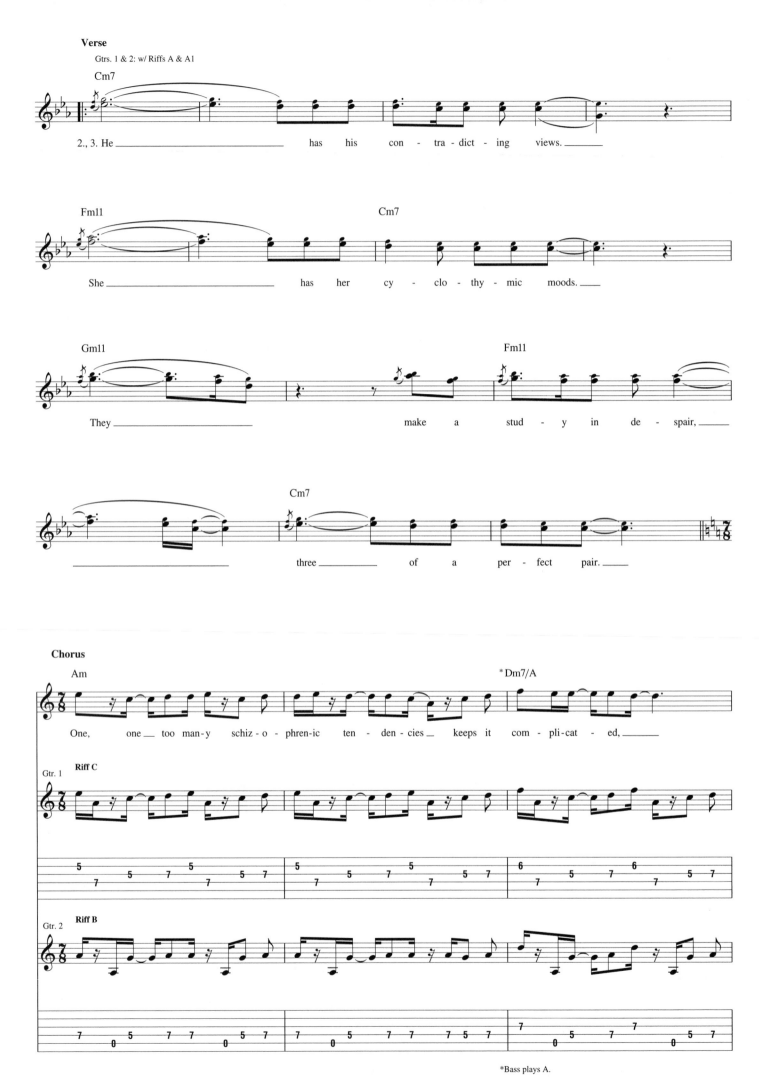

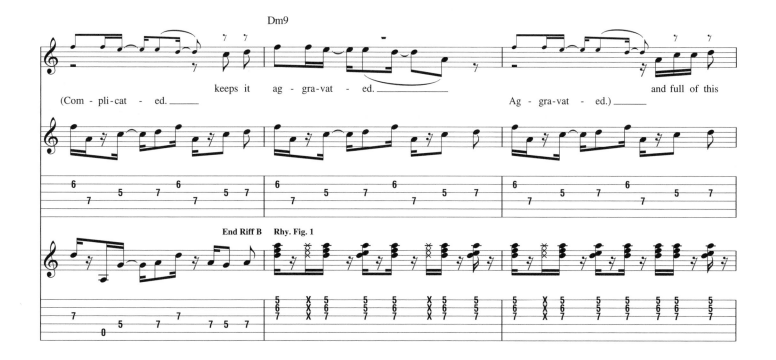

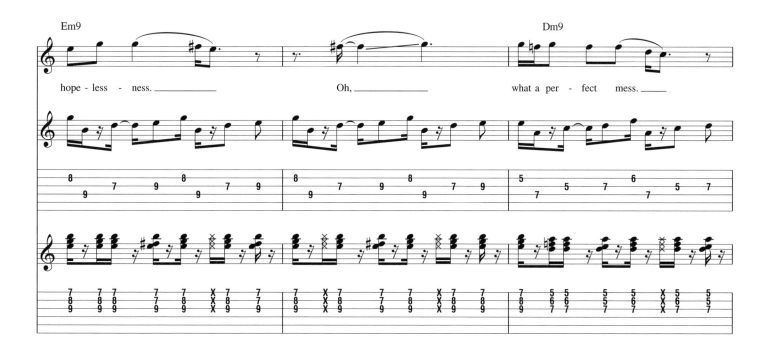

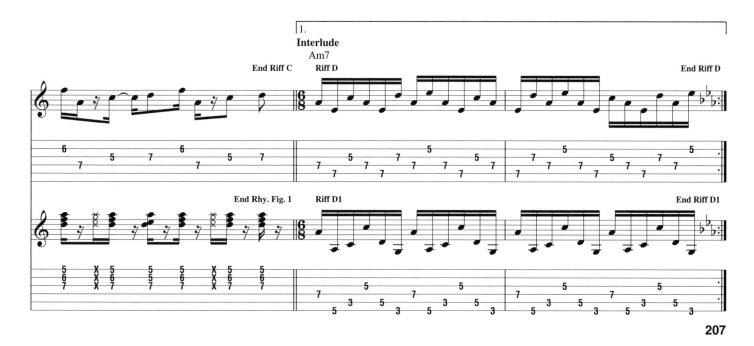

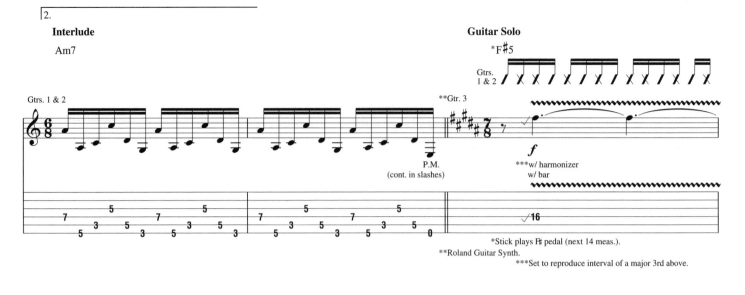

**Interlude**

Am7

**Guitar Solo**

*F#5

*Stick plays F# pedal (next 14 meas.).
**Roland Guitar Synth.
***Set to reproduce interval of a major 3rd above.

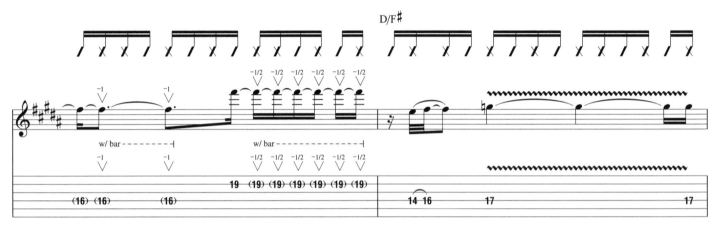

D/F#

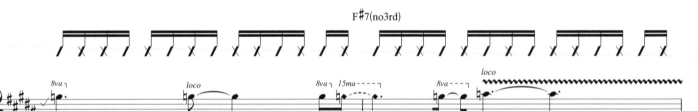

F#7(no3rd)

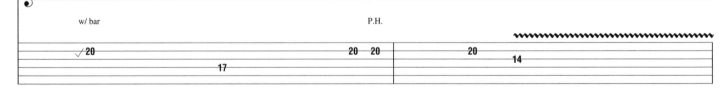

F#5 type 2

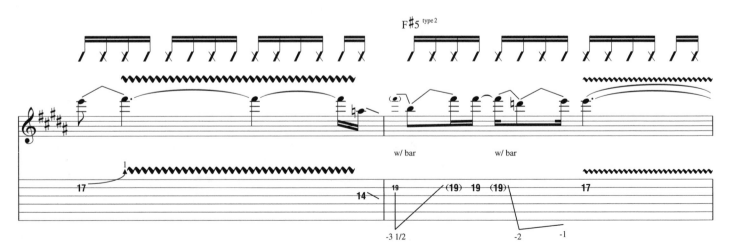

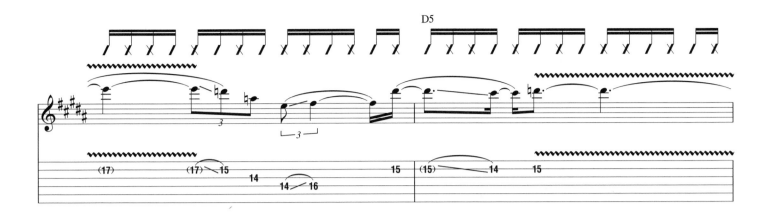

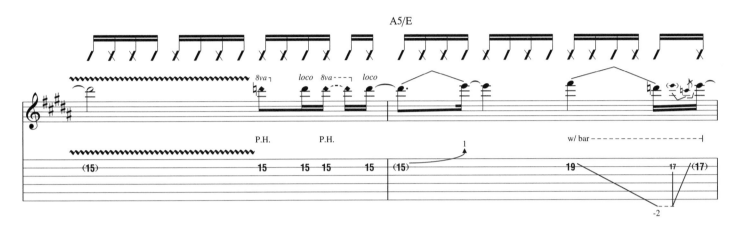

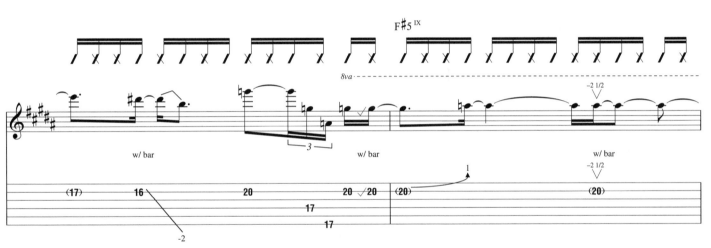

**Chorus**

Gtr. 1: w/ Riff C
Gtr. 2: w/ Riff B

Am

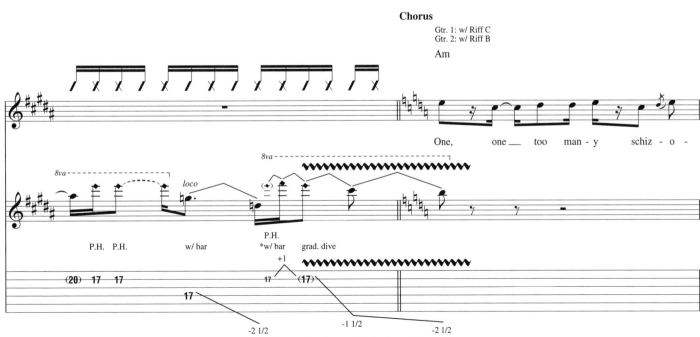

One, one too man-y schiz-o-

*Pull bar up, then dive and vib. simultaneously.

Gtr. 3 tacet

Dm7/A

phren - ic ten - den - cies___ keeps it com - pli - cat - ed, _____ keeps it

Gtr. 2: w/ Rhy. Fig. 1

Dm9                                                                    Em9

ag - gra - vat - ed, _____ and full of this hope - less - ness. _____

*Gtr. 4 (dist.)

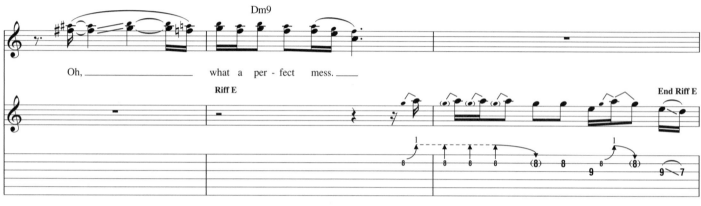

mf

*Bkwds. gtr. arr. for gtr.

Dm9

Oh, _____ what a per - fect mess. ___

Riff E                                                            End Riff E

## Chorus

Gtr. 1: w/ Riff C
Gtr. 2: w/ Riff B
Gtr. 4 tacet

Am                                                                     Dm7/A

One,    one___ too man - y schiz - o - phren - ic ten - den - cies___ keeps it com - pli - cat - ed, ___

Gtr. 2: w/ Rhy. Fig. 1

Dm9

(Com - pli - cat - ed. ___)    keeps it so___ ag - gra - vat - ed. ___    Ag - gra - vat - ed.) ___    and full of this

Em9                                         Gtr. 4: w/ Riff E                Dm9

hope - less - ness. ___    Oh, ___    what a per - fect mess. ___
                           (Oh, ___    what a per - fect mess.) ___

Play 6 times & fade

## Outro

Gtrs. 1 & 2: w/ Riffs D & D1

Am7

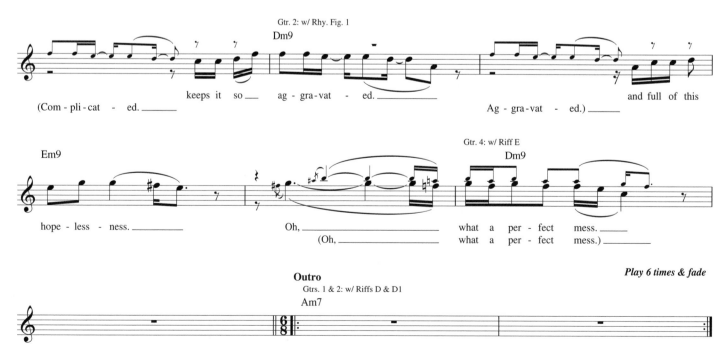

from Fates Warning - *Perfect Symmetry*

# Through Different Eyes

### Words and Music by Matheos

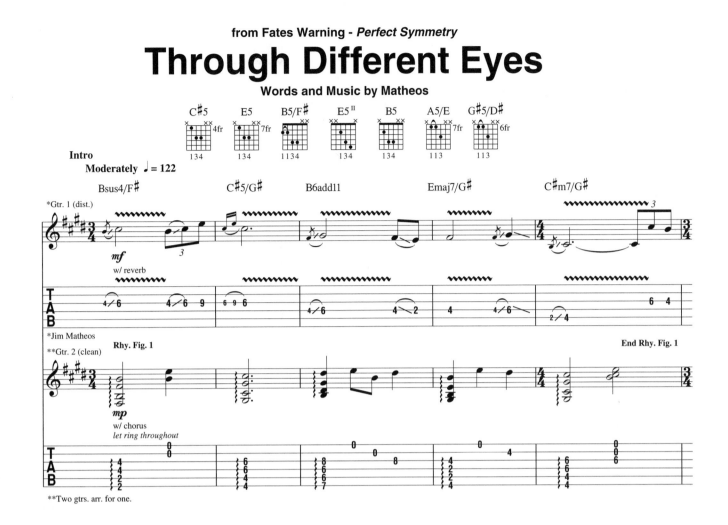

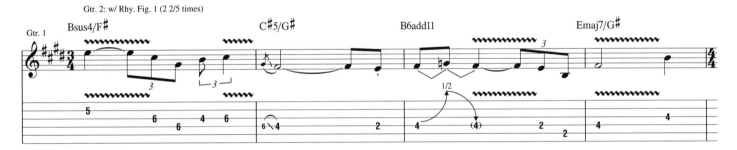

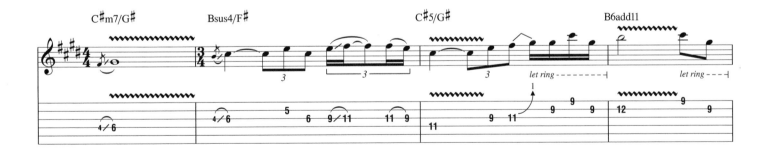

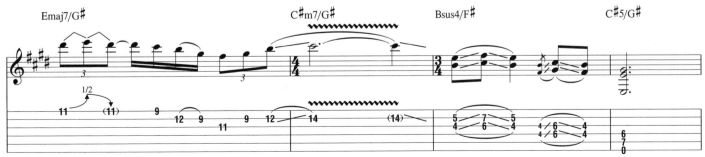

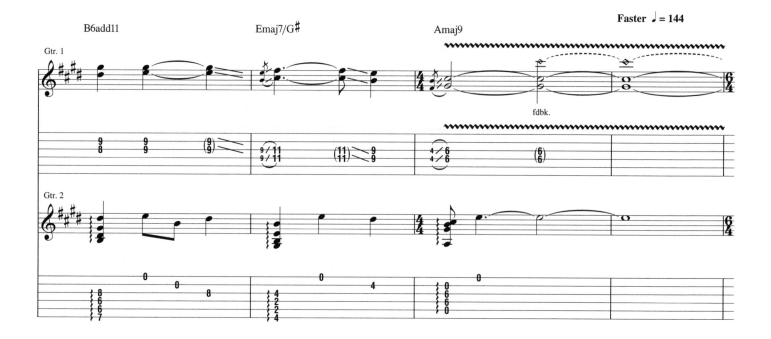

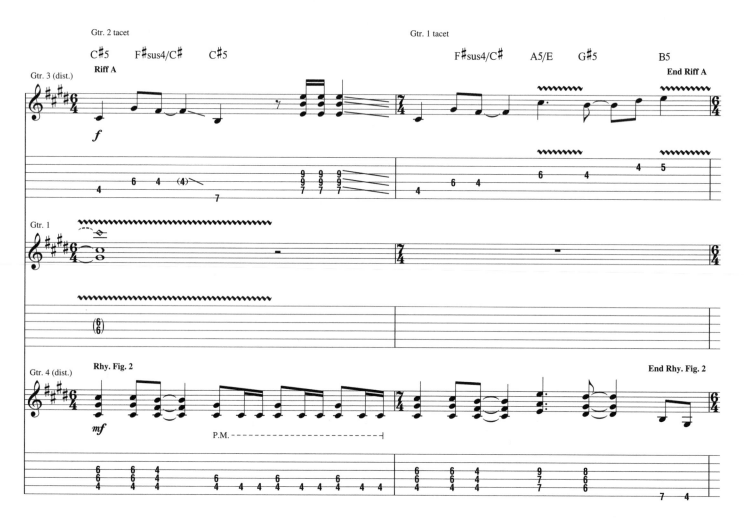

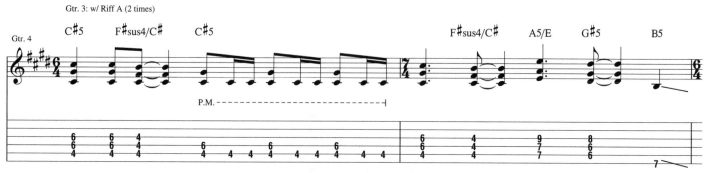

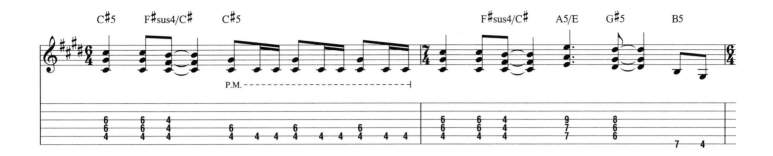

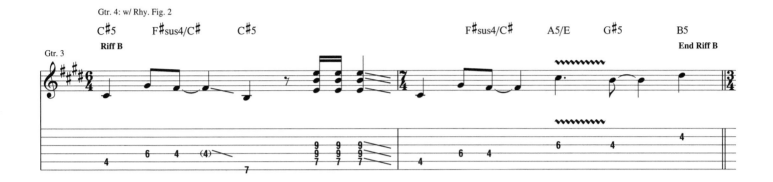

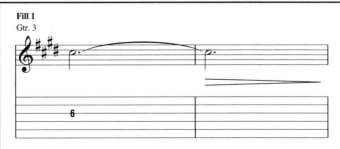

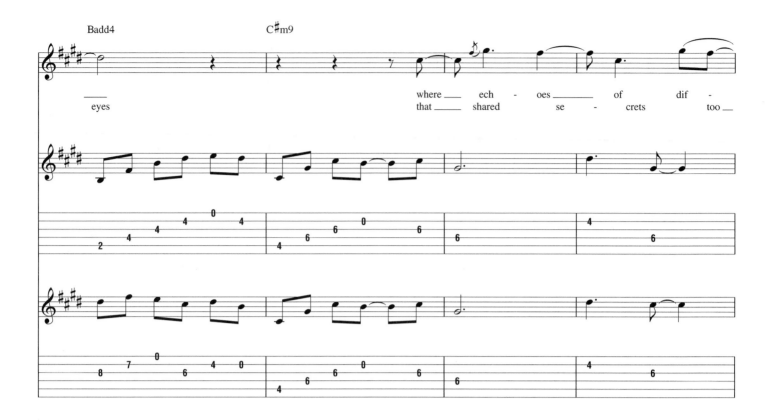

Gtrs. 5 & 6: w/ Riffs C & C1

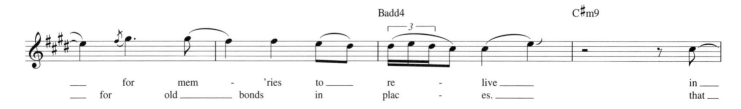

**Guitar Solo**

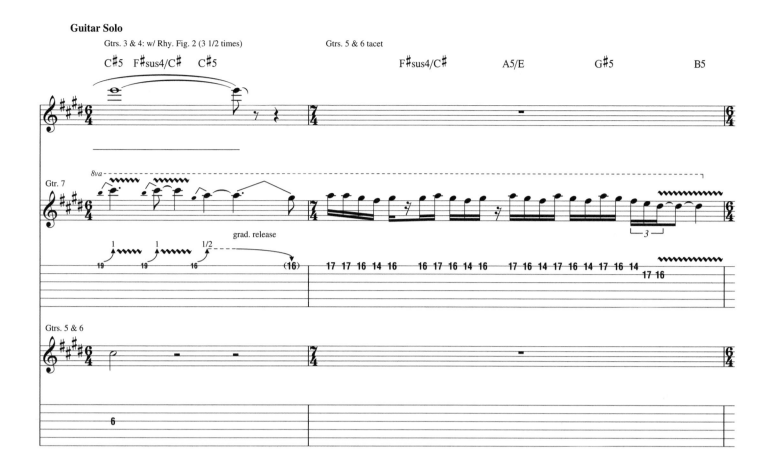

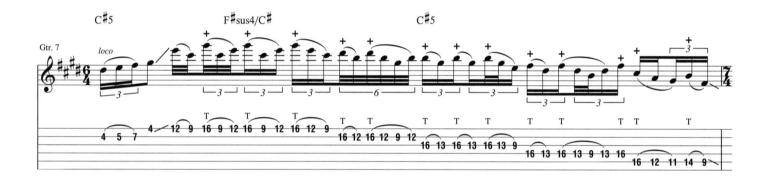

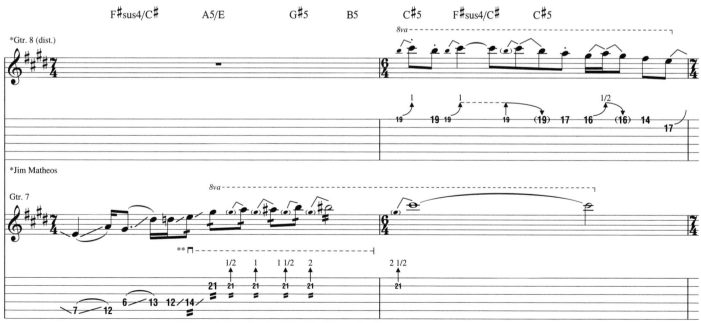

**Downpick sixteenth-note triplets while sliding and bending.

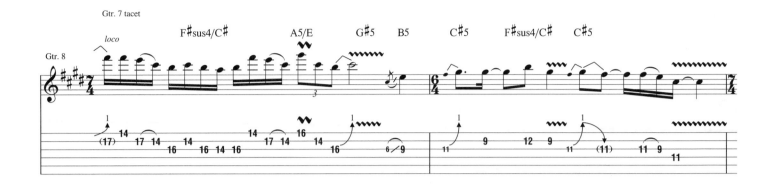

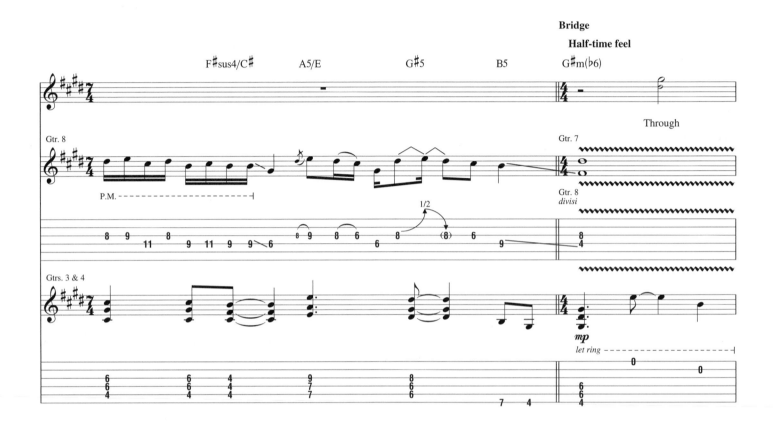

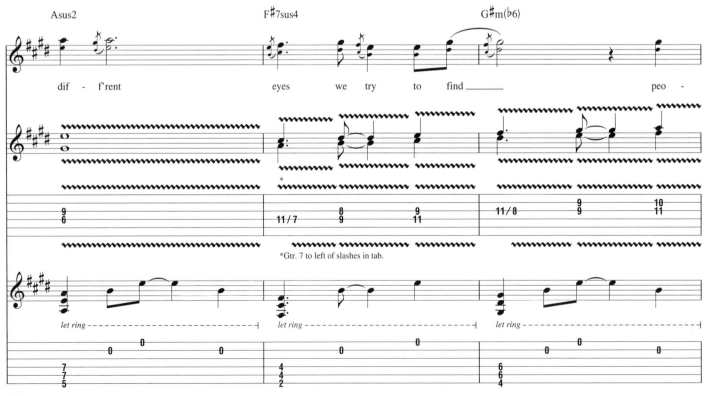

# Time

**Words and Music by Roger Waters, Nicholas Mason, David Gilmour and Rick Wright**

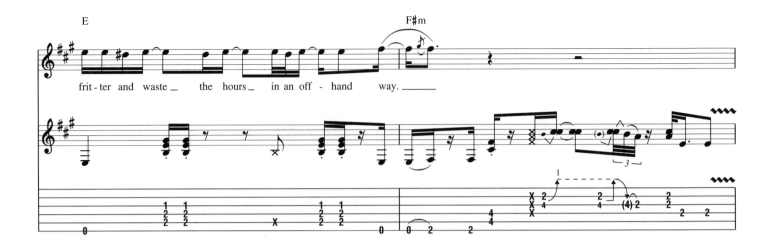

frit-ter and waste _ the hours _ in an off - hand way. _____

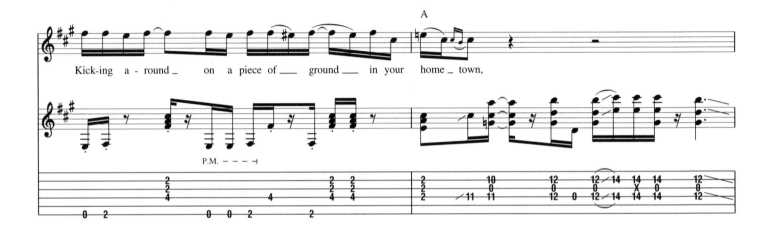

Kick-ing a - round _ on a piece of ___ ground ___ in your home _ town,

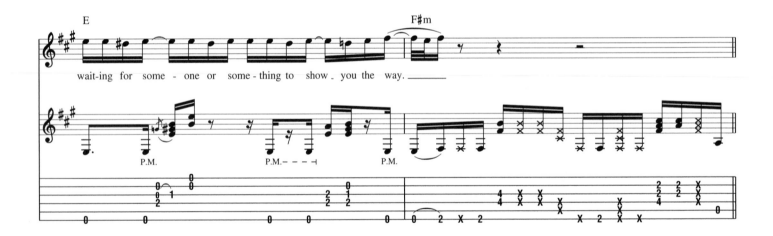

wait-ing for some - one or some - thing to show _ you the way. _____

**Bridge**

Dmaj7

**Voc. Fig. 1**

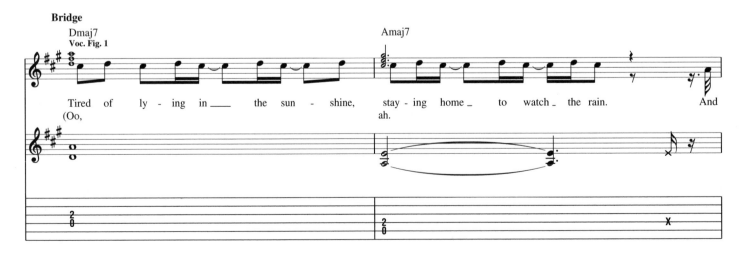

Tired of ly - ing in ___ the sun - shine, stay - ing home _ to watch _ the rain. And
(Oo, ah.

222

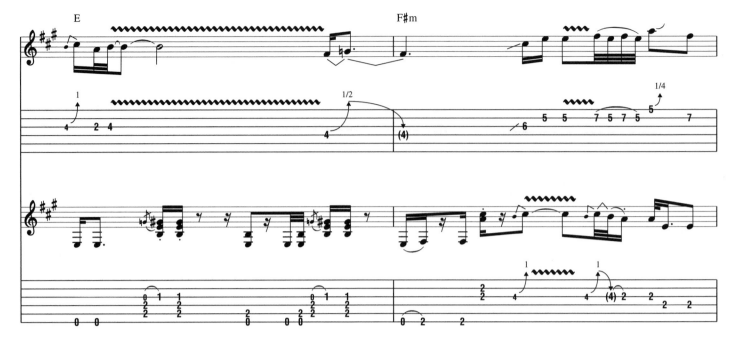

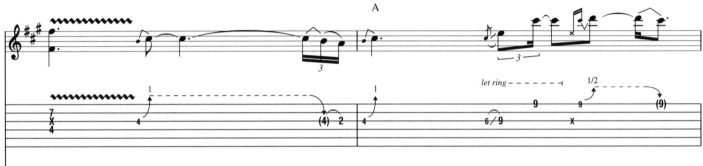

* Harmonic located between 2nd & 3rd frets.

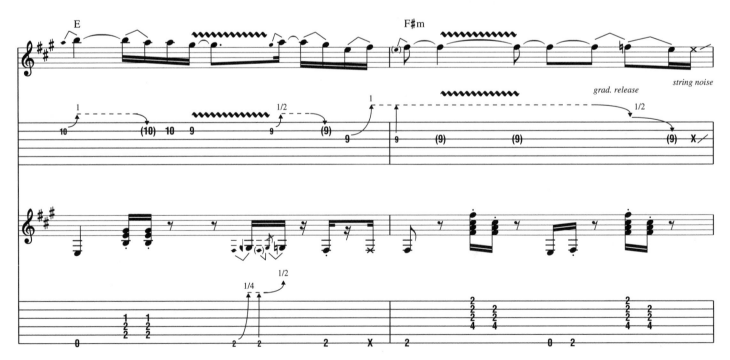

## Interlude

Bkgd. Voc.: w/ Voc. Fig. 1

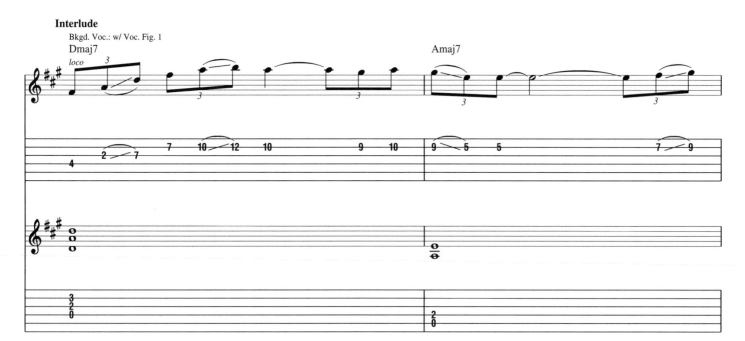

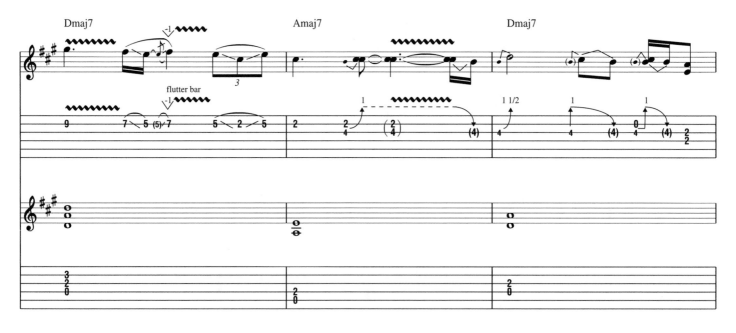

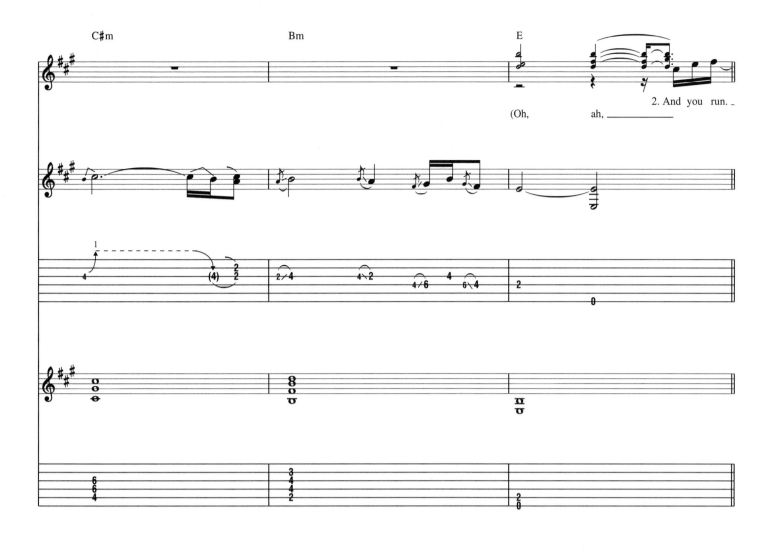

2. And you run. _
(Oh, ah, _____)

**Verse**

Gtr. 2 tacet

_____ you run _____ to catch up _____ with the sun _____ but it's sink - ing.
ah.)                                                                          (and)

let ring–

rac-ing a-round ___ to come up be-hind ___ you a-gain. _____ The

sun is the same ____ in a rel-a-tive way, _ but you're old - er,

short-er of breath, _ and one day clos-er to death. _

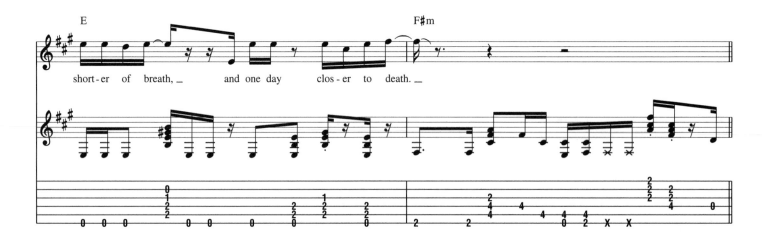

**Bridge**

Ev-'ry year is get-ting short-er, nev-er seem _ to find _ the time. _

(Oo, _____ ah.

(Yeah, _____

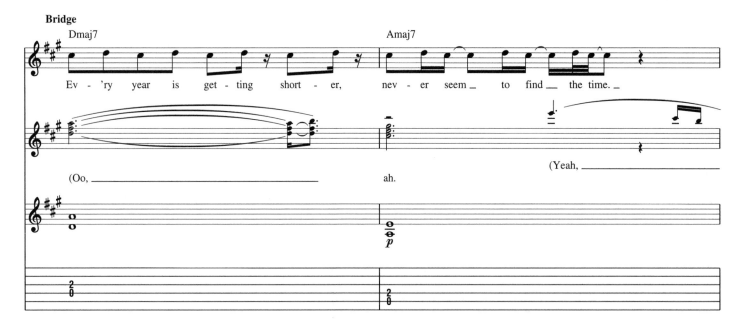

Plans that ei - ther come _ to naught or half a page. _ of scrib-bled lines.

Oo, ah. Oh. _____

Hang - ing on in qui - et des - par - a - tion _ is the _ Eng - lish _ way. The

Oo, _____ ah.
(Oh.)

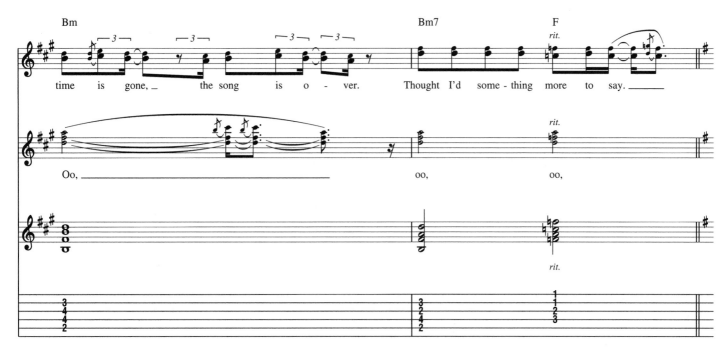

time is gone, _ the song is o - ver. Thought I'd some - thing more to say. _____

Oo, _____ oo, oo,

**Breathe (Reprise)**

**A tempo**

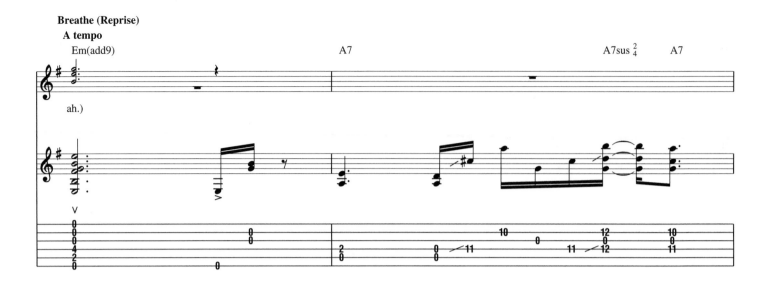

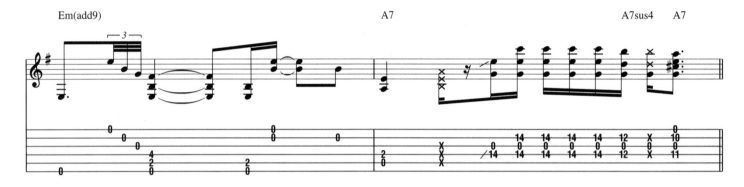

**Verse**

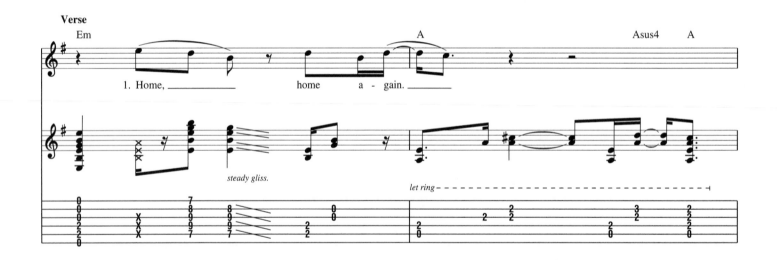

1. Home, _____ home a - gain. _____

*steady gliss.*

*let ring - - - - - - - - - - - - - - - - - - - - - - - - - - - -*

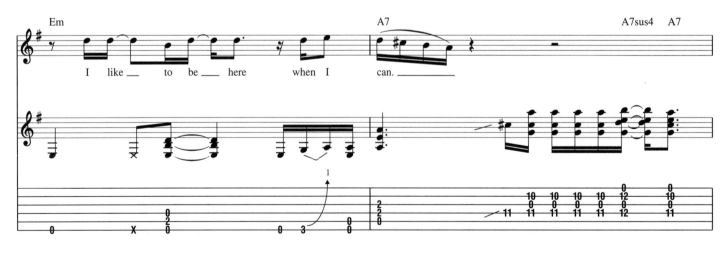

I like \_\_ to be \_\_ here when I can. _____

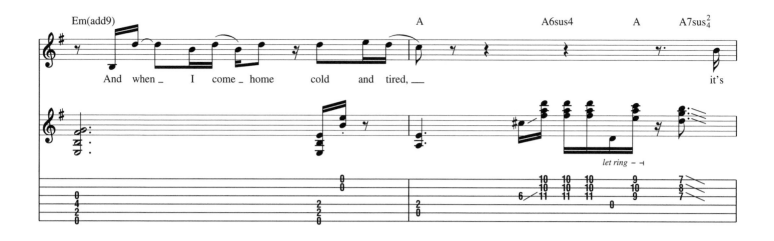

And when __ I come __ home cold and tired, __                                    it's

good __ to warm __ my bones __ be - side __ the fire. __

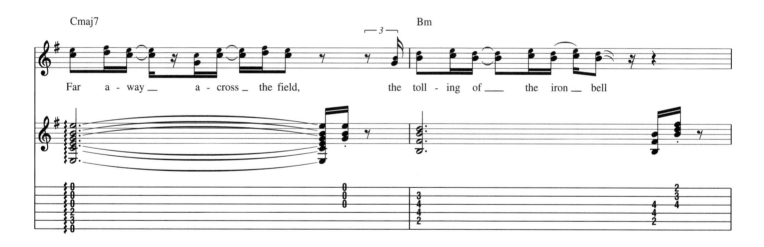

Far a - way __ a - cross __ the field,          the toll - ing of __ the iron __ bell

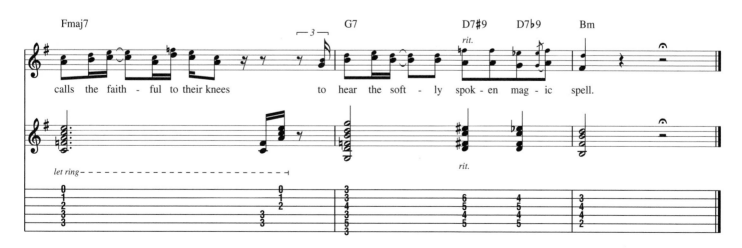

calls the faith - ful to their knees          to hear the soft - ly spok - en mag - ic spell.

from Genisis - *Duke*

# Turn It on Again

### Words and Music by Tony Banks, Phil Collins and Mike Rutherford

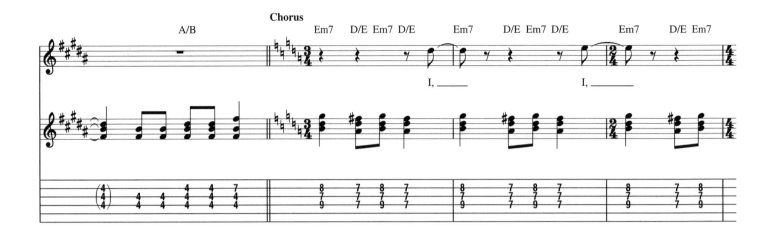

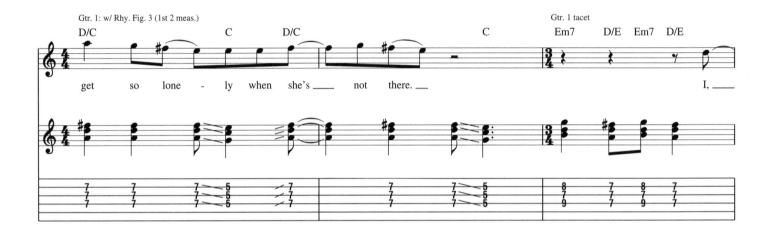

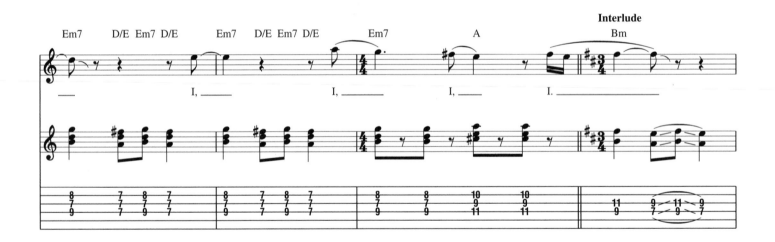

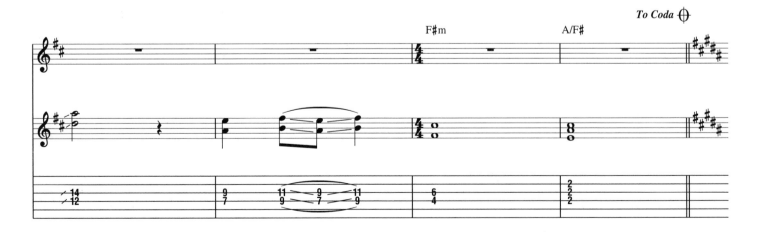

from King Crimson - *In the Court of the Crimson King*

# 21st Century Schizoid Man

**Words and Music by Robert Fripp, Michael Giles, Greg Lake, Ian McDonald and Peter Sinfield**

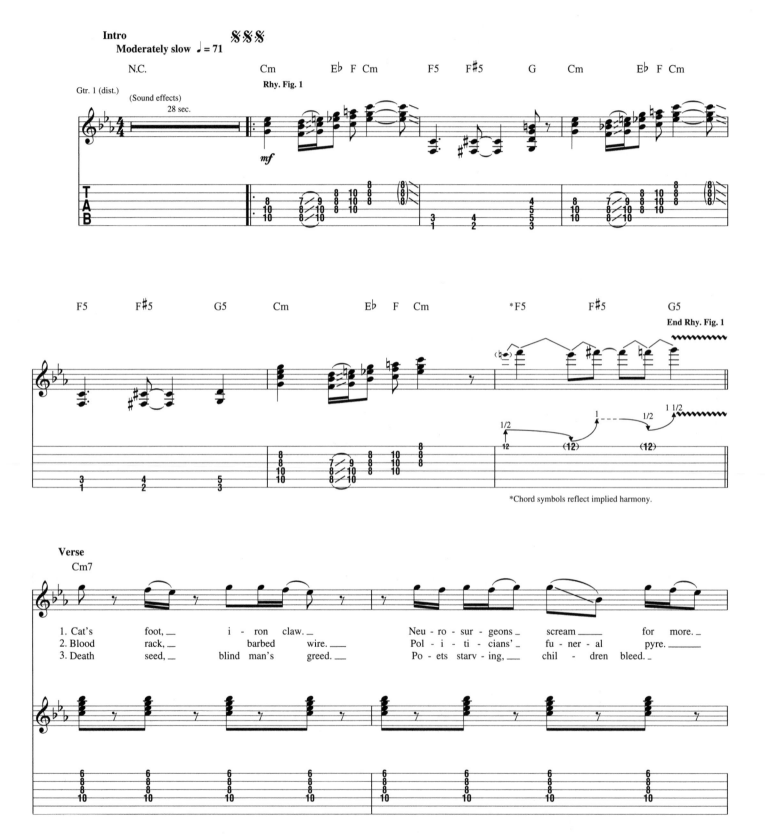

*Chord symbols reflect implied harmony.

1. Cat's foot, __ i - ron claw. __ Neu - ro - sur - geons __ scream ____ for more. __
2. Blood rack, __ barbed wire. __ Pol - i - ti - cians' __ fu - ner - al pyre. __
3. Death seed, __ blind man's greed. __ Po - ets starv - ing, __ chil - dren bleed. _

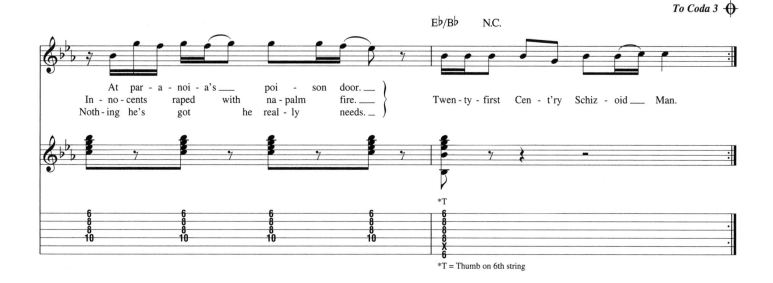

At par - a - noi - a's___ poi - son door.___
In - no - cents raped with na - palm fire.___
Noth - ing he's got he real - ly needs.___

Twen - ty - first Cen - t'ry Schiz - oid___ Man.

*T = Thumb on 6th string

**Interlude**

Rhy. Fig. 2

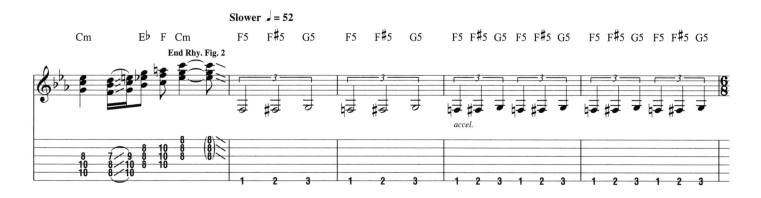

**Slower** ♩ = 52

End Rhy. Fig. 2

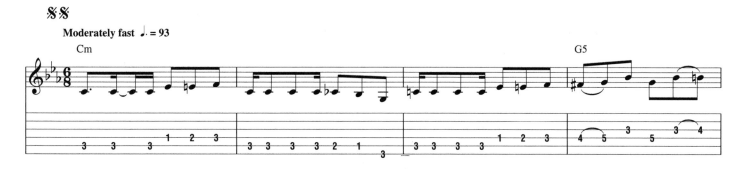

accel.

𝄋 𝄋

**Moderately fast** ♩. = 93

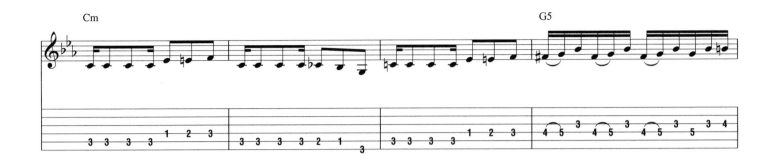

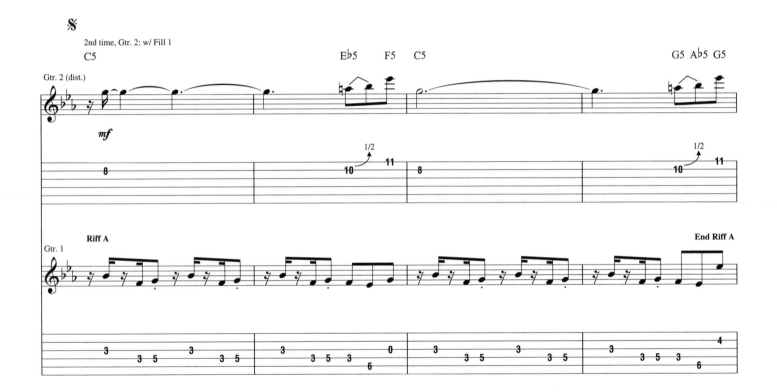

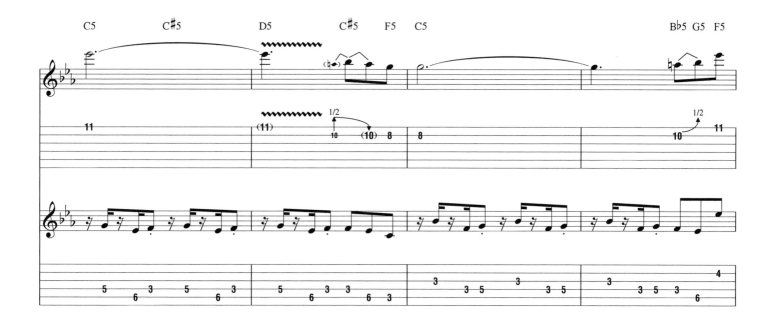

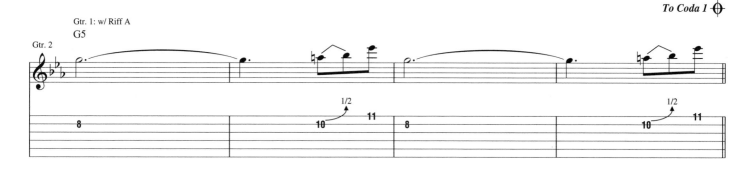

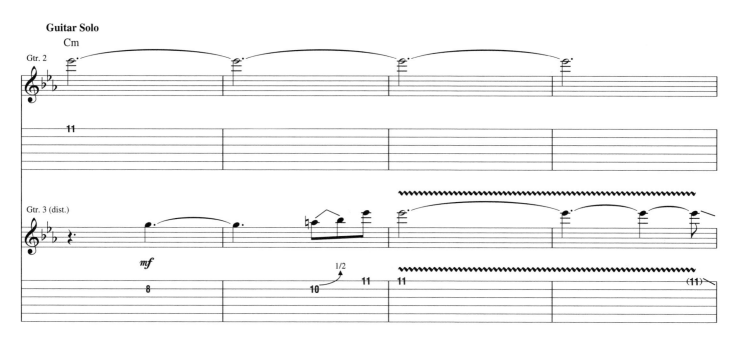

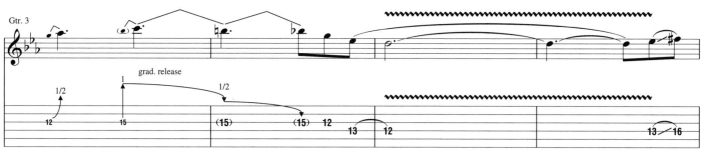

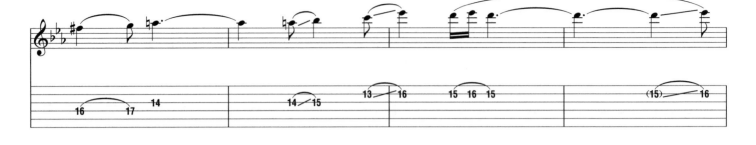

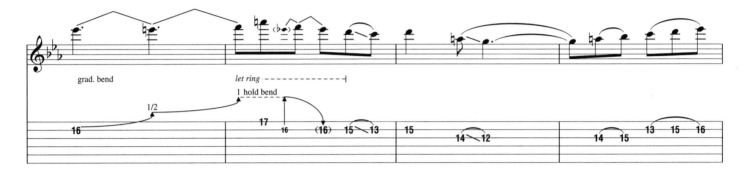

grad. bend

let ring - - - - - - - - - - - - - - - -

1/2

1 hold bend

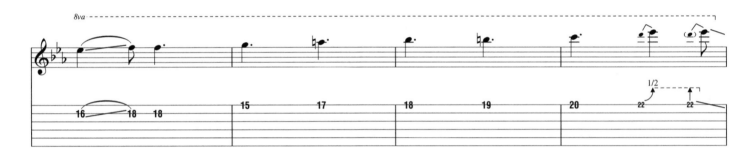

8va - - - - - - - - - - - - - - - - - - - - - - - - - - - - - - - - - - - - - - - - - - - - - - - - - - - - - - - - - - - - - -

1/2

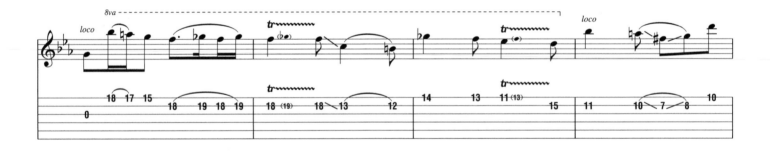

8va - - - - - - - - - - - - - - - - - - - - - - - - - - - - - - - - - - - - - - - - - - - - -

loco

loco

tr

tr

tr

tr

*- - - - - - - - -

*Played ahead of the beat.

1 - - - - - - - - - - - - - - -

*3rd string only.

**Saxophone Solo**

Cm

*D.S. al Coda 1*

Gtr. 3 tacet

**30**

Gtr. 2

$\oint$ **Coda 1**

Gtr. 2 tacet

G5

N.C.

Gtr. 1

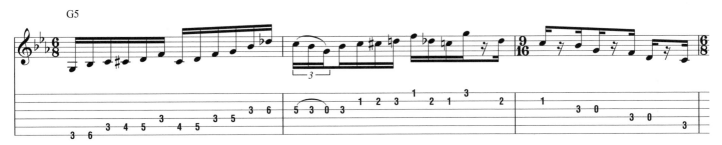

G5

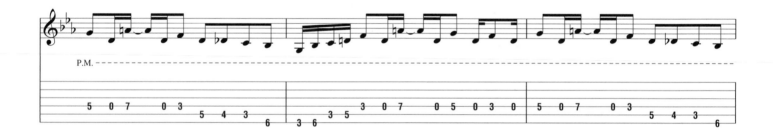

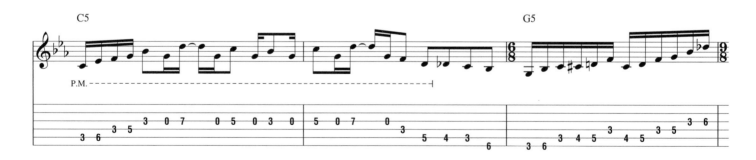

*D.S.S.S. al Coda 3*
*(no repeat)*

### ⊕ Coda 2

### ⊕ Coda 3

**Interlude**

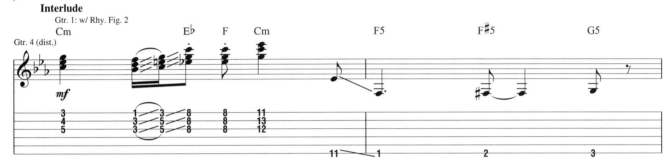

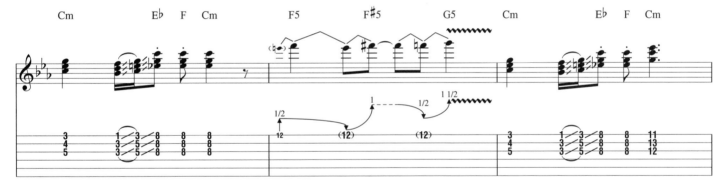

**Slower** ♩ = 52

from Kansas – *Leftoverture*

# The Wall

**Words and Music by Kerry Livgren and Steve Walsh**

\*Piano arr. for gtr.
\*\*Violin arr. for gtr.

Gtr. 1: w/ Rhy. Fig. 1

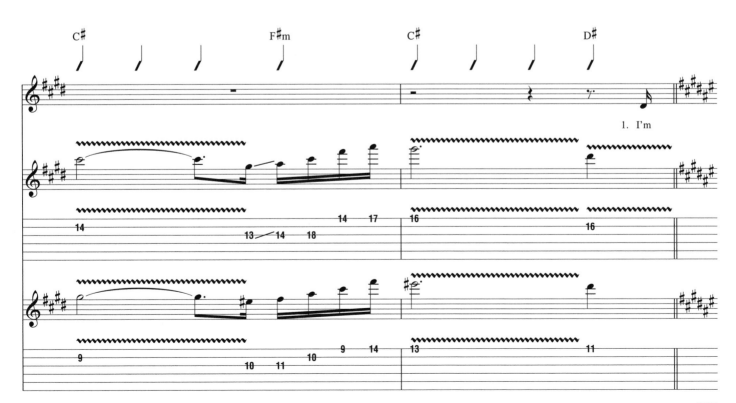

**Verse**

Gtrs. 1, 2 & 3 tacet

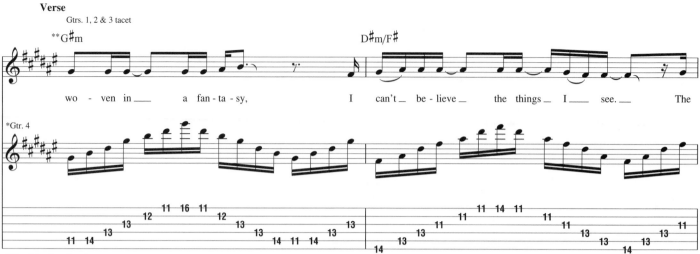

*Harpsichord arr. for gtr.
**Chord symbols reflect implied harmony.

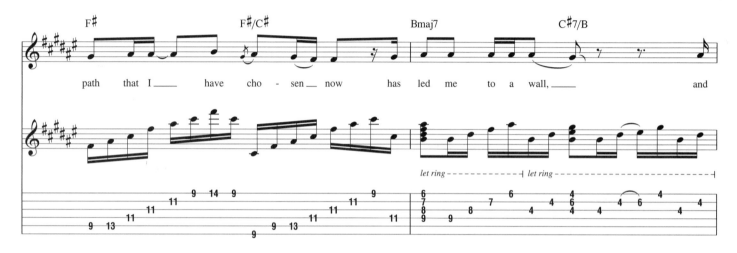

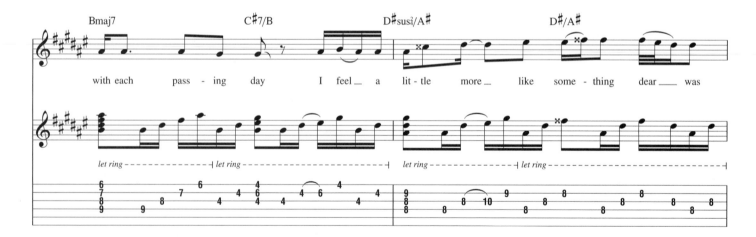

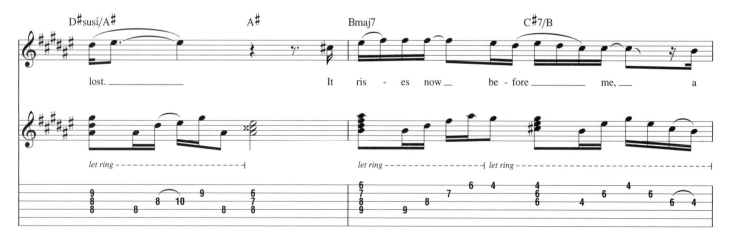

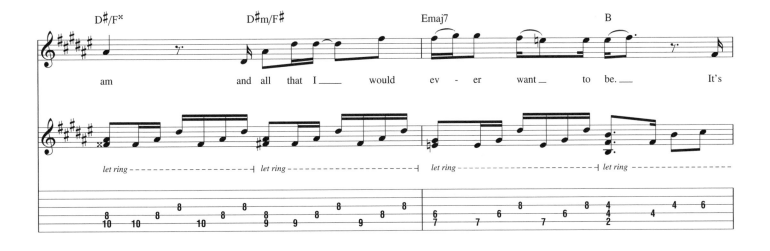

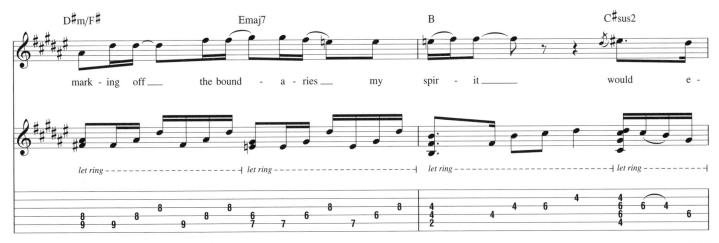

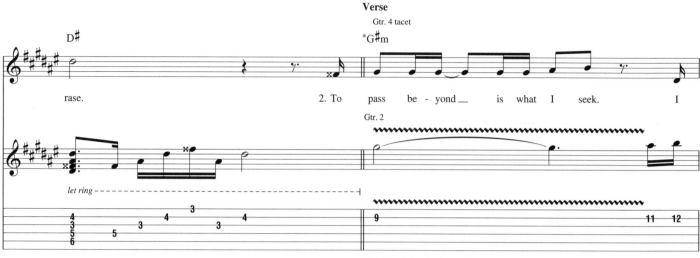

Verse

Gtr. 4 tacet

D#                                         *G#m

rase.                                    2. To  pass  be - yond __  is  what  I  seek.  I

Gtr. 2

let ring

*Chord symbols reflect overall harmony.

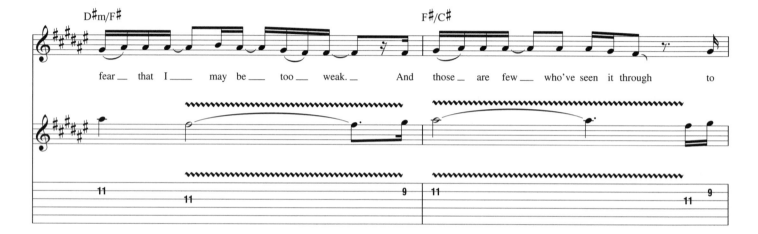

D#m/F#                                     F#/C#

fear __  that  I __  may  be __  too __  weak. __  And  those __  are  few __  who've seen it through      to

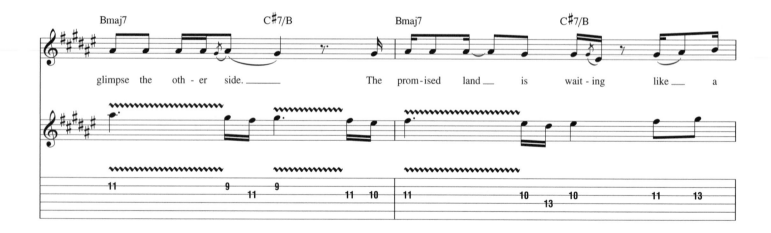

Bmaj7                    C#7/B              Bmaj7                   C#7/B

glimpse  the  oth - er  side. ___          The  prom - ised  land __  is  wait - ing  like __  a

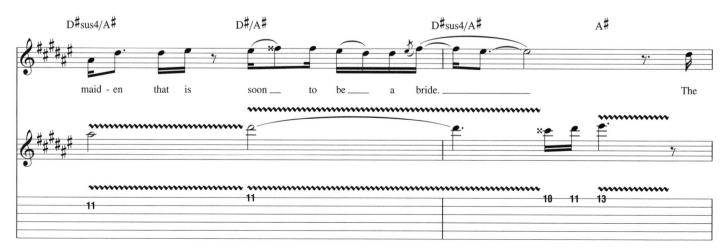

D#sus4/A#                D#/A#                        D#sus4/A#                A#

maid - en  that  is  soon __  to  be __  a  bride. _____              The

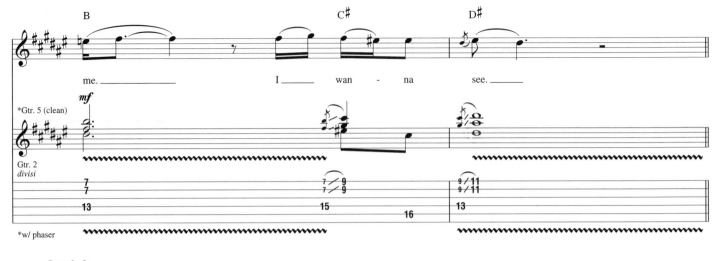

me. _____ I _____ wan - na see. _____

*Gtr. 5 (clean) *mf*

Gtr. 2
*divisi*

*w/ phaser

**Interlude**

Gtr. 2 tacet

Gtr. 5

N.C. Bmaj7          F#add9/A#          A°7

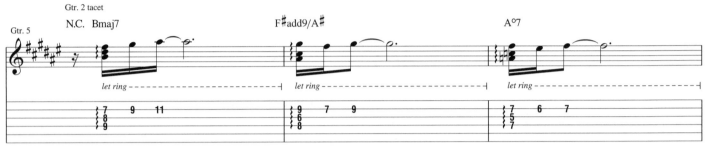

let ring - - - - - - - - - -   let ring - - - - - - - - - -   let ring - - - - - - - - - -

**Guitar Solo**

Gtr. 1: w/ Rhy. Fig. 1
Gtr. 2: w/ Riff A
Gtr. 5 tacet

C#/G#          G#sus4     G#          Gtr. 3  C#m

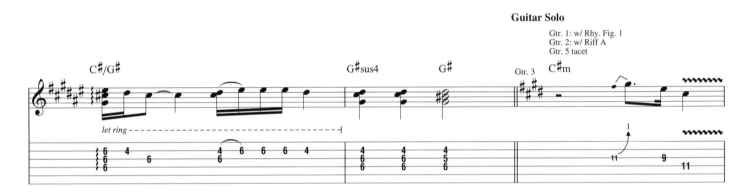

let ring - - - - - - - - - - - - - - - - - - - - -

G#m          C#m          G#m

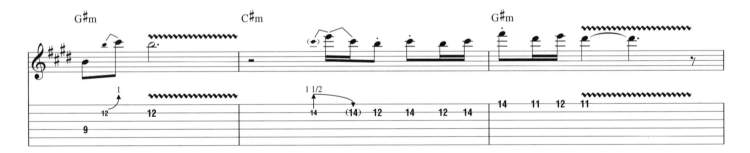

E          D          C#          D#

Gtr. 1

Gtr. 3

Gtr. 3

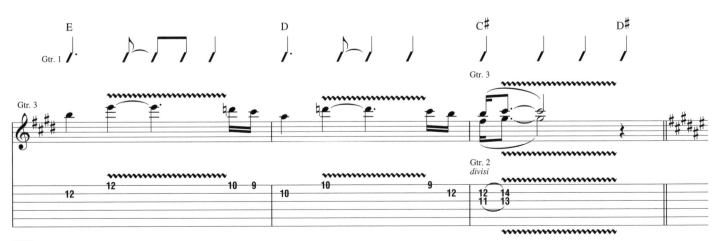

Gtr. 2
*divisi*

**Verse**

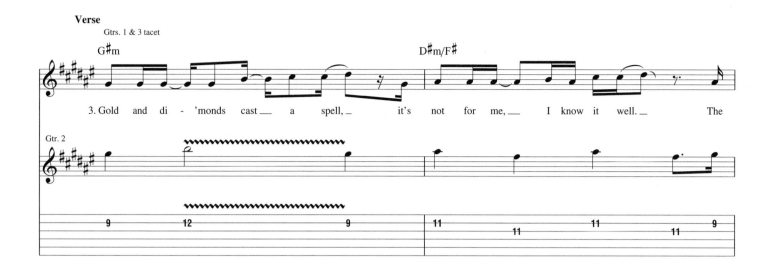

3. Gold and di - 'monds cast __ a spell, __ it's not for me, __ I know it well. __ The

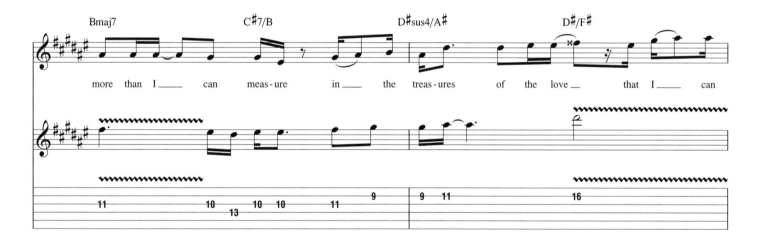

rich - es that I seek __ are wait - ing on the oth - er side. _____ There's

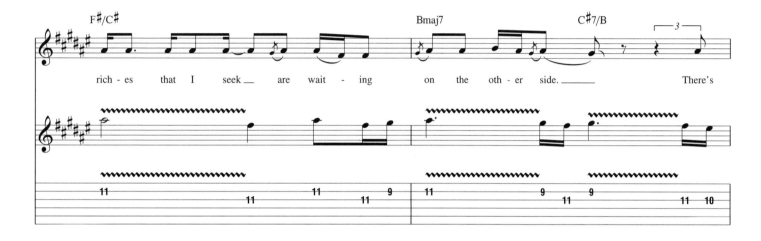

more than I __ can meas - ure in __ the treas - ures of the love __ that I __ can

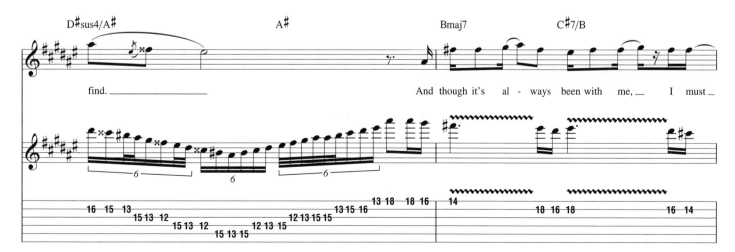

find. _____ And though it's al - ways been with me, __ I must __

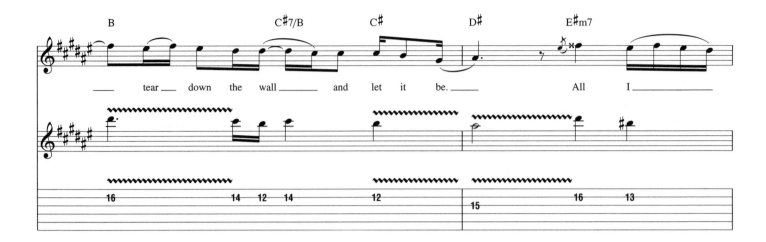

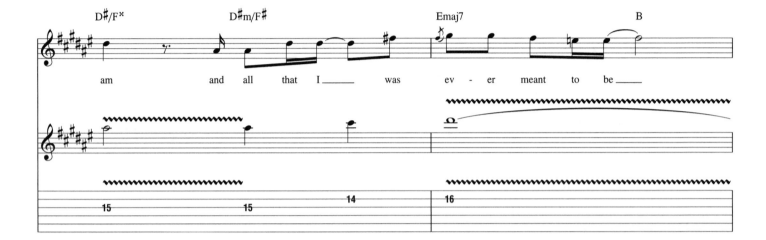

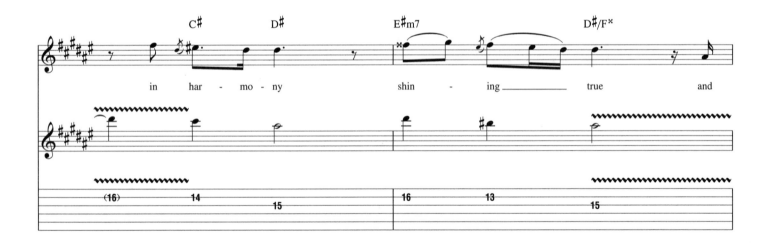

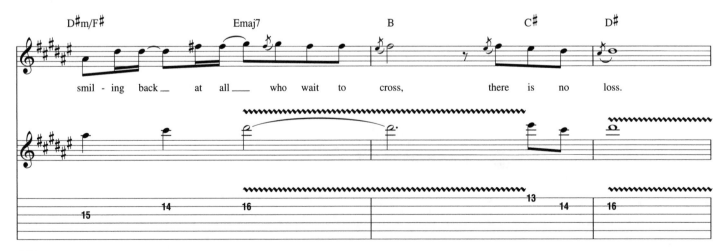

**Outro**

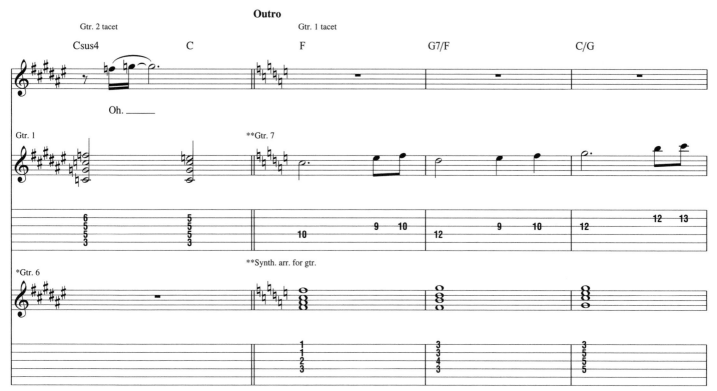

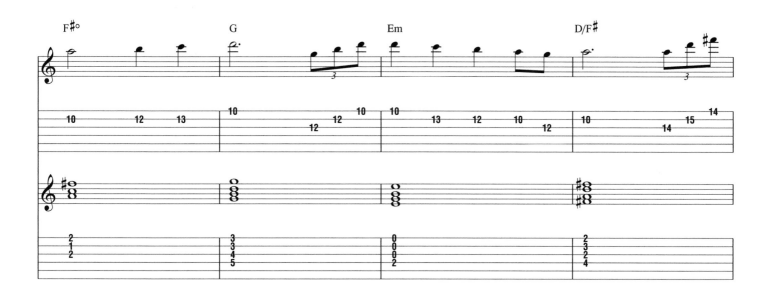

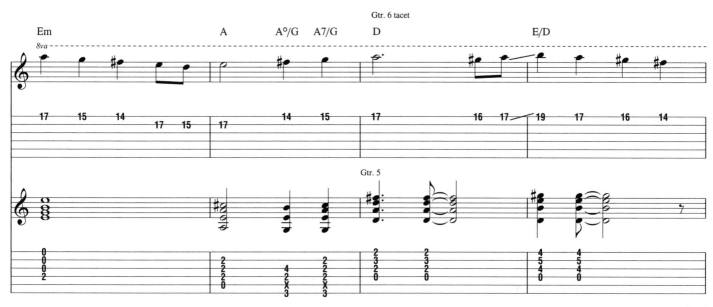

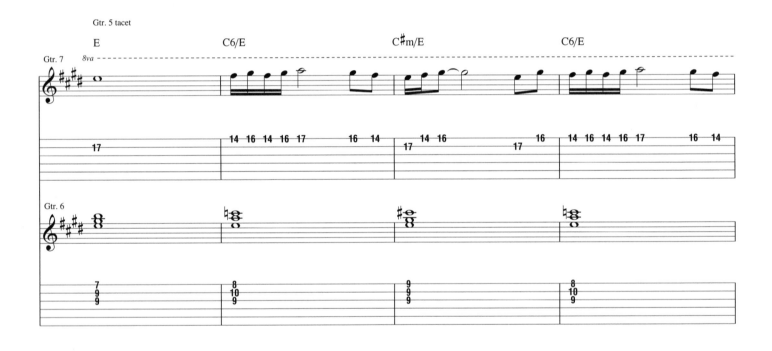

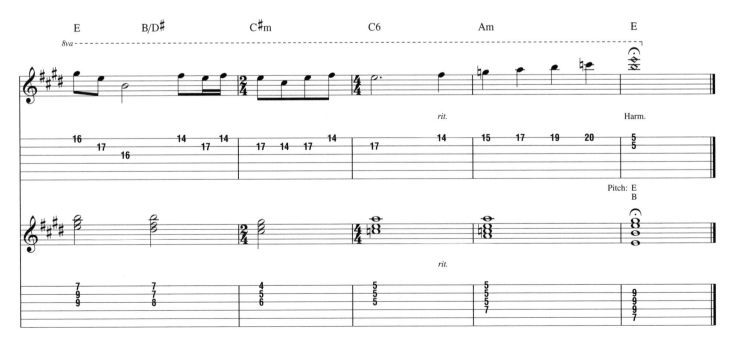

254

from Genesis - *Archive 1967–1975*

# Watcher of the Skies

**Words and Music by Tony Banks, Phil Collins, Peter Gabriel, Steve Hackett and Mike Rutherford**

**Interlude**

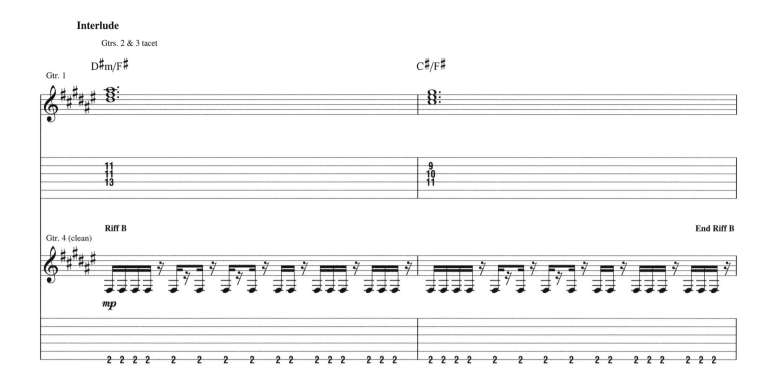

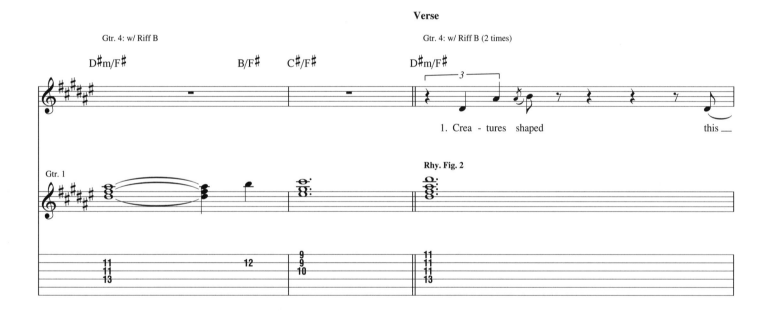

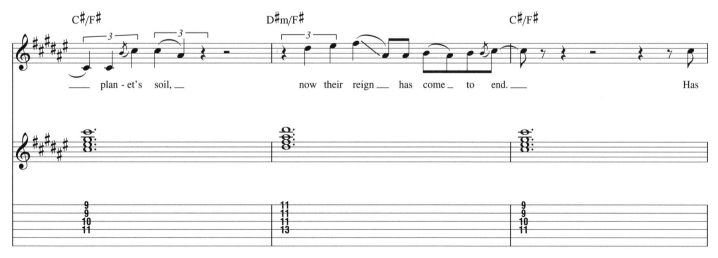

**Chorus**

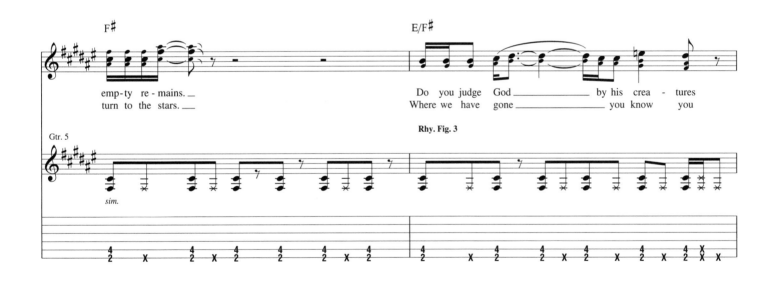

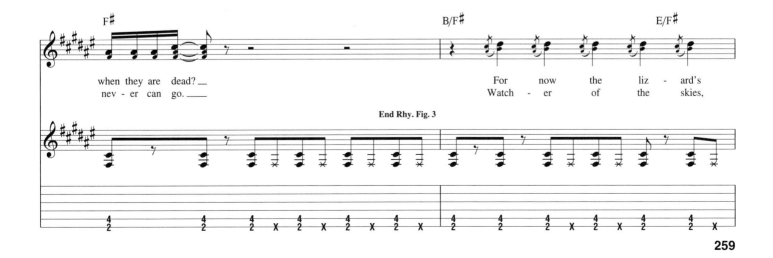

259

shed-ding his tail. ___
watch-er of all, ___

This is the end ___ of man's long
this is your fate ___ a - lone, this

Gtrs. 1 & 5 tacet

un - ion with Earth. ___

2. From

Gtr. 1

Gtr. 6

Gtr. 5
*divisi*

wah-wah off

Gtr. 4
*divisi*

**Verse**

Gtr. 1: w/ Rhy. Fig. 2
Gtr. 4: w/ Riff B (3 times)

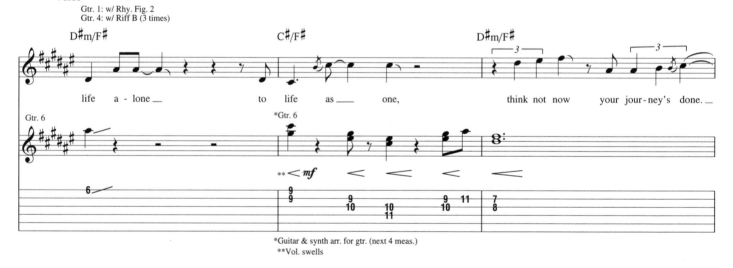

life a - lone ___ to life as ___ one, think not now your jour-ney's done. ___

Gtr. 6

*Gtr. 6

**< *mf*

*Guitar & synth arr. for gtr. (next 4 meas.)
**Vol. swells

For though your ship ___ be stur - dy, no mer-cy has ___ the sea. Will you sur-

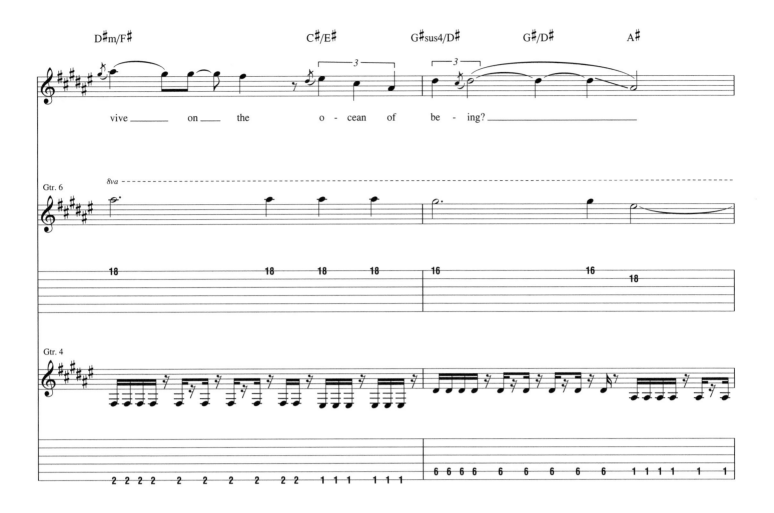

vive _____ on ____ the ____ o - cean of be - ing? _____

**Chorus**

Gtr. 1: w/ Rhy. Fig. 1 (1st 3 meas.)
Gtrs. 2 & 3: w/ Riff A (1 1/2 times)
Gtr. 6 tacet

Come an - cient chil - dren,

*Sung ahead of the beat.

hear what I say. ___  This is my part - ing coun - cil for

**Interlude**

you on your way. ___

Gtr. 1

Gtr. 6

*let ring - - - - -*

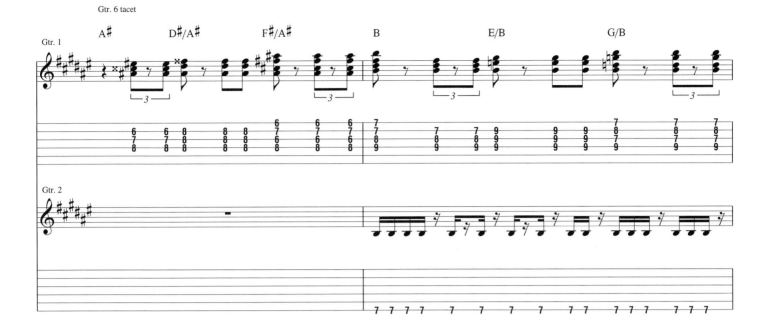

*D.S. al Coda*

*Gtr. 5 to left of slashes in tab.

 **Coda**

**Outro**
Gtr. 1: w/ Rhy. Fig. 1 (till fade)
Gtr. 5: w/ Rhy. Fig. 3 (till fade)

fate is your own.___

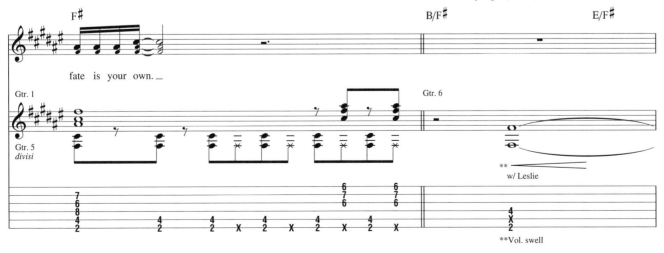

**w/ Leslie

**Vol. swell

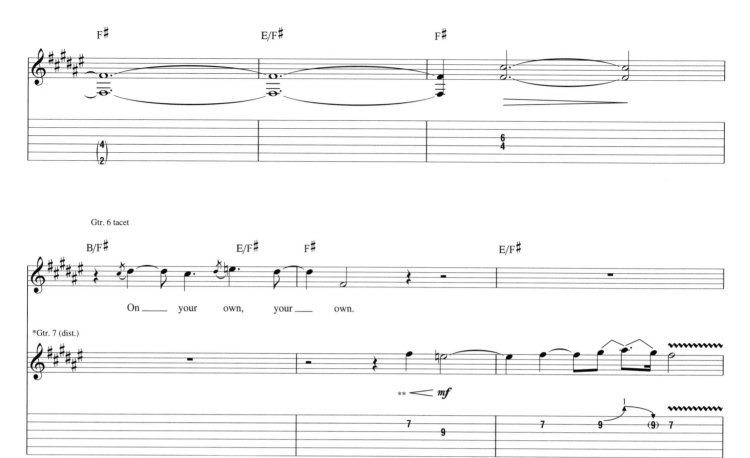

Gtr. 6 tacet

On ____ your own, your ____ own.

*Gtr. 7 (dist.)

** < mf

*Bkwds. gtr. arr. for gtr.

**Vol. swell

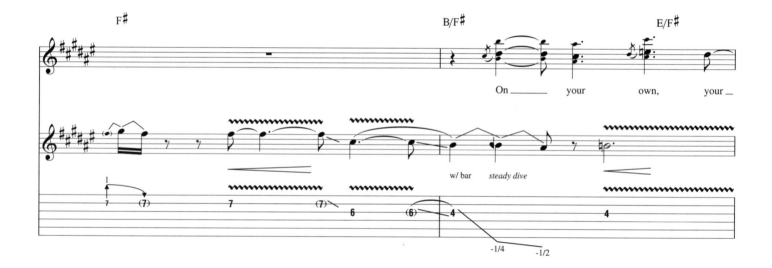

On ____ your own, your __

w/ bar  *steady dive*

-1/4    -1/2

**Begin fade**

**Fade out**

____ own.

1/2    1

# When the Heart Rules the Mind

### Words and Music by Steven James Howe and Stephen Richard Hackett

*Chord symbols reflect implied harmony.

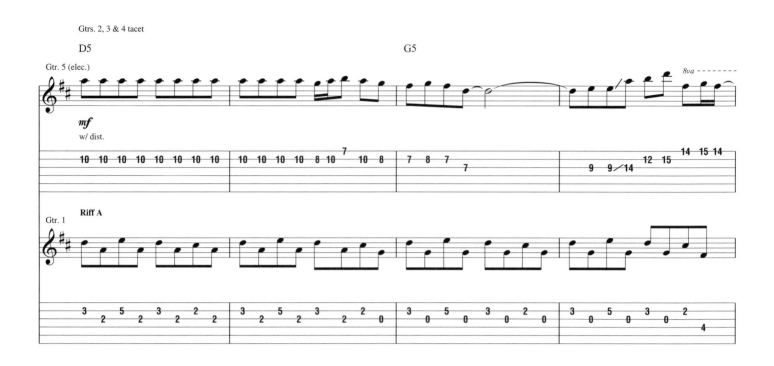

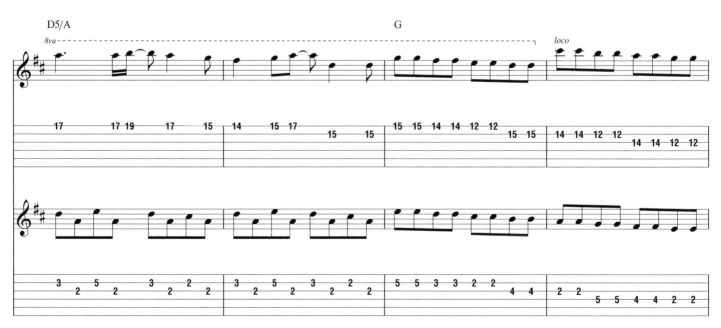

*Gtr. 1 to left of slash in tab.

**Verse**

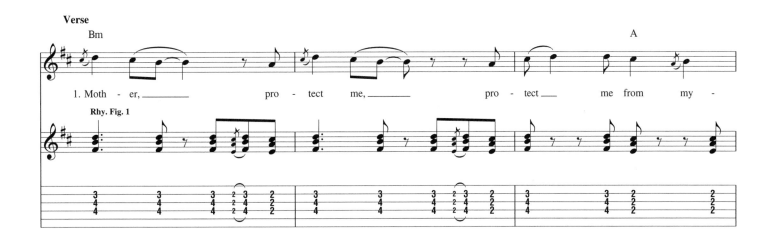

1. Moth - er, _____ pro - tect me, _____ pro - tect ___ me from my -

Gtr. 6: w/ Rhy. Fig. 1 (2 times)

self. _____ Late - ly _____ I can't tell _____ who

real - ly are my friends. _____ Burn - ing _____ the

can - dle, _____ the can - dle at both ends.

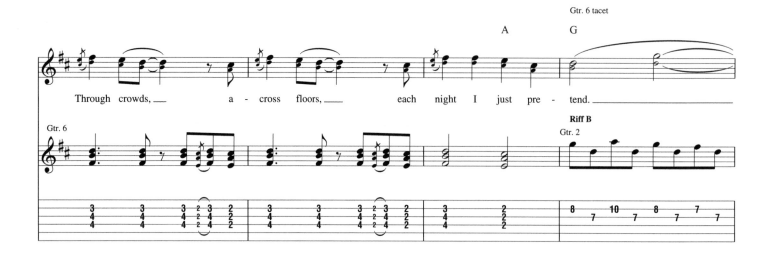

Through crowds, ____ a - cross floors, ____ each night I just pre - tend. ____

When the heart rules ____ the mind, ____

one look and love is blind. ____ When you want the dream ____ to last, ____

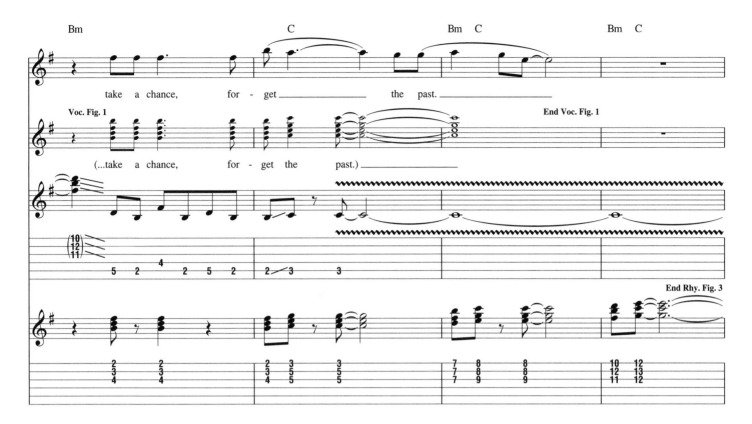

take a chance, for - get the past.

(...take a chance, for - get the past.)

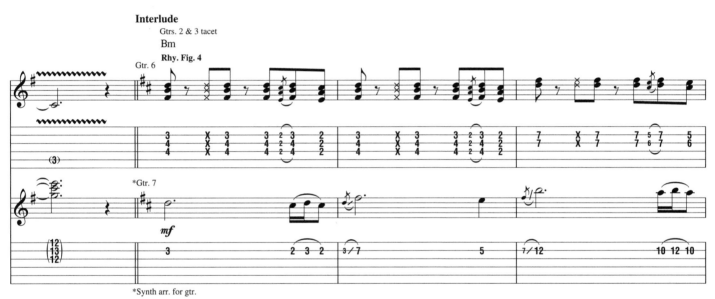

**Interlude**
Gtrs. 2 & 3 tacet
Bm

*Synth arr. for gtr.

**Verse**
Bm

2. Watch - ing the ac - tor,

takes the stage by storm.___ Steal - ing___ the lime - light___

Rhy. Fig. 5

End Rhy. Fig. 5

Gtr. 6: w/ Rhy. Fig. 5 (1 1/2 times)

Gtr. 6: w/ Rhy. Fig. 4 (1 1/2 times)

while _ we're in the wings.___ Some - times,___ the

Gtr. 7

Gtr. 8 (elec.)

*f*
w/ dist. & reverb

slight P.M.

Gtr. 8 tacet

he - ro___ must play the un - der - dog.___ But I don't___ feel _

Gtr. 7

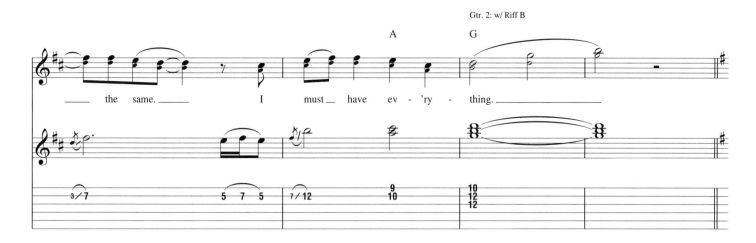

**Chorus**

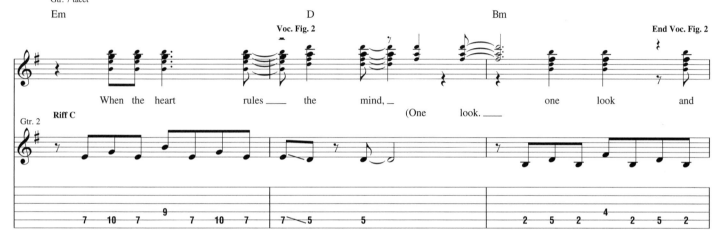

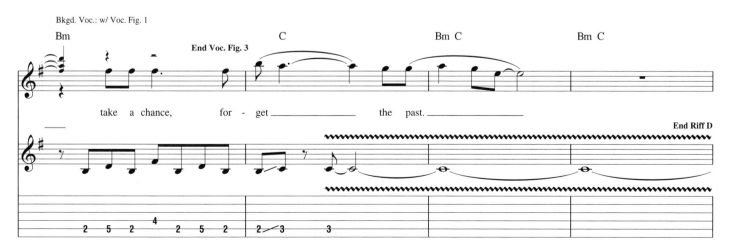

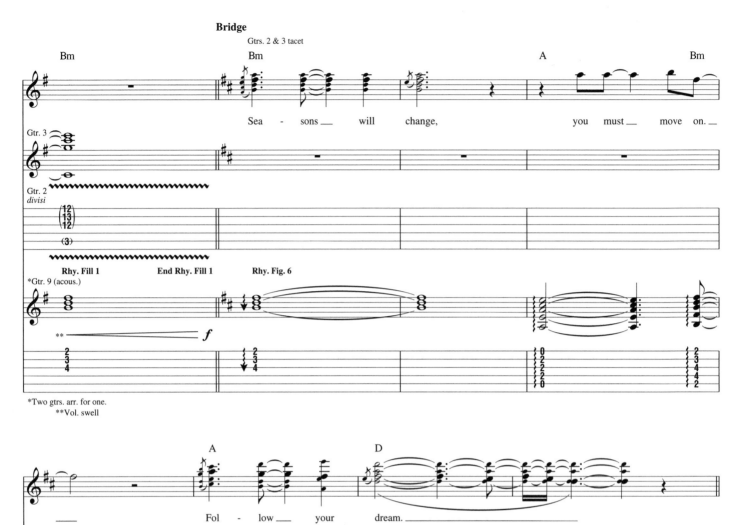

*Two gtrs. arr. for one.

**Vol. swell

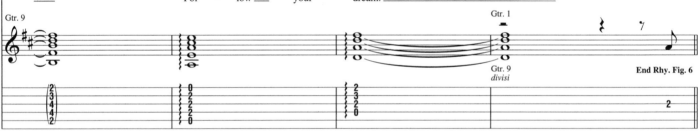

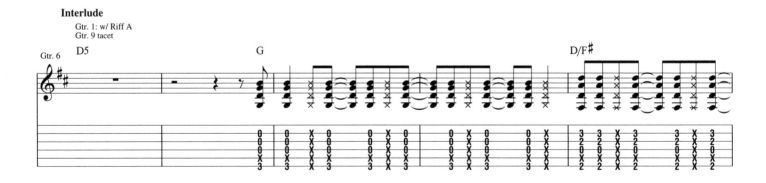

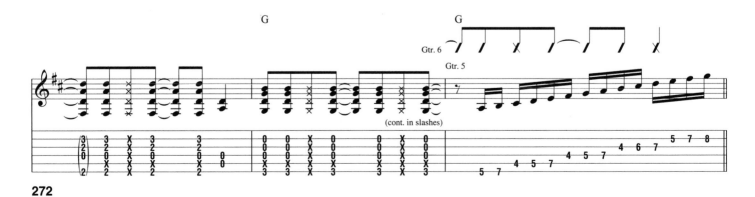

## Guitar Solo

Gtr. 1: w/ Riff A

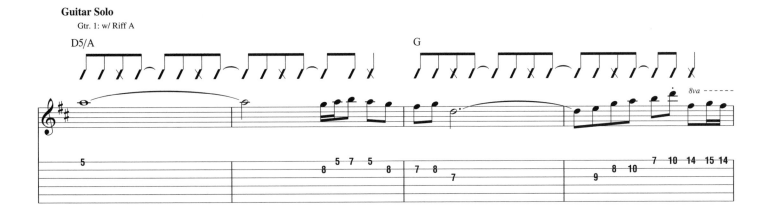

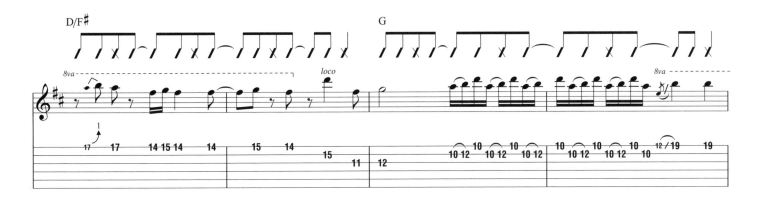

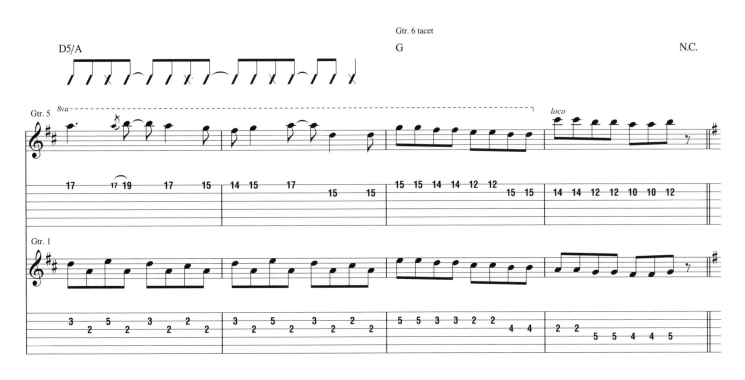

## Interlude

Gtrs. 1 & 5 tacet

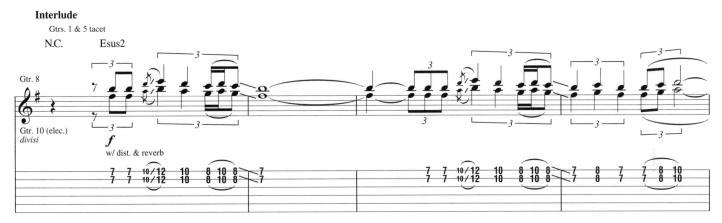

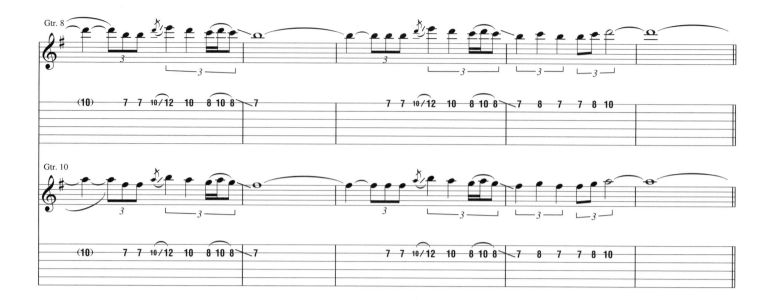

## Chorus

When the heart    rules _ the    mind, _          one    look    and    love    is    blind. _____          When    you    want    the

dream _ to    last, _                take    a    chance,    for - get    the    past. _____          When    the    heart    rules _

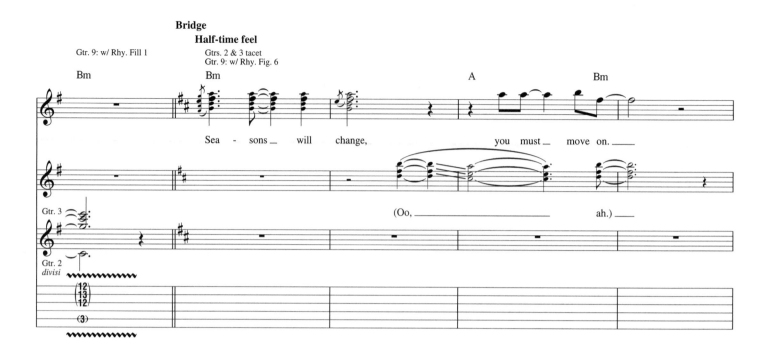

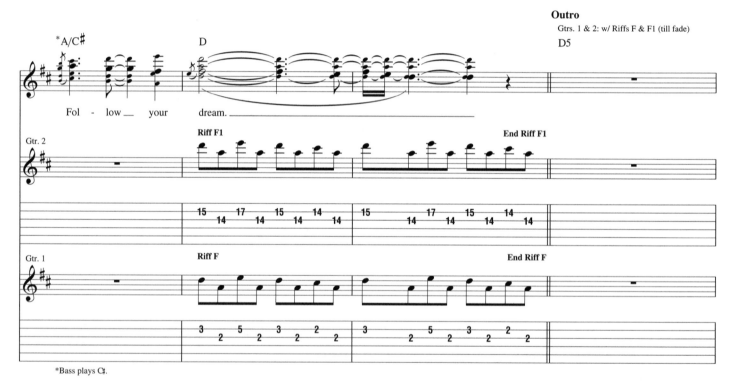

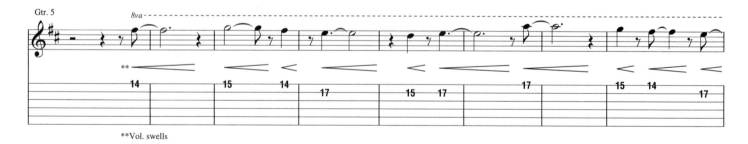

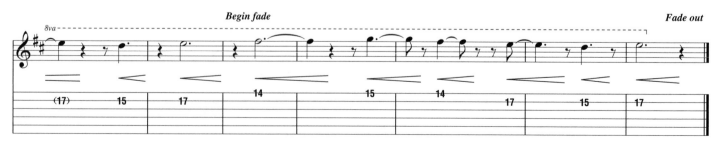

from Opeth - *Damnation*
# Windowpane
**Words and Music by Mikael Akerfeldt**

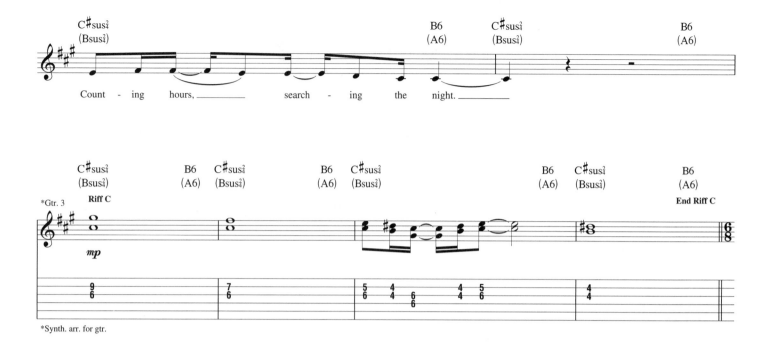

Count - ing hours, _____ search - ing the night. _____

*Gtr. 3    Riff C

End Riff C

*Synth. arr. for gtr.

**Guitar Solo**

Gtr. 1: w/ Riff A (8 times)
Gtr. 3 tacet

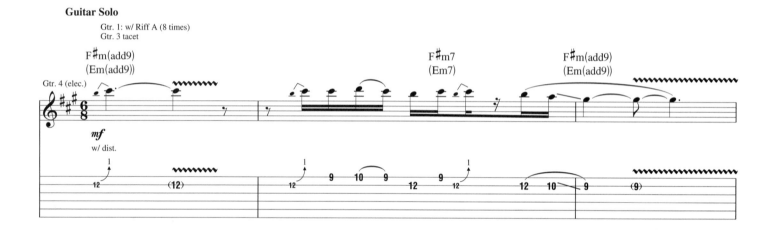

Gtr. 4 (elec.)

*mf*
w/ dist.

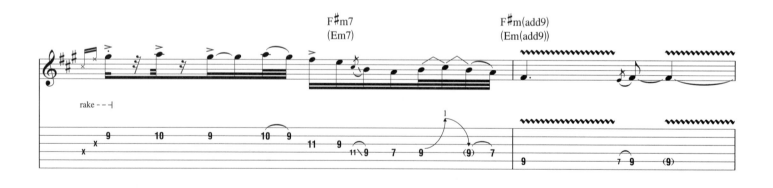

rake - - -|

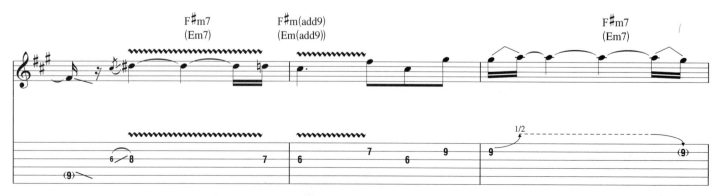

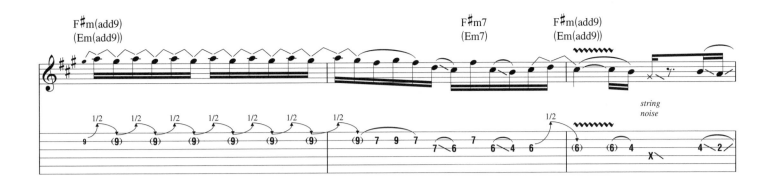

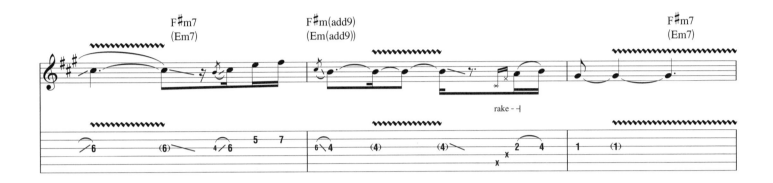

**Verse**

Gtr. 2: w/ Riff B (6 times)
Gtr. 4 tacet

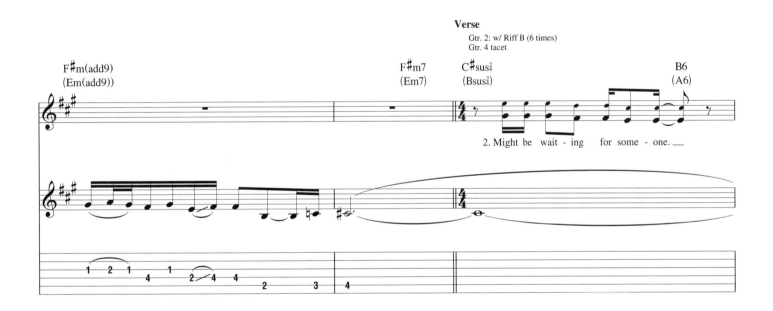

2. Might be wait - ing for some - one. __

Might be there for us __ to see. __

fdbk.

Pitch: G♯

**Bridge**

Gtr. 2: w/ Rhy. Fig. 1

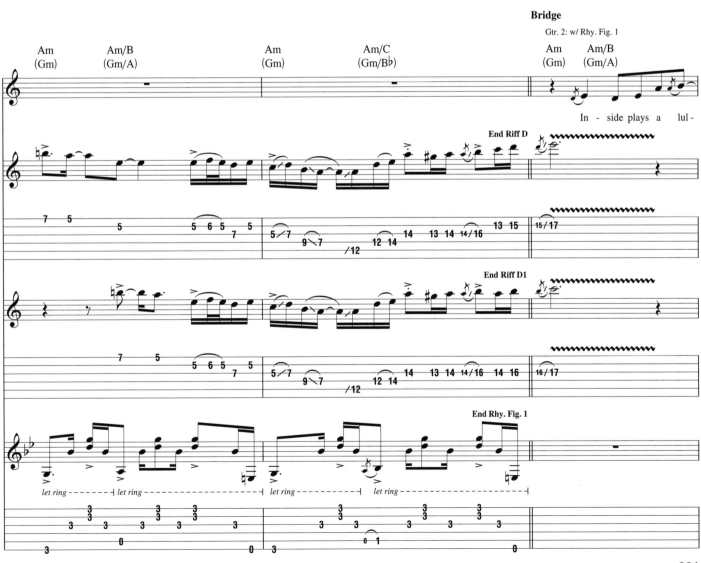

In - side plays a lul-

End Riff D

End Riff D1

End Rhy. Fig. 1

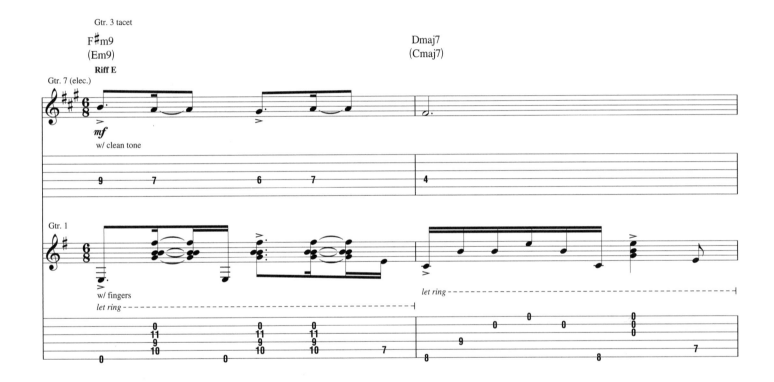

Gtr. 3 tacet

**F#m9**
**(Em9)**

**Dmaj7**
**(Cmaj7)**

**Riff E**

Gtr. 7 (elec.)

*mf*

w/ clean tone

Gtr. 1

w/ fingers

*let ring*

*let ring*

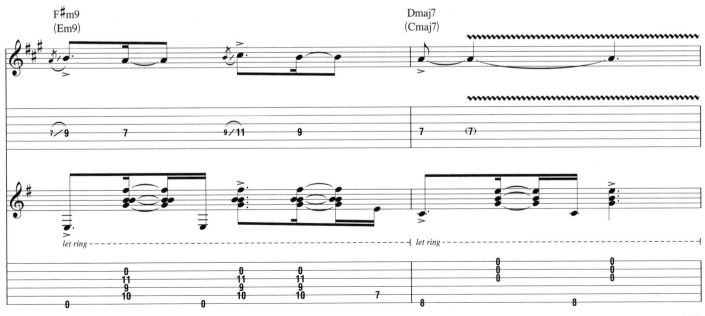

**F#m9**
**(Em9)**

**Dmaj7**
**(Cmaj7)**

*let ring*

*let ring*

284

**Guitar Solo**

Gtr. 1: w/ Rhy. Fig. 2 (2 times)

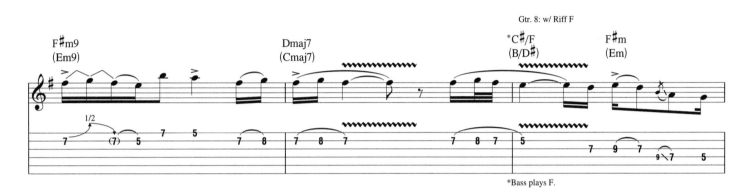

*Bass plays F.

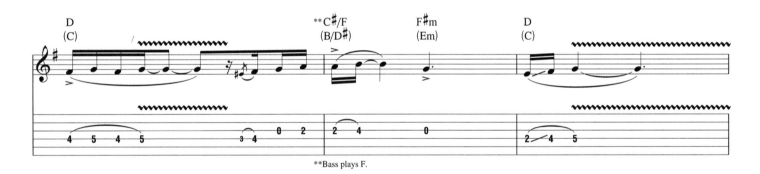

**Bass plays F.

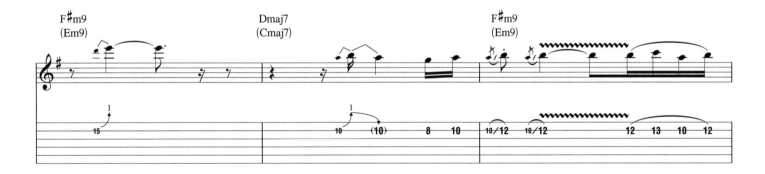

Gtr. 8: w/ Riff F

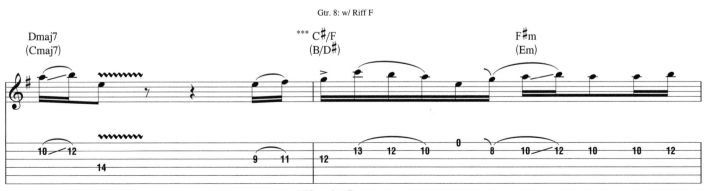

***Bass plays F.

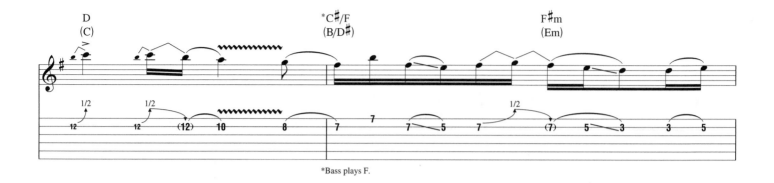

*Bass plays F.

**Interlude**

Gtr. 9 tacet

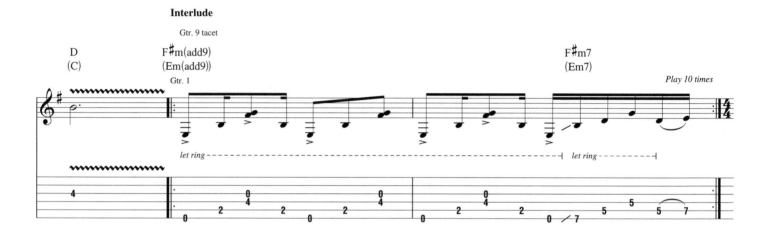

**Verse**

Gtr. 1 tacet
Gtr. 2: w/ Riff B (9 times)

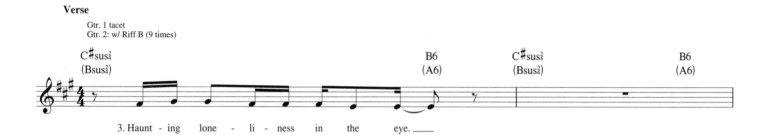

3. Haunt - ing lone - li - ness in the eye. ____

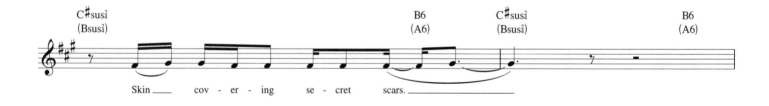

Skin ____ cov - er - ing se - cret scars. ____

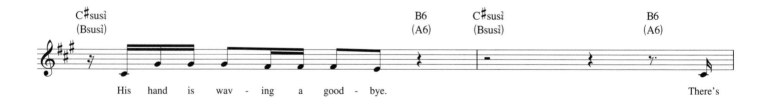

His hand is wav - ing a good - bye.              There's

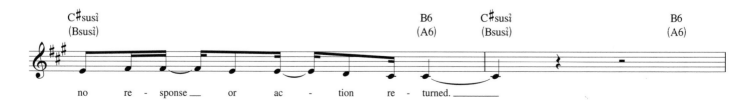

no re - sponse ____ or ac - tion re - turned. ____

286

Gtr. 3: w/ Riff C (2 1/2 times)

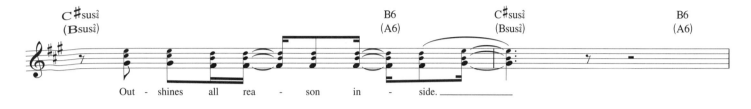

There is deep prej - u - dice in me. ___

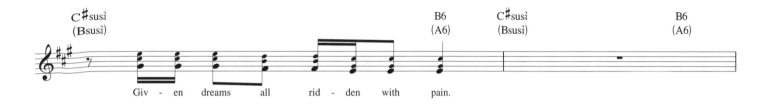

Out - shines all rea - son in - side. ___

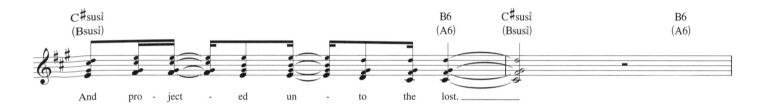

Giv - en dreams all rid - den with pain.

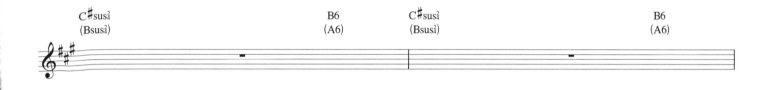

And pro - ject - ed un - to the lost. ___

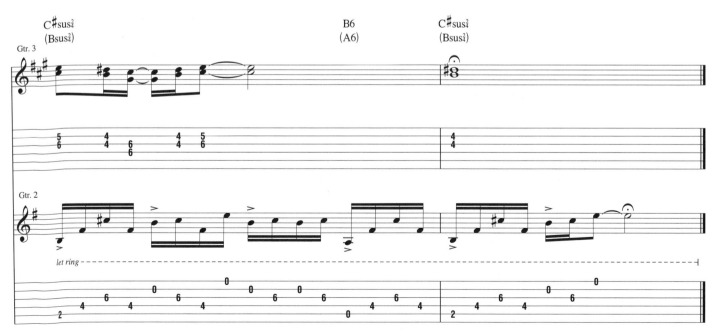

# Guitar Notation Legend

Guitar music can be notated three different ways: on a *musical staff*, in *tablature*, and in *rhythm slashes*.

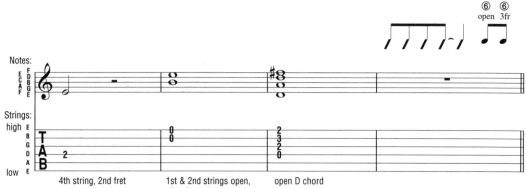

**RHYTHM SLASHES** are written above the staff. Strum chords in the rhythm indicated. Use the chord diagrams found at the top of the first page of the transcription for the appropriate chord voicings. Round noteheads indicate single notes.

**THE MUSICAL STAFF** shows pitches and rhythms and is divided by bar lines into measures. Pitches are named after the first seven letters of the alphabet.

**TABLATURE** graphically represents the guitar fingerboard. Each horizontal line represents a string, and each number represents a fret.

4th string, 2nd fret | 1st & 2nd strings open, played together | open D chord

---

**HALF-STEP BEND:** Strike the note and bend up 1/2 step.

**WHOLE-STEP BEND:** Strike the note and bend up one step.

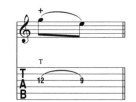

**GRACE NOTE BEND:** Strike the note and immediately bend up as indicated.

**SLIGHT (MICROTONE) BEND:** Strike the note and bend up 1/4 step.

---

**BEND AND RELEASE:** Strike the note and bend up as indicated, then release back to the original note. Only the first note is struck.

**PRE-BEND:** Bend the note as indicated, then strike it.

**VIBRATO:** The string is vibrated by rapidly bending and releasing the note with the fretting hand.

**WIDE VIBRATO:** The pitch is varied to a greater degree by vibrating with the fretting hand.

---

**HAMMER-ON:** Strike the first (lower) note with one finger, then sound the higher note (on the same string) with another finger by fretting it without picking.

**PULL-OFF:** Place both fingers on the notes to be sounded. Strike the first note and without picking, pull the finger off to sound the second (lower) note.

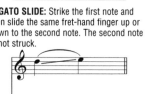

**LEGATO SLIDE:** Strike the first note and then slide the same fret-hand finger up or down to the second note. The second note is not struck.

**SHIFT SLIDE:** Same as legato slide, except the second note is struck.

---

**TRILL:** Very rapidly alternate between the notes indicated by continuously hammering on and pulling off.

**TAPPING:** Hammer ("tap") the fret indicated with the pick-hand index or middle finger and pull off to the note fretted by the fret hand.

**NATURAL HARMONIC:** Strike the note while the fret-hand lightly touches the string directly over the fret indicated.

**PINCH HARMONIC:** The note is fretted normally and a harmonic is produced by adding the edge of the thumb or the tip of the index finger of the pick hand to the normal pick attack.

---

**PICK SCRAPE:** The edge of the pick is rubbed down (or up) the string, producing a scratchy sound.

**MUFFLED STRINGS:** A percussive sound is produced by laying the fret hand across the string(s) without depressing, and striking them with the pick hand.

**PALM MUTING:** The note is partially muted by the pick hand lightly touching the string(s) just before the bridge.

**RAKE:** Drag the pick across the strings indicated with a single motion.

---

**TREMOLO PICKING:** The note is picked as rapidly and continuously as possible.

**VIBRATO BAR DIVE AND RETURN:** The pitch of the note or chord is dropped a specified number of steps (in rhythm), then returned to the original pitch.

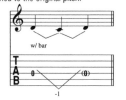

**VIBRATO BAR SCOOP:** Depress the bar just before striking the note, then quickly release the bar.

**VIBRATO BAR DIP:** Strike the note and then immediately drop a specified number of steps, then release back to the original pitch.